Victory without Peace

Victory without Peace

AMERICAN FOREIGN RELATIONS IN THE TWENTIETH CENTURY

DAVID F. TRASK

Professor of History, State
University of New York at Stony Brook

JOHN WILEY & SONS, INC.
New York · London · Sydney

For Elizabeth Brooks Trask

Preface

This little book is a kind of primer for readers of open mind and spirit who wish to reconsider America's past in international life. It outlines the manifold ways in which America's participation in world politics has been affected not only by the unique quality of the national experience but also by the pattern of world history. I have tried to write about those aspects of the American story relevant to an understanding of the contemporary world crisis, believing as I do that each of us by careful thought might contribute in some small but vital way to the recovery of peace with honor.

Lake Caspian   DAVID F. TRASK
Greensboro, Vermont

Contents

List of Maps

Victory without Peace

CHAPTER I

Prologue to Empire

WHEN THE GREAT powers met at Vienna in 1814 to decide the future course of Europe, their leaders hoped above all to preclude another adventure in hegemony comparable to that of Napoleon just past. Terrible memories of Austerlitz, Jena, and other great battles constantly goaded the statesmen of Europe to unexampled feats of negotiation. Above all else their hope was to restore the balance of power, insuring once and for all that no single state might threaten the sovereignty of all the others. To be sure, representatives of certain states, like the Tsar Alexander of Russia, hoped to aggrandize at the expense of defeated enemies, and that ingenious minister of Louis XVIII, Talleyrand, schemed to rescue France from permanent destruction. Nevertheless, the predominant desire of all delegations at Vienna was to insure against another season of political danger like that of the Napoleonic wars. When the work of Metternich, Castlereagh, Hardenberg, and the others was completed, they had seriously compromised the immediate future of various European ideologies, especially those of a nationalist or democratic nature, but they had made a peace which was to maintain itself quite successfully for a hundred years.

The peacemakers of 1814–1815 were ultimately successful not because they favored "legitimacy" or opposed "self-determination" but because they insured that no European state could hope to establish its power generally over the entire continent. This boundary or that might alter; this nation or that might gain or lose within the general system of European politics, but no nation of any importance had to fear total subjugation. Despite the upheavals of 1830 and 1848, or even the Prussian victory over France in 1871, nothing shook the foundations of 1815 sufficiently to precipitate another general war during the rest of the century. Europe was, to all intents and purposes, a stable continent. The "liberties of Europe," by which the diplomats of 1815 meant freedom from conquest by any one power, had once again been guaranteed, as they had been before at Westphalia in 1648.

The successes of Vienna held enormous portent for the rest of the world. The relative stability of Europe contributed significantly to the successful outcome of revolutionary enterprises taking place in the New World. The reconstitution of the European balance tended to curb expansionist appetites in Europe proper and to direct colonizing activities to Africa and Asia rather than the western hemisphere. For the Americas during the nineteenth century the net result was vastly reduced European influence.

If 1815 had such momentous consequences for Europe, it was also a year of fundamental import to a small nation, hardly mentioned at Vienna, across the broad expanse of the Atlantic Ocean. Events at Vienna ended the likelihood of any serious European threat to the sovereignty of the United States of America until the twentieth century. The remarkable stability of the European balance of power was an essential precondition of American accomplishment during the nineteenth century. As long as those European nations with sufficient power to threaten American security were locked in the European balance, they could hardly contemplate extensive imperial enterprise in the western hemisphere, any more than they could undertake hegemonizing wars in Europe itself. Energies which might have been expended in the exploitation of the Americas were diverted instead to social and economic challenges at home or to overseas expansion.

It was true that Great Britain, for example, did possess sufficient naval power to conquer anywhere it pleased in the Caribbean Sea, a conceivable base for an attack on North America. The United States certainly lacked sufficient power to prevent British incursions in Latin America wherever the Admiralty might decide to impose its will. But what then would happen to Britain's position *vis-à-vis* the European continent? Had Britain concentrated its fleet in the Caribbean, a rival European power or group of powers might have threatened the British position in Europe or even in Asia.

Comparable considerations affected France, although that nation proved less circumspect. At various times, French leaders dreamed of great American empires, but such dreams inevitably turned to dust. In 1862, Napoleon III launched an effort to conquer Mexico but was forced to withdraw by 1867, realizing that a combination of Mexican resistance, criticism at home, and European dangers seriously compromised the overall security of France. Had Napoleon managed to preserve the regime of the Austrian Maximilian, it might have greatly undermined American security, but in this instance the United States merely expressed disapproval; it was not forced to move beyond verbal opposition. Other pressures than those exerted by the government in Washington insured the liquidation of what might have been a truly frightening threat to the United States.

The one real moment of opportunity for European success in the New World came during the 1860s when the United States was disastrously torn by internal political turmoil. The onset of the Civil War presented Napoleon III with his opportunity in Mexico, but fortune smiled upon the United States as well as on the western hemisphere generally, for at this very time Europe was itself seriously shaken by the national consolidation of two great continental states—Germany and Italy. Events at home worked against any considerable penetration into the western hemisphere by ambitious European adventurers. Once again, European conditions preserved the sovereignty of the young American republics, chief among which was the United States.

* * *

Since no truly serious European dangers presented themselves during the nineteenth century, the Americans were left largely to their own devices and could take advantage of truly unusual opportunities. To the west of the initial settlements along the Atlantic seaboard stretched a vast hinterland, inhabited for the most part by relatively primitive aborigines who could not offer more than temporary resistance. Europe, far from the scene and preoccupied with its own concerns, could hardly pose more than tenuous opposition to the absorption of the American hinterland by the United States. The westward movement of the American people stimulated a second great national preoccupation during the nineteenth century—the creation of a truly vast and diversified national economy.

The diplomatic history of the United States during the nineteenth century is often treated as an aspect of westward expansion and economic development because these interrelated phenomena in fact largely shaped the nation's foreign policy. Even before the events of 1815, perspicacious Americans recognized the realities of the long century stretching before them. If Europe could not interfere effectively with American interest and aspiration in the New World, why should Americans concern themselves with Europe? Why get involved in extracontinental affairs for no good reason? There was more than enough to occupy them at home. Said Washington: "It is our true policy to steer clear of any permanent alliance with any portion of the foreign world, so far, I mean, as we are now at liberty to do it." Jefferson expressed the same sentiment in more benevolent but equally positive language. "[H]onest friendship with all nations, entangling alliances with none."

Throughout the nineteenth century, the successors of Washington and Jefferson respected the injunctions of their founders. The policy of isolation during time of peace and neutrality during time of war served the national interest well. Unfortunately for the future, few Americans realized that the effectiveness of isolation and neutrality depended not simply on abstinence from European politics but also upon the maintenance of European equilibrium. Always before, when Europe became involved in general warfare, the New World had perforce been drawn in—at the time of Philip II, during the hegemonial enterprises of Louis XIV, and most recently during the Napoleonic conquests. As it happened, no comparable attempt disturbed the course of the nineteenth century after 1814, and Americans became accustomed to believe that in all situations, including general warfare in Europe, the policy of "no entangling alliances" would suffice to insure American security and progress.

The practice of disengagement from Europe found its roots not only in political realities but also in profoundly influential psychic tensions. To understand the depths of the American commitment to avoidance of Europe and Europe's ways, it helps to reflect on the wording of certain passages in Washington's Farewell Address of 1796. In speaking of the advantages inherent in the federal union of states, the General noted, among other things, that it gave "an exemption from those broils and wars between themselves which so frequently afflict neighboring countries not tied together by the same governments, which their own rivalships alone would be sufficient to produce, but which opposite foreign alliances, attachments and intrigues would stimulate and imbitter." Or again: "Against the insidious wiles of foreign influence (I conjure you to believe me, fellow-citizens) the jealousy of a free people ought to be *constantly* awake, since history and experience prove that foreign influence is one of the most baneful foes of republican government." And finally: "Why, by interweaving our destiny with that of any part of Europe, entangle our peace and prosperity in the toils of European ambition, rivalship, interest, humor, or caprice?"

It is certainly true that Washington was here arguing against the French alliance contracted in 1778, attempting to discredit the insistence upon its maintenance argued by the growing Jeffersonian opposition, but behind these sentiments lurked moving historical experiences which gave the passages special force. Washington's phrases reveal a profound emotional as well as pragmatic rejection of Europe which stemmed from the history and experience of the American settlers. After all, the very enterprise of colonization represented a massive rejection of Europe. The colonists had come to America from all parts of Europe not simply because they were attracted by American delights but also because they were repelled by European dangers. Those who built America were, preeminently, the disinherited of

Europe. The settlers naturally drew a strong moral and even spiritual distinction between Europe and America. Europe was evil; America was good.

This clear distinction gradually hardened into something like a Manichean view of the western world, especially as the colonial experiment matured into success. Europe became equated with the Old Adam, incorrigibly corrupt and decadent, whereas the United States was naturally incorruptible and pristine. The outcome of the revolutionary experience during the latter years of the eighteenth century lent additional justification to this moralistic, indeed quasi-religious, formulation. After all, had not the Puritan Fathers come to establish a city upon a hill to reconstitute that republic of virtue rejected by seventeenth-century England? The seeming triumph of American arms during the War of 1812 only served to confirm the national illusion that a special providence had directed the settlers to the New World and that it continued to watch over and prosper the nation.

If the distinction between decadent Europe and pristine America ran silent in the hearts of most Americans, it ran deeply indeed. Long after its rational basis had dissipated, if indeed it ever had a reasonable foundation, Americans clung to the concept with remarkable tenacity. That tenacity reflected those moral and spiritual distinctions between the Old World and the New burned into the national psyche by the painful experience of rejection and separation which had taken place in the distant American past and which was fructified by the constant arrival of new immigrants. Today we have considerable knowledge of the manifold constraints on adult behavior imposed by childhood experience. As it is with individuals, so it is for nations as well.

It was, then, not simply the obvious political wisdom of isolation which suggested its adoption as national policy at the outset of the national experience; it was also the burden of generations of accumulated resentment. By and large, as the nation grew beyond the Appalachians into the great valley of the Mississippi and even further into the Trans-Missouri West, it seemed natural to attribute national progress to the policy of isolation. That isolation not only seemed to preserve the nation from European entanglements of no particular political utility to the fledgling republic but it also protected America's virtue.

For a hundred years and more after the achievement of national independence Americans felt themselves constantly improving in wisdom and stature, and in favor with God and man. They too easily believed that a special virtue preserved them from the outcomes of European life. In these circumstances, it was difficult indeed to recognize the truth of the matter—that Americans were frequently guilty of

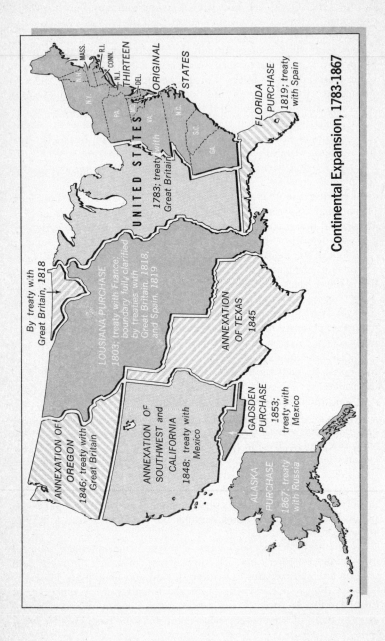

Continental Expansion, 1783-1867

ANNEXATION OF OREGON
1846; treaty with Great Britain

By treaty with Great Britain, 1818

LOUISIANA PURCHASE
1803; treaty with France; boundary fully clarified by treaties with Great Britain, 1818, and Spain, 1819

ANNEXATION OF SOUTHWEST and CALIFORNIA
1848; treaty with Mexico

GADSDEN PURCHASE
1853; treaty with Mexico

ANNEXATION OF TEXAS
1845

UNITED STATES

THIRTEEN ORIGINAL STATES

1783: treaty with Great Britain

MASS.
N.H.
R.I.
CONN.
N.Y.
N.J.
PA.
DEL.
VA.
N.C.
S.C.
GA.

FLORIDA PURCHASE
1819; treaty with Spain

ALASKA PURCHASE
1867; treaty with Russia

6

the very sins they so easily attributed to Europe. The winning of the West, for example, is a tale wherein the most superficial student may observe on all sides that very "ambition, rivalship, interest, humor, or caprice" which Washington attributed to Europe and ruled out of the American future.

No national assumption was more redolent of inconsistency than the concept of "manifest destiny" by which Americans increasingly justi-fied the process of continental imperialism. The diplomacy of expan-sion which began with the Jay Treaty in 1794 and continued until the annexation of Alaska in 1867 frequently required unsavory diplomacy in respect to whatever nation might stand in the way, be it England, France, Spain, Mexico, or indigenous American Indian tribes, but all was justified in the name of manifest destiny, a destiny symbol-ized by a screaming American eagle whose widespread wings overshad-owed those areas marked for conquest. Even as their public men enlarged upon the glories of American liberality toward other nations, their practical men refuted the oratory. If the injured raised questions about American methods, they soon learned that their tormentors firmly believed that what was good for America was equally good for them. They were forced to accept arguments which explained away the inconsistency between American words and American deeds by reference either to the inevitability or the benevolence of American expansion.

If carping Europeans continued their biting criticisms of New World theory and practice, the Americans became increasingly secure in their national myths and national ways. The nineteenth-century progress of the Republic was itself sufficient proof to negate those nay-sayers from across the sea who wondered increasingly whether the American republic was not going the way of previous experiments in official virtue. As the century ran its course, Americans were ever more firmly convinced that the policy not simply of political but also of spiritual separation from Europe was a fundamental prerequisite of national progress. Only rarely did shrewder observers recognize that American security and progress was a function not merely of national energy and competence but of historical accident—the existence of a remarkably stable European balance which insured against serious challenges to the course of the bumptious young republic. America enjoyed a remarkably protected childhood by comparison with most nations. It gained from the events of the Congress of Vienna and after what C. Vann Woodward has aptly called "free security." Much was conferred upon America by the onset of the nineteenth-century balance in Europe—much more than was conferred upon Europe by the United States. However inadvertant a gift, it was perhaps the most important of Europe's contributions to the well-being and improvement of American life.

* * *

If any particular evolution predominates in the history of American foreign relations during the nineteenth century, it is the growth of Anglo-American understanding. Despite the tradition of hatred for Great Britain stemming from the real or presumed abuses of the colonial era, the Revolution, and the abortive War of 1812, a number of compelling influences suggested from the very outset of national independence that both countries would benefit greatly from friendly relations. For the most part, American and English interests and aspirations were either complementary or noncompetitive. Both countries depended for security primarily on control of the seas. Each sought out and cultivated the other as a market for exports. Both were concerned with the preservation of the European balance of power because in the nature of things the disruption of that delicate equilibrium would normally militate against their national interests, conceived in both strategic and commercial terms. In competition with each other, the two nations would certainly create political opportunities for their enemies. In combination, they were formidable adversaries indeed because together they could dominate the Atlantic Ocean.

The outcome of this "natural alliance" during the years after the end of the stupid War of 1812 was a long and generally successful series of negotiations which eliminated numerous potential causes of Anglo-American controversy and created a tacit but nonetheless imposing Anglo-American understanding. Both countries found it to their advantage to seek accommodations through peaceful negotiation rather than warfare. If the association was hardly a love match, it was a profitable liaison of convenience. In the period 1815–1818 the two countries negotiated a series of "friendly conventions" which restored trade relations and demilitarized the Great Lakes area. In 1842 and 1846, by means of the Webster-Ashburton and Oregon negotiations, they settled a critical dispute over the location of the Canadian-American boundary. In these negotiations the interests of Canada were frequently sacrificed, but British ministers regularly deemed this outcome a reasonable price to pay for continuing American friendship. After the Civil War a dangerous Anglo-American dispute stemming from the depredations of a Confederate sea raider obtained in Britain, the *Alabama*, was successfully resolved by negotiation and arbitration. The same procedure settled an explosive controversy over the Venezuelan boundary near the end of the century.

In fact, the pervasive development and influence of the Anglo-American understanding across the nineteenth century suggests that even in its heyday the policy of isolation was largely a myth. However disguised or unacknowledged, the Anglo-American understanding was an entanglement of major utility to the United States, and it was equally advantageous to Great Britain. The consocation did not, of course, mean that the United States would come to the aid of Britain in troublous times, or that the British would lend assistance to the United States in the event of a war with a third power, but it did mean that neither would embarrass the other unduly in moments of danger. Even during the Civil War the British cabinet ultimately resisted the blandishments of the Confederacy, realizing in the end that its fundamental advantage lay in maintaining correct relations with the Union.

* * *

Throughout the nineteenth century until its very end the Americans gave far less attention to surrounding seas and adjacent continents —especially to the Caribbean-Latin American and Pacific-East Asian regions—than to their own continent. Preoccupied with geographic expansion and economic development in North America, they only grudgingly turned to other parts of the world. Nevertheless, strategic alarms sometimes drew their attention to the rest of the western hemisphere, and commercial ambitions on occasion attracted them to the Pacific Ocean. It remains true that the history of American activity in Latin America and East Asia as well as in surrounding waters during the nineteenth century is important not so much because of its impact at the time but rather because it laid the basis for an enlarged interest during the next century. The American overseas empire acquired at the conclusion of the century was, of course, located in just these areas; its addition represented the culmination of historical forces gathering strength quietly across the first hundred years of the national experience.

Americans early appreciated the importance of restricting external influence in the western hemisphere. European possessions provided bases for potential aggression against the United States as well as other American nations. The great independence movements sweeping across Latin America after 1810 speedily eliminated Spanish and Portuguese control of Latin America, much as the events of 1775 and after had vastly reduced the possessions of Great Britain to the north. Americans were generally pleased by the expulsion of Spain from most of Latin America because they recognized that their own security and influence in the hemisphere were vastly enhanced by the exclusion of powerful antagonists.

The Monroe Doctrine, announced in 1823, was in part a reaction to a specific policy situation, the possibility that the Quadruple Alliance might help Spain to recover its lost American empire, but it was also a response to larger considerations of national security and progress. When originally pronounced, the Doctrine had remarkably little influence on anybody. It was all but forgotten in a short time, only to experience several revivals until it became an article of national faith after the Civil War. Its initial significance resides in its enunciation of general principles as early as 1823 which slowly matured into enforceable national policy in accord with the later efflorescence of American power. Everyone now knows that the Doctrine shaped by John Quincy Adams and President James Monroe announced that the United States would oppose any further European colonization in the New World and would in return avoid involvement in European politics if American interests were not involved. As such it was a logical extension of the combined principles of isolation and neutrality, asking of Europe that it behave toward the United States as the United States proposed to behave toward Europe.

In addition to the noncolonization principle in the Doctrine, Monroe's statement also included a ringing reaffirmation of American democratic idealism. It not only pronounced against colonization but also against the importation of an alien "political system." The Doctrine was actually not a policy for Latin America so much as a policy for dealings with Europe in connection with hemispheric affairs. No intimation of the right of unilateral intervention in Latin-American countries was included in the original statement, nor was there a promise of assistance except when United States interests were threatened.

European powers ignored the Doctrine for much of the nineteenth century when it suited their convenience. France and Britain in particular were regular violators of its prohibitions. Britain annexed the Falkland Islands in the 1830s without American objections, and later expanded its influence along the Mosquito coast of Central America. The French and British together invaded the La Plata region in the period 1838–1850 without engendering a major American protest. During the Civil War Spain reannexed Santo Domingo and also intervened in Chile. As in the case of Napoleon's Mexican project, noncolonization was maintained more because of external developments than because of action by the United States. In addition, Latin Americans often opposed or ignored the pronouncement of 1823, suspecting that it was either valueless or dangerous to them.

By whatever device, the strategic position sought by the United States through the Monroe Doctrine remained relatively secure. If various European powers aspired to recolonize the western hemisphere, they were kept from doing so by numerous political realities aside from the opposition of the United States. To be sure, Great Britain in many ways could enforce the Monroe Doctrine. Its fleet effectively commanded the Atlantic Ocean and was fully capable of preventing any serious incursions in Latin America by continental powers. If Great Britain refrained from colonization, it was not because it lacked an interest in Latin America. That maritime nation rapidly displaced Spain as the principal trader to Latin America and almost monopolized its markets until the twentieth century with no serious challenge from the United States. Although in 1823 and at later points Americans revealed an interest in expanding their Latin-American commerce, economic opportunities of far greater importance and attractiveness lay much closer to home. Strategic rather than commercial concerns predominated in the minds of those who expounded "Monroeism" in 1823 and later, a circumstance which would not alter appreciably until 1889, when James G. Blaine inaugurated the modern Pan American system by proposing to create a hemispheric common market. Blaine's project was an effort to capture the Latin-American market for American business, but it quickly came to naught and nothing comparable to it has ever achieved acceptance.

The political stability prevailing in Europe and in the western world generally during the nineteenth century, combined with the political weakness of the Latin-American republics, insured that no serious threat to the United States would emanate from Latin America any more than from western Europe during the fruitful years of America's first century.

If America concerned itself with Latin America in order to insure its strategic position *vis-à-vis* Europe, its early activity in the Pacific and East Asia stemmed essentially from commercial considerations. Once the west coast had been added to the country by means of the Oregon Treaty of 1846 and the Treaty of Guadaloupe Hidalgo in 1848, the United States achieved a sound strategic footing with respect to the Orient—an "empire on the Pacific." The acquisition of the Pacific coast had been motivated largely by a desire to realize an old American dream—the dream of a great trade to the fabled East. Memories of the Old China Trade lay just behind a large number of American diplomatic enterprises in the Pacific-East Asian region, whether it was the negotiation of favorable commercial treaties with China in 1844 and 1858, the opening of Japan to western trade in 1853–1854, or the penetration of Korea in the late nineteenth century. The territorial acquisitions of the United States in the Pacific after the Civil War —Alaska, Midway Island, and Samoa—reflected a desire to perfect commercial communications with various regions in the western

Pacific rather than imperial aspirations. Strategic concerns, while manifest in the sporadic agitation for the annexation of the Hawaiian Islands, were distinctly subordinate to commercial concerns, if only because no measurable strategic danger to American security came from Asia until the twentieth century.

Despite continuing American interest in the trade of the Orient, the hoped-for commerce never materialized in any considerable volume. As in the case of Latin America, Europeans dominated the markets of the western Pacific. Nevertheless, the knowledge of the Pacific acquired during the nineteenth century did contribute to a growing involvement which provided a basis for a vastly expanded commitment at the very end of the nineteenth century.

* * *

The unparalleled success of the United States in its early years was not entirely a consequence of inner strength, but the Americans had good reason to boast of their national accomplishment as the nineteenth century passed its zenith. A remarkably favorable international situation was a considerable advantage, but those who guided the foreign policy of the young republic, like those who presided over its domestic affairs, did not fail to seize opportunities presented to them. Americans were up and doing, and they laid the foundations for even more imposing accomplishment. The American future seemed assured. Who would then dispute the claim that Uncle Sam was ten feet tall? The events of the latter part of the nineteenth century, especially after the conclusion of the Civil War, only confirmed the optimism of earlier years even as they solidified a number of pleasant but potentially dangerous national myths.

CHAPTER II

Intimations of Empire

DESPITE THE EFFORTS of certain historians in recent years to instruct them differently, most Americans persist in the illusion that the national experience in the nineteenth century was unique, a phenomenon largely if not entirely divorced from the experience of other peoples in the western world. Certainly the Civil War was a peculiarly searing national experience, easily the most far-reaching decision in our history. Its outcome confirmed the vision of national union inherent in the Constitution. But was it an entirely special experience? A brief look elsewhere suggests that it was not. Comparable outcomes proceeded in Europe from both the German and the Italian search for national unity. The establishment of the Dual Monarchy combining Austria and Hungary was a reflection of the tendency toward the establishment of consolidated nation-states throughout the western world. And even in the East, Japan moved in the same direction during the Meiji restoration.

Once past its greatest internal crisis, the United States threw itself vigorously into the associated processes of industrialization and urbanization, but similar trends were apparent in many other nations. The United States was not the only country to experience the phenomenon of industrial capitalism or the cultural revolution associated with the growth of great cities. Its supposed innovations in modern civilization found their analogues in many other societies, including the perfection of democratic governance. If the United States departed significantly from the pattern of most European powers in any striking way before the *fin de siècle*, it was in its refusal to contemplate projects of overseas expansion as a normal and natural aspect of national sovereignty and aggrandizement.

For some twenty years around midcentury there had been a burst of interest in overseas expansion, particularly into immediately adjacent seas. An expansionist movement called "Young America" attracted numerous followers, including a dynamic Senator from Illinois named Stephen A. Douglas. Young America aspired principally to assist the

13

cause of democracy wherever it needed help, but it was peculiarly dedicated to a series of expansionist projects, particularly in the Caribbean. More pragmatic organizations echoed its sentiments. The slave-smelling Democratic Party of the Fifties hoped to divert attention from the divisive issue of slavery extension by encouraging an interest in overseas adventures. Democratic Presidents one after another lent support to quixotic experiments in empire including the Ostend Manifesto of 1854 which called for the annexation of Cuba, the filibustering of William Walker in Central America, and an abortive attempt to acquire the Hawaiian Islands.

The trend continued for a time even after the Civil War. The first Republican Secretary of State, William H. Seward, strove mightily to accomplish at least some of the projects envisioned by his political antagonists in the Democratic Party before the war, but he succeeded only in purchasing Alaska from the Russians and in occupying Midway Island. In other aspirations, like the purchase of the Danish West Indies, his ambitions were dashed by a combination of overt opposition and general lack of interest. The failure of President U. S. Grant to seize Santo Domingo in 1871 marked the culmination of the early postwar turn away from expansionist projects in the Caribbean and the Pacific.

For a generation thereafter American involvement in international affairs reached its lowest point. Diplomatic historians, who naturally prefer periods of high activity, have given this period little attention until recent years. Textbooks quickly review the relatively dull diplomacy of the era between the settlement of the *Alabama* claims in the early 1870s and the Anglo-American controversy over the Venezuelan boundary dispute of 1895, hurrying on to the exciting events which precipitated the Spanish-American War. What accounts for this decrease in the intensity of American foreign relations, a trend symbolized by the declining importance of the Secretary of State in the President's cabinet?

The most obvious explanation lies in the preoccupation with economic expansion at home after the Civil War. The nation was active. The signal accomplishments of American industry at this time obscure the striking agricultural revolution of the same period. Great movements of people—whether from Europe to America, from the country to the city, or from the East to the West—absorbed the energies of millions. The construction of great transcontinental railroads from the Mississippi valley to the west coast was only the most eye-catching episode in a marvelous transportation revolution. Even more than before the Civil War domestic opportunities drew energies away from international affairs. Party platforms paid increasing obeisance to the isolationist formulas of the Founders and monotonously attributed national success to the nation's strict observance of those tenets, a trend reflective of a pervasive lack of interest in international activity.

Sometimes a nation must accept international obligations and involvements despite its desire, but the United States was a fortunate isle. As it happened, the "nadir" in American foreign relations coincided with a period of relative stability in Europe, a function of settlements following the Franco-Prussian War. The absence of international tension allowed the Americans to turn away from international politics as they desired. The Age of Imperialism was beginning, that noisome scramble for colonial fiefs in Africa and Asia which preoccupied the great powers of Europe in the years after 1870, but this development would hardly endanger the national interest of the United States unless it impinged on Latin America. In a very real way, the imperial enterprises of Europe in Africa and Asia enhanced American security in the short run because they tied down potential European rivals in distant tropic climes. Once again, European circumstances contributed significantly to the continuing success of nonentanglement theory. And so the Americans launched themselves into the Gilded Age, assiduously pursuing the national religion of the dollar, and easily dismissing international politics as of little or no account.

* * *

Ironically, the very domestic enterprises of such great concern to Americans during the generation after the Civil War ultimately contributed to the repudiation of isolation and neutrality as the cornerstones of American foreign policy. The enormous national growth of the period 1865–1900 rapidly lifted the United States into the ranks of the great powers. When a nation is a small power, or even a "middle power," it may pursue a policy of nonentanglement with some degree of success, perhaps even great success, as in the case of the United States during its first hundred years. But this is possible if, and only if, the general international setting permits it. Such was largely the case during the period 1815–1900. If the enormous reaches of the Atlantic and Pacific Oceans contributed importantly to the success of "no entangling alliances," the striking absence of major international instability during these years is the principal reason for the maintenance of American isolation and neutrality.

Small (or middle) powers may avoid undue international involvements under certain favorable circumstances, but it is impossible for great powers to follow this line. If they do so, it is usually at great peril. The reason is perfectly obvious. When a nation becomes "great," which is to say huge or important, what it does inevitably affects the lives and fortunes of many others, and what other nations do is of equal importance to it. This is not customarily the case with lesser powers, but there is no way out of this situation for those powers considered "great." With great-power capability and status comes unavoidable international involvement on a large scale. For great powers there is no real choice about whether to engage in extensive international operations. The only choice lies in the realm of who, what, where, when, and how. Because the United States rapidly acquired the capabilities of a great power during the latter years of the nineteenth century, it just as quickly lost that freedom to ignore international obligations and involvements to which it attributed so much national success.

Everybody talks about "great power," but few bother to define the term with any degree of precision. Just what is meant by "great-power capability?" What are the measures of power? To be considered a great power, a nation must normally possess certain attributes, at least in some degree, particularly a considerable and efficient population, a large and well-located homeland, a diversified and productive economy, and a stable but creative society and polity. By the 1890s the United States had acquired all these characteristics.

A large and efficient population provides the human resources for the manifold activities of a great power. In 1790, there were approximately four million Americans, but by 1890 a century of remarkable growth had increased the population of the United States to about 63,000,000. Among the established great powers of the time, only Russia with about 115,000,000 people surpassed the population of the United States. The American total compared favorably with those of Britain and France (about 40,000,000), Germany (47,000,000), and Italy (31,000,000). Of course, numbers are not enough by themselves to meet the requirements of power. Both China and India, more heavily populated than any of the great powers of the time, faced problems of illiteracy, disease, and poverty which deprived them of the degree of human ability demanded of peoples who would sustain great-power status. The Americans were not only great in numbers; they were also relatively efficient in comparison with the people of any other nation.

The United States by 1890 was larger in size than any other power except Russia, and it was peculiarly well located in terms of other great land-masses. Bounded on two sides by great oceans, at the north by sparsely settled Canada and the Arctic wastelands, and at the south by the relatively weak nations of Latin America, no great power could claim a more defensible homeland. The oceans provided desirable commercial connections to all the world, but they served as gigantic moats across which conquerors could hardly move with ease. The United States commanded the entire western hemisphere and was well located with respect to the great "world island" of Eurasia.

A statistical survey of the American economy by 1890 or so further confirms the pattern of power suggested by the most cursory study of demography and geography. Only Great Britain ranked with the United States as an industrial power and no nation surpassed American agriculture. The United States possessed an unparalleled store of natural resources, a mature system of transportation and communication, and efficient commercial and financial establishments. The wheat of the Middle West and the cotton of the South served world markets as well as those available at home. American iron and steel production, perhaps the most critical industrial index, surpassed all other nations, and New York was almost ready to challenge London as the leading commercial and financial center of the world. No country remotely approached the United States in railroad mileage or in the quantity and quality of its telephone, telegraph, and postal services.

Only in one respect did the United States lag behind the standards of the great powers. Its military establishment was smaller and less well equipped than those of a large number of other countries. The armed services had grown in strength and efficiency across the nineteenth century, but the long era of "free security" had worked against a special emphasis on military and naval power. Nevertheless, the American wars of the nineteenth century, occurring about once in each generation, had tended to revitalize soldierdom and sailordom after periods of declining efficiency. It should not be forgotten that the Civil War was the greatest of military conflicts between the Napoleonic Wars and World War I. During the 1880s the inadequacies of the American navy had created some concern, and an active program of modernization and construction had produced a small but active fleet, one vessel of which was the shining battleship *Maine*. The army remained small, numbering hardly more than about 28,000 regulars at the beginning of the Spanish-American War, although it included a number of intrepid young officers like John J. Pershing. But if the forces in being were relatively inconsequential by comparison with most of the other great powers, other nations realized that the United States was indeed a military power to be contended with because its tremendous latent strength could be mobilized rapidly in the face of an external challenge.

Finally, the United States benefitted immeasurably from its unusually stable but nevertheless dynamic political and social systems. The Civil War had decided the great political question of the century—the tension between the principles of national supremacy and states' rights. The horrible war had at least brought about a remarkable political consensus. If American elections were frequently lively, it was not because they were contested over strikingly divisive issues. European observers like Lord Bryce unanimously marveled at the lack of clear distinctions between the great national parties, a sure sign of unusual national unity. Although the nation encountered a series of novel and distressing social issues associated with the rise of a unique urban-industrial civilization, these by no means approached critical intensity—certainly not the intensity characteristic of the "social question" in most European countries. Thoughts of revolution were unheard of in America. Despite unusual political stability, the degree of economic and social opportunity extant in nineteenth-century America contributed to the maintenance of a notable national dynamism. Americans remained startlingly creative in social and political as well as in technological and entrepreneurial contexts. The country was both secure and energetic, surely in this respect the equal or better of any other around the world.

All of these capabilities became apparent at breath-taking speed in the latter years of the Victorian era. They came into being so rapidly that they were present to the senses well before Americans generally recognized them for what they were—a proof of America's ability to assume the roles and functions of a great power. It could be only a matter of time before the nation moved onto the world stage—before it entered fully into world history. Once possessed of those capabilities which made it a great power, an indisputable reality by the 1890s, the nation could no longer hope to maintain the luxury of diplomatic isolation and neutrality. It would shortly be required to decide among the various political options open to the great powers of the time, any one of which required a measurable degree of international entanglement, certainly far more than the nation had as yet accepted. Extensive engagement in world politics is an immutable concomitant of great-power capability and status. Shortly the Americans would be required to discard old traditions and to elaborate new policies in accordance with their changed circumstances.

* * *

One of the possible options open to the United States—one of the ways by which it might conceivably make its presence known among the great powers—was to launch itself upon a career of overseas expansion. Some precedent existed upon which to build, especially the midcentury flurry of activity in both the Caribbean and the Pacific.

Contemporary European activity in Africa and Asia provided a further model and stimulus. Perhaps also the "official" closing of the American frontier by the census-takers of 1890 had its impact on imaginations seeking new worlds to conquer. At any rate, even before the nation had fully acquired the attributes of a great power, a small but talented group of opinion leaders across the country undertook to agitate for overseas expansion. Diverse in backgrounds, commitments, and expectations, this "imperial cadre"—for that was what it was, a putative leadership echelon for empire—undertook to sell the country on overseas expansion. This is not to say that the group was carefully organized, fully conscious of its purpose, or conspiratorial in nature. However, its enterprises, whether cooperative or individual, constituted a burgeoning propaganda for imperial adventure.

The leading members of the imperial cadre usually represented specific interest groups, but their collective voice was what the ordinary citizen heard as it was refracted through the various mass media of the day, especially the public print and the podium. The newspaper, the journal of opinion, the public oration, and the sermon, all these vehicles offered themselves to energetic salesmen of expansion. Some, like the liberal clergyman Josiah Strong, utilized all of these possibilities and more. At the outset of its campaign, the imperial cadre often encountered indifference and opposition, but as time passed and America approached great-power capability, its message became more insistent and more frequently heard. It appears that the contest between imperialists and anti-imperialists was entered by relatively small numbers, but they were an enormously influential element. Even in the most imposing debate, a few contribute while the many listen. If the audience did not fully comprehend what it heard, it was being stirred by the same forces which moved the imperial cadre. By 1898 the people had been thoroughly exposed to a wide variety of arguments in behalf of empire.

Among the most influential and enterprising members of the imperial cadre was a vigorous naval officer named Alfred Thayer Mahan, an intellectual anomaly in a notoriously thick-headed service, whose numerous writings provided a cogent body of strategic arguments in behalf of an imperial enterprise. Navalists like Mahan believed that the nation must acquire a series of insular possessions in surrounding seas in order to provide bases to protect the American shore and also to support a fleet capable of protecting an expanded American commerce on the high seas. In this connection they contemplated the prospect of annexing Hawaii and various Caribbean isles. They were especially interested in the construction of an interoceanic canal under American control across the Central American isthmus in order to shorten maritime communications. Associated with these beliefs was the feeling that the traditional defensive concept of naval strategy entertained by most Americans since colonial times was outmoded. A great fleet capable of attacking other fleets could, of course, exert much broader influence than one designed primarily to guard the approaches to the western hemisphere.

The arguments of Mahan and others attracted a talented group of supporters, including well-placed politicians like Henry Cabot Lodge and Theodore Roosevelt, who were constantly in the public eye and never averse to instructing the nation in what came to be known as the "large policy"—a policy of energetic national aggrandizement including empire. The strategic arguments of Mahan's school proved especially compelling because they played on the fears of the populace while at the same time obfuscating the question of whether the acquisition of empire was at variance with traditional American democratic values. Those who advanced strategic arguments for empire could justify their position on the high ground of "national interest," to which all other considerations must remain subordinate. Their definitions of national interest, of course, did not always correspond with those of their critics, but nice distinctions of this sort rarely attract much attention.

Another customary justification for empire was a commercial argument—the claim that empire was essential to the economy in general and an expansion of overseas commerce in particular. Many Americans were obsessed with the pace and variety of the nation's economic development, and they had begun to wonder whether production might not outrun the market, thus precipitating serious recessions. Others wondered where they would secure raw materials to feed into the mighty maw of American industry, once the rape of the American bounty was completed. Still others desired protected investment opportunities in order to make use of excess capital acquired in domestic business operations. Less frequently heard was an especially chilling claim that social unrest at home might follow in the wake of economic stagnation. Observing the course of European imperial activities, the proponents of a commercial rationale for empire argued that colonial powers universally excluded economic competitors from their domains. The United States might find itself with no overseas outlets for trade unless it acquired its own empire and did to others as they did unto American traders.

And then there was also the political argument for empire that the United States must acquire overseas possessions if it wished to husband its present power. No argument was more imposing than the claim of the imperial cadre that nations must expand or die. This claim, supported by the contemporary popularity of a spurious philosophical analogy from Darwinian biology (that body of theory known as social Darwinism), was easily grasped and devastating in impact. The slogan of expansion or death held forth the promise of achievement through action; quiescence seemed to foreshadow degradation. If power resided in continuing geographic expansion, and the only places to grow lay across broad oceans, then why waste time? The race for the remaining imperial plums was already on; the United States must move rapidly if it wished to preserve its future.

Despite the cogency of this triad of arguments—strategic, economic, and political—they were without a peculiar kind of attractiveness; they lacked ethical or moral appeal. Americans, in common with most other peoples, like to feel that what they do is not simply expediential but also "good." Many who might reject "realistic" arguments would respond to moralistic appeals. To meet this demand the imperial cadre developed a second triad of justifications for expansion which perhaps made a stronger impression on the general audience than more calculating blandishments. Propagandists settled particularly on racial, religious, and ideological appeals to the highminded in their audience.

The racial argument depended on the view that the "inferior" or "dark" races of the world desperately required the advice and counsel of lighter, "superior" racial stocks, particularly the white Anglo-Saxons of western Europe. Supported by the impressive credentials of social Darwinists like Herbert Spencer and John Fiske, the exciting call to "take up the white man's burden" hit at the national vanity of Americans, even as it appealed to their passion for uplift. Perhaps, also, the contemplation of the white man's burden offered surcease from a nagging feeling of guilt, a consequence of the nation's persecution not only of the Negro but also of the Indian. Few proponents of empire failed to cite the necessity of educating the "backward peoples" of the world in Anglo-Saxon ideas and ideals as a service to civilization.

Another appeal of an ethical character hit at the formal religiousity of the country—the national assumption that Americans were a profoundly religious people. Of course, American religion was pervasively Protestant at the time; the Catholics and Jews were yet to have a truly important impact. The national conviction was that Protestantism was the truly "spiritual" branch of Christianity, superior to all other faiths, Christian or otherwise. Was not the world waiting for the sunshine? If "spiritual" Christianity possessed the qualities attributed to it by Americans, then what was more logical than to assume that the faith should be at once propagated far and wide? Not a few churchmen recognized the pitiful accomplishment of the energetic but unsuccessful missionary enterprises to which Americans had lent enthusiastic support throughout the century. Would not the dominion of Christ be more rapidly expanded under the aegis of Christian imperialists? American pulpits fairly rang with such arguments in the late Victorian Age; no institution lent more dignity to the cause of empire than the little church across the square where empire builders in clerical collars acted out imperial fantasies on warm Sunday mornings in May.

A final appeal catered to the universal faith in the efficacy of American democracy. Americans had long since convinced themselves that their government was the final, perfect form of political philosophy and practice. Much too facilely, perhaps, their scholars and publicists gave all credit for national success to the workings of democratic institutions proliferated at all levels of government. If democracy had worked so well in America, would it not be equally beneficent elsewhere? Democracy would follow the flag, serving as ideological manure. If spread sufficiently around the empire, liberty and justice (under God) would spring up all over the place. An American empire would differ from all others because it would be tutored in the sacred democratic texts of Washington, Jefferson, Jackson, and Lincoln.

No one at the time suggested that the imperial cadre ultimately achieved its objective not because their arguments had great force, imposing as they were, but because the idea of empire might well have catered to that elemental tendency to atavism which some argue is inherent in the race. Perhaps the most attractive appeal of empire was that it presented an opportunity to "civilize 'em with a Krag." Civilization confers untold benefits upon mankind, but it also tends to preclude certain antisocial urges, sadistic in nature, which seem to affect everyone. If unacceptable in polite society, these urges must find expression in covert ways. Could it have been that forbidden impulses expressed themselves during the 1880s and 1890s through the project of imposing the national will on less powerful peoples incapable of effective resistance? How better to find "a place in the sun" and at the same time cater to inner sadism than to place a boot on the throat of a benighted heathen on some tropic isle? Who could imagine a better way to accomplish "good" and also get one's thrills than to eviscerate the cruel Spaniard, symbol of all that was decadent in the Old World?

The imperial cadre cogently presented its multiple case for expansion to a populace which would have been astounded at the thought that what it conceived as the work of civilization was in fact a manifestation of a most primitive prehistoric heritage. If America seemed still to slumber in the 1890s—if the imperial cadre at times despaired of success—Americans were quietly listening. Events were soon to play into the hands of those who had striven for so long to elicit a responsive chord from the general public.

*   *   *

In 1893 a serious economic downturn overwhelmed the country, and all concern, at least for a season, turned inward on the ensuing Panic. Interest in expansion naturally declined in that moment of domestic disaster. These were the years of "Gold Bugs" and "Pops," of Coxey and Hanna, and above all of McKinley and Bryan—years of imposing national division and debate. But if the Panic temporarily sidetracked expansionist sentiment, it ultimately stimulated a new kind of jingoism. Many intelligent souls of all political persuasions sensed in the turmoil of the times the possibility, unthinkable before, of political and social upheaval dangerous to the established order of things. This prospect was, of course, most alarming to those minions who dealt in the currency of the status quo. Shrewd politicos knew well that nothing vitiates internal dissension like external dangers, real or presumed. Had not the redoubtable Seward proposed a foreign war in 1861 to head off civil conflict on the assumption that conflict with England would provide a cause to which all Americans could repair? There were those who were willing to lend their support to any enterprise which might still social protest. To some advanced "expedientials," even war was preferable to Bryan.

America had become increasingly bumptious during a decade or so before the Panic of 1893. This tendency was in part a manifestation of repressed inferiority feelings concerning Europe which had long oppressed the people. The baiting of European nations, especially England, was nothing new. Twisting the lion's tail, after all, was an ancient and honorable American sport. But there was something original in the new bumptiousness. It reflected a desire to use America's newfound power. In 1895 Secretary of State Richard Olney had occasion to inform the British Empire in no uncertain terms that it must adhere strictly to the terms of the Monroe Doctrine, particularly in connection with a dispute between England and Venezuela over the location of the British Guiana-Venezuela border. Olney informed Lord Salisbury that America's will was fiat in the New World. Despite his deplorable manners, Olney's claim was close to the truth; America's tacit dependence on Britain was at an end. In the future, Britain would depend increasingly on assistance from the United States, a fact poignantly brought home when Salisbury ultimately agreed to America's demand that the Venezuelan boundary dispute be submitted to arbitration. In one fell swoop Olney both summarized and expanded the Monroe Doctrine. The Venezuelan dispute was suffused with portent for the future. It was an appropriate prelude to the events which culminated in the explosion of 1898, that fateful decision for empire which launched the nation on its career as a great power.

In 1895 a revolution against Spain once again broke out in Cuba. Cubans had rebelled before, notably during the period 1868–1878, but few Americans had paid much attention. The insurrection of 1895 was something else again. Of course, the great mass circulation press headed by William Randolph Hearst and Joseph Pulitzer had not been active during the earlier excitement. It is also true that American investments in Cuba were neither as extensive nor as threatened in 1868 as in 1895 and after. Interest in an interoceanic canal had not been as rife in earlier years. And yet, these differences hardly account for the fervor with which the American people of all political persuasions quite generally embraced the cause of the Cuban *insurrectos.*

Of course, many conservative politicians had long been proponents of expansion and, like Senator Lodge, had often urged the adoption of a "large" foreign policy. More surprising was the chorus of liberal support for an intervention in behalf of the Cubans. Many fine humanitarian instincts had been frustrated in the 1890s. Domestic reform, whether urban or rural, had come a cropper as of 1896. The "first battle" of William Jennings Bryan had been lost, and the reformers who had gained inspiration from the "battle of the standards" suddenly found themselves without a cause, their enemies once again firmly in power. The plight of the Cubans offered an outlet for aspirations unfulfilled at home. For widely divergent reasons, then, conservatives and liberals could join hands in support of *Cuba libre.* The destruction of Spanish power in the Caribbean attracted conservative interest. The elimination of Spanish oppression had a comparable appeal to frustrated domestic reformers, hopeful of accomplishing for Cuba what they had failed to gain for disadvantaged groups in the United States.

But no amount of expediential or humanitarian motivation can account fully for the outburst of 1898; it can be understood sufficiently only if the new-found power of the United States is taken into account. That power, latent, must find expression, and an opportunity presented itself in Cuba. If the Americans were disingenuous, they were hardly unique in disguising less than noble aspirations in the mantle of a humanitarian endeavor. The imperial alternative had been shouted across the land by a generation of skilled molders of opinion. How easy to respond to that call if it became a great crusade.

First Cleveland and then his successor McKinley called for Spanish reforms to relieve the hard lot of the Cubans, especially in the wake of the reconcentration policy developed by the Spanish General Weyler. The Spanish might well have preserved their control of Cuba for awhile had they offered major concessions to the Cuban revolutionaries at the proper time, but the shaky Spanish monarchy was in great difficulties at home. The government could not contemplate a massive retreat in the face of combined Cuban and American pressure because craven surrender might topple the dynasty.

By 1898 the situation had become critical. Spain hoped to counter growing American insistence on action by obtaining pledges of assistance from European powers, but although many expressed sympathy none was willing either to affront the United States or to endanger its European standing by committing some of its power to the support of Spain in the western hemisphere. The European balance, stable for many years, was beginning to fall apart, and in these circumstances individual nations were prone to look to their own interests. Spain was caught on the horns of an insoluble dilemma; it could neither propitiate the Cuban rebels nor accumulate sufficient support to deter American intervention.

If the general public in the United States increasingly called for stern measures, their leaders were quite circumspect. The ponderous Cleveland did not want war. He sought to avoid intervention, but a rising tide of opinion forced him to indicate with increasing vigor to Spain that American forbearance could not continue indefinitely. His successor, the cautious McKinley, also adopted a policy of restraint but was swept inexorably along by a growing tide of public emotion. As the circle narrowed, the likelihood of provocative incidents increased, and in due course they occurred — most dramatically the sinking of the battleship *Maine* in Havana harbor by causes still unknown.

McKinley haltingly came to the crossroads. In March and April Spain refused to accept an American ultimatum, the key provision of which was a requirement of Cuban freedom, the one thing no Spanish government could voluntarily accept. McKinley's war message allowed Congress to vote for war in April 1898 but not before including in the war resolution a self-denying ordinance — the Teller Amendment. In it the United States foreswore any intention to annex Cuba. Spain resignedly accepted the challenge, determined to preserve the national honor by offering at least token defense of its Caribbean possessions which included Puerto Rico as well as Cuba.

The Spanish-American conflict, that "splendid little war" of 1898, began of all places in the Far East. Admiral George Dewey, commanding a modest flotilla of American ships, sailed into Manila Bay, the principal port of the Spanish-held Philippine Islands, and sank a

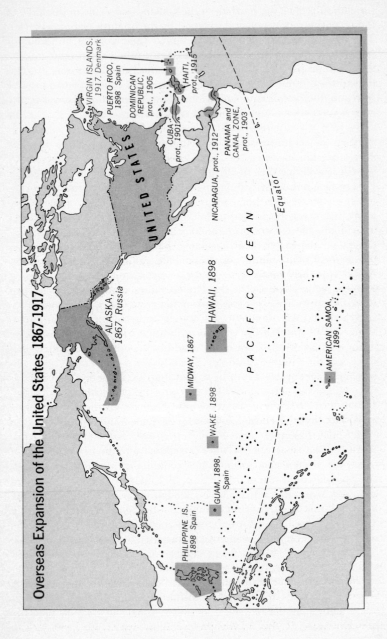

Overseas Expansion of the United States 1867-1917

VIRGIN ISLANDS, 1917, Denmark

PUERTO RICO, 1898, Spain

DOMINICAN REPUBLIC, prot., 1905

HAITI, prot., 1915

CUBA, prot., 1901

NICARAGUA, prot., 1912

PANAMA and CANAL ZONE, prot., 1903

UNITED STATES

ALASKA, 1867, Russia

MIDWAY, 1867

HAWAII, 1898

WAKE, 1898

GUAM, 1898, Spain

PHILIPPINE IS., 1898 Spain

AMERICAN SAMOA, 1899

PACIFIC OCEAN

Equator

miserable little collection of Spanish ships in order to prevent them from sailing across the Pacific to the war zone in the Caribbean. Here was a romantic achievement indeed. Dewey was the man of the hour, but he was temporarily at a loss to do anything about his naval victory because he lacked sufficient troops to occupy the islands. He had to be content for the moment to cooperate with Filipino insurrectionists who, like their Cuban counterparts, hoped for independence and welcomed American assistance in freeing themselves from Spanish control. Quite soon, McKinley authorized the dispatch of land forces in order to occupy the main island of Luzon, a decision which could hardly have been motivated by a desire to insure the independence of the Philippines.

A second major development of the war in the Pacific was the annexation of the Hawaiian Islands by joint resolution of the Congress. This device circumvented the constitutional provision for the acceptance of treaties which required a two-thirds vote in the Senate. This action culminated fifty years of interest in the strategically situated islands, a half-century during which American planters and other business interests had gained a predominant influence in the local government and had developed an increasing desire for annexation by the homeland. Only a half-dozen years before the annexation of 1898, a little *coup,* aided by the American minister in residence, had unseated the old Hawaiian monarchy and installed a planter-dominated republic. The revolutionary regime immediately signed a treaty of annexation with the United States, but President Cleveland objected to the irregular proceedings which had accompanied the overthrow of Queen Lilioukalani and withdrew the treaty from the Senate. Hostilities with Spain renewed the project. The annexation of 1898 was justified largely as an emergency war measure, but it derived from many years of agitation.

The achievements of 1898 in the Pacific were now complete; the American flag flew proudly over the Hawaiians, the Philippines, and the little island of Guam. The dream of a century past was suddenly realized; a complete line of communications now linked the American west coast with the fabled ports of the Orient. To such ends was the heady idealism of April turned in a few short months. A war which had begun as a high-minded crusade for Cuban freedom was rapidly converted into an excuse for an extraordinary imperial grab in regions far removed from the principal theater of war.

While these events took place, an American army laboriously formed in Florida and a naval blockade sealed off Cuba. A Spanish naval squadron, outmanned and outgunned, managed to slip into the port of Santiago, only to find itself hopelessly bottled up. Late in June an American force straggled ashore near Santiago, and after a few skirmishes took the city, from whence the Spanish vessels had fled on July 3rd only to be destroyed by the blockading squadron of the United States. Puerto Rico also fell to an American army; a "moonlight excursion" to that island encountered little or no resistance. Only 379 troops perished as direct result of combat injuries in all theaters of the Spanish War, although truly monumental incompetence in both the army and navy contributed to a gruesome toll of over 5000 additional deaths from other causes, particularly tropical disease.

Spanish honor having been satisfied, the French ambassador in Washington was able to arrange a truce on August 12th; the sordid little struggle was at an end. The armistice provided for Cuban independence and the annexation of Puerto Rico and an island in the Ladrones (ultimately Guam) by the United States. Fortunately, Senator Teller had mentioned only Cuba in his self-denying ordinance. In autumn a peace conference convened in Paris. The only issue of substance before the peacemakers was the disposition of the Philippine Islands.

President McKinley, congenitally cautious, found it difficult to decide whether the United States should annex the far-off archipelago. Characteristically, he backed and filled on the issue but finally settled his mind by the time-honored device of putting his ear to the ground. A speaking tour into the West convinced him that the American people wished to annex the islands, not just Luzon as some had proposed but the entire group. McKinley himself had claimed that he could not have come within two thousand miles of locating the islands on a globe when they were first attacked by Dewey, but, in common with many other Americans, his geography had improved considerably by the fall of 1898. The smell of empire was deep in the nostrils of the President and the people.

The outcome of the war suggests that conquest was what America had wanted all the time, even if it had deceived itself that it had gone to war for entirely altruistic motives—to secure freedom for Cuba. McKinley later claimed that divine instruction had come to him while deep in prayer at the White House, ordering the annexation of the Philippines, but he took into account a number of mundane motives as well. The commercial benefits were obvious. So was the likelihood that if the United States did not take the islands, they would be absorbed by an imperial power, probably Germany, or perhaps even Japan. Therefore on December 10, 1898, the peace commissioners in Paris signed a treaty which ceded the Philippines in entirety to the United States, a bitter pill for Spain which was sweetened a bit by a cash payment of $20 million.

One task remained; the Senate must give its consent to the treaty. If its presentation to the Senate precipitated an acrimonious debate, the outcome was a foregone conclusion. To be sure, an organization born in New England, the Anti-Imperialist League (which rapidly established branches elsewhere in the country), made a gallant fight of it. Opponents of empire like Senator George Frisbie Hoar of Massachusetts relied primarily on basic constitutional arguments. They claimed that America was founded on the principle of consent of the governed, and that the Filipinos should have the right to choose their own governance. The annexation of the Philippines ignored the obvious fact that the Filipinos themselves, led by the patriot Aguinaldo, had every desire to establish their independence. Aguinaldo's army became increasingly restless as American forces established control of the Islands. The anti-imperialists asked how the Americans could violate the very principles which had presumably justified their intervention in Cuba a few short months before. To support the constitutional case against annexation, the anti-imperialists offered a series of additional arguments. Certain purists argued that annexation was inconsistent with the Monroe Doctrine. Southern racists were concerned about the color of many Puerto Ricans and Filipinos. Only a few noted the strategic problems created by the acquisition of territory many thousands of miles away from the American shore.

However valid these arguments, they were easily overwhelmed by full-throated expansionist orators like Senator Albert Beveridge of Indiana, whose famous speech entitled "The March of the Flag" rang the changes on every conceivable argument for annexation including the old canard of "manifest destiny." Constitutional quibbles did not sway the Senate. William Jennings Bryan, erstwhile aspirant to a second defeat at the hands of McKinley in the forthcoming election, might have seriously embarrassed expansionists by making a strong fight against the treaty, but he choose to refuse battle. Was he hoping by this device to create a popular issue on which to wage the campaign of 1900? In any case, enough opponents of the administration in the Senate voted with the majority to guarantee consent by a vote of 57 to 27. Had one vote changed, the treaty would have failed, but a new Senate was about to be seated in which the Republican gains in the midterm elections of 1898 would have asserted themselves, so the victory was more decisive than the vote seemed to indicate. Just before the final ballot, news arrived that Aguinaldo had taken the field against his liberators, a challenge which may have influenced the behavior of some Senators.

The Philippine insurrection turned into a much longer, bloodier, and costlier struggle than the Spanish-American War itself. Aguinaldo's guerilla tactics proved difficult to counteract. Some 70,000 troops required over three years to break the back of Filipino resistance. All the elements of irony were present in this inglorious scene. Not a few foreign observers pointed out that American methods in the Philippines were starkly reminiscent of those attempted by Spain in Cuba before 1898. All that defenders of the McKinley policy could do to circumvent this particular criticism was to remind the country that consistency, after all, was the vice of small minds.

* * *

For better or worse, the United States had leaped upon the world scene by the simple device of wresting away from Spain that nation's imperial possessions in the Caribbean and the western Pacific. Cuba attained its independence, or so it appeared, and therefore the original purpose of the intervention had been achieved, but much more was accomplished. Opponents of the imperial grab ignored a crucial reality. The old foreign policies were dead beyond recall; the nation had outgrown them. To the extent that opponents of the "large policy" refused to take into account the changed circumstances of the United States—its acquisition of great-power capability and status— they were open to the accusation of irrelevance. America could no longer play the role of sleeping giant; its newfound power had awakened the nation. The anti-imperialists developed no real alternative to the expansionist projects of 1898, and this failure insured their defeat. Very soon, opponents of empire did discern a possible new role for the Republic in the affairs of the world as an alternative to imperialism. The United States, they argued, might instead become an exponent of international cooperation rather than conquest, of peaceful negotiation of differences rather than decision by the sword. These ideas, heard broadly once before in the land during the Age of Jackson, were widely disseminated on the occasion of the first Hague Peace Conference held in 1899, but for the moment the nation was committed to working out its imperial ambition. Imperialism was hardly all play and no work. The American people would soon discover that empire was fraught with all manner of dangers and embarrassments, but time was needed to make this discovery.

For the moment, then, the nation experienced an imperial interlude. That interlude came at a time of massive change both in Europe and Asia. Across the Atlantic, the balance of power was undergoing a test that it ultimately failed, and beyond the wide Pacific the ancient kingdom of China was on the verge of revolution, creating opportunities for aggrandizement by imperial Japan, now ready to assert its modernity through expansionist enterprises on the Asiatic mainland. In short, the circumstance which had so favored the growth of the United States during the nineteenth century—the absence of political dangers to the western hemisphere from either end of Eurasia—was about to alter. However unwittingly, the American pursuit of empire in the Caribbean and the Pacific at the outset of the new century contributed to the onset of cataclysmic conflict in western Europe and in eastern Asia within a generation—the beginning of that pattern of uncontrolled violence which is the principal hallmark of world history since about 1900.

CHAPTER III

Imperial Interlude

ABOUT 1900 OR SO, Europe entered into a series of striking re-alignments, responding to a growing imbalance of power which portended another dreadful season of warfare. At the crux of the difficulty was Wilhelmine Germany, dissatisfied with its position in Central Europe and hopeful of further national aggrandizement. Diplomats once again confronted the possibility of a new threat to the liberties of Europe. Throughout the nineteenth century, the British had successfully "held the European balance," avoiding permanent continental alliances. Their policy of "splendid isolation" from the great European land powers had been perhaps the most important factor in maintaining continental stability. By the turn of the century this tradition had become bankrupt. With Germany on the advance, Britain launched upon a search for supportive alliances and under-standings in order to restore its security. Some British statesmen inclined to the so-called "natural alliance" with Germany, but this option proved unavailable. Concerned also about Asian pressure exerted by Russia, their traditional diplomatic antagonist, the British contracted an alliance with Japan in 1902. In 1904 they inaugurated a new European policy, increasingly directed against Germany, by negotiating the *Entente Cordiale* with France. Three years later, Britain arranged an accord with Russia, no longer an immediate threat to colonial interests in Asia because of its defeat by Japan in 1905 and revolutionary disturbances at home during the same year.

Thus was forged the "Triple Entente"; Britain, France, and Russia were now aligned in a loose coalition against that group of interior powers in Europe known as the "Triple Alliance" — Germany, Austria-Hungary, and Italy. After 1907 the two coalitions entered upon a collision course. No great power remained to hold the balance after Britain abandoned that role. If the Triple Alliance complained of "encirclement" by the exterior coalition, the latter was increasingly convinced that Germany and its friends were bent on aggression. Events after 1907 — particularly the second Moroccan crisis, a series of

Balkan wars, and a massive armaments race—constantly increased the likelihood of a dramatic passage at arms.

Developments across the Atlantic vastly affected the United States, although few Americans at the time grasped their significance for the Republic. The continental crisis precluded European interference with the Latin-American projects of the United States in the wake of the Spanish war. There the United States set out to establish preponderance—a polite word for hegemony—to which the countries of Latin America could offer no extensive resistance. The European situation also forced those nations with measurable commitments in the Far East—particularly Britain, France, Germany, and Russia—to withdraw much of their power from that region. As Japan began its aggressions in East Asia, the United States found itself largely alone as China's champion, a responsibility it had hardly anticipated in 1898.

However distasteful to Americans, difficulties in East Asia could be endured as long as Europe remained at peace, but a final confrontation between the Triple Alliance and the Triple Entente was in the making. If some American observers like the shrewd Lewis Einstein realized that Europe was verging on war, most persisted in the illusion that the United States could ride out the storm by merely adhering to its traditional policies of isolation and neutrality. However, events dissipated this convenient but entirely fallacious assumption. The Americans forgot that God helps those who help themselves. The world soon precipitated itself into a cycle of violence which profoundly altered the direction of world history; it also vastly affected the course of national development in the United States.

None of this was readily apparent in those halcyon years immediately succeeding the Spanish-American War, when the United States blithely undertook to consolidate its late imperial conquest. In 1900, Billy Bryan made a "second battle" for the Presidency, hoping to ride into office on the wings of an anti-imperialistic reaction. The outcome assuredly demonstrated the futility of this strategy. McKinley campaigned on "the full dinner pail," and the boy orator of the Platte found no effective antidote. Voters responded to the general economic recovery of the day and to the national self-congratulation over the victories of '98. If the election was no mandate for additional overseas expansion, it erected no barriers against exploitation of the empire in being.

As it happened, McKinley did not long survive re-election. He was cut down by an anarchist bullet in Buffalo in 1901. His successor was none other than perhaps the most enterprising member of that imperial cadre which had agitated so extensively for empire before 1898. Theodore Roosevelt's storied charge up San Juan Hill had confirmed his image as an exponent of the "strenuous life" — "manly" resolve and "virile" deeds. His Presidency did nothing to dissipate his reputation for action. If sometimes he appeared to be "about six years old," as alleged by one of his European friends, he was most of the time a shrewd, calculating executive whose years in the White House were characterized more by caution than swagger. Chance had placed in power a spirit particularly concerned with the American empire, and he did not fail to maximize the opportunities presented to him.

* * *

Even before Roosevelt assumed office, the United States had begun to repudiate its pledges of 1898 to Cuba. An army of occupation remained in the Pearl of the Antilles, commanded by General Leonard Wood. If it cleaned up the island and built some nice little schools, it also confirmed America's influence. Cuba had long intrigued American statesmen because it lay athwart lines of communication from the eastern seaboard to the west coast and commanded much of the maritime access to Central America. To insure that Cuba would present no future difficulties to the United States, a gifted secretary of war, the influential Elihu Root, in 1901 helped to compose the Platt amendment (named after its senatorial sponsor, Orville Platt of Connecticut). The document seriously compromised Cuba's sovereignty. Among other things it gave the United States control of the island's foreign relations, a right of unilateral intervention to combat domestic discord, and a lease on the strategic harbor of Guantanamo bay. The Cubans hardly courted these obligations, but they soon discovered that withdrawal of American troops was contingent upon their acceptance. The United States had imposed a virtual protectorate upon the new nation; in so doing it violated the letter and the spirit of the Teller amendment.

The Cuban protectorate was part of a general preparation for the construction of an interoceanic canal across the Central American isthmus. At the same time Roosevelt sought to purchase the Danish West Indies, but the plan misfired when the legislature of Denmark (under German pressure) refused the bargain. This set back did not deter T.R., who was anxious to proceed rapidly. The United States had just succeeded in abrogating restrictive clauses in the ancient Clayton-Bulwer treaty of 1850 with Great Britain, which had obligated the signatories to cooperate with each other in the construction of any future isthmian canal. The Hay-Pauncefote Treaty of 1901 authorized exclusive American development of an interoceanic connection. After much disputation among proponents of rival routes across Central

America, T.R. attempted to obtain a lease across the Panama, the northern province of Colombia. Secretary of State John Hay duly negotiated an agreement which granted the necessary concession. Much to Roosevelt's disgust, the Colombian Senate proved refractory, perhaps hoping to hold up the United States for more money. The Hay-Herran Treaty of 1903 was rejected unanimously in its chambers.

Never one to hesitate when his duty was clear, Roosevelt indirectly implicated himself in a plot by Panamanian revolutionaries to obtain independence from Colombia. The resourceful Philippe Bunau-Varilla, chief engineer of the defunct New Panama Canal Company which had failed in an attempt to build a canal during the 1880s, hoped to peddle the remaining assets of his firm to the United States for $40 million. He provided liaison between the Panamanian revolutionaries and T.R. Early in November 1903, the revolution took place, and American naval vessels conveniently prevented Colombian troops from putting it down. Only four days after the revolution, the United States extended *de facto* recognition. A week later Roosevelt received the first Panamanian minister, none other than the French national Bunau-Varilla, who promptly negotiated a treaty giving the United States its desired rights and privileges. In 1911, T.R. incautiously trumpeted: "I took Panama and let Congress debate." No more accurate description of his course has yet been written. However unorthodox, his policy realized a dream of centuries, a canal across Darien, and it also added a second quasi-protectorate to the American collection in the Caribbean.

Despite his success in Panama, Roosevelt was worried. He had just emerged from a disturbing encounter with a number of European powers, including Britain and Germany, who attempted in 1902 to collect some defaulted debts owed to them by Venezuela. Roosevelt resolved the second Venezuelan crisis by arranging an arbitration before the Hague tribunal, but he remained fearful that future Caribbean defalcations might provide a convenient pretext for European violations of the Monroe Doctrine. He had determined to make the Caribbean an American lake; its control was essential to the defense of the Panama Canal. These considerations preceded a fateful extension of Monroeism—the Roosevelt Corollary. In 1904 the President included a remarkable passage in his annual message, arrogating to the United States the right of unilateral intervention in Latin American countries unable to keep their houses in order. "Chronic wrongdoing," the President claimed, gave the United States the right to exercise an "international police power" in the western hemisphere in order to preserve the Monroe Doctrine. Here was bold policy indeed, a pert reflection of America's new-caught sense of power in international affairs. Monroe and Adams must have rotated in their graves. Never had they contemplated anything remotely comparable to the Roosevelt Corollary, but times had distinctly changed.

An opportunity to exercise an international police power in the Caribbean soon presented itself. In 1905 the Dominican Republic went the way of Venezuela by repudiating certain European obligations. T.R. promptly ordered an intervention. To reconstruct Dominican finance and to satisfy European creditors, he organized a customs receivership to collect and disburse Dominican revenue which was derived principally from tariffs. The Dominican Republic soon joined Cuba and Panama in the stable of American fiefs in the Caribbean. The Roosevelt Corollary opened a whole new field of endeavor to the United States Marine Corps, which became a frequent visitor in the Caribbean as the principal agent of unilateral intervention. Whatever Latins or Europeans may have thought about the legitimacy of these operations, no one could contemplate serious opposition. Roosevelt had launched a policy of hegemony in the Caribbean, and the Corollary of 1904 was its official announcement.

If Roosevelt's Latin American policy had been motivated by strategic considerations, that of his successor, the portly William Howard Taft, reflected an additional interest—the desire of some Americans to wrest control of Latin American trade and commerce from Europe. Secretary of State Philander C. Knox launched an abortive experiment in "dollar diplomacy," a policy supposedly designed to enlarge United States influence in the Latin American economy by encouraging private investment in Latin American enterprise. Taft may have deemed the practice a means of confirming the strategic predominance of the United States in the region, but his critics considered this explanation a cover for downright exploitation. Unfortunately for the dollar diplomats, their dabbles in the Caribbean failed to bear much fruit. To begin with, the Senate proved uncooperative, refusing consent to the Knox-Castrillo convention of 1911 which provided for American penetration of Nicaragua. In addition, all too many *norteamericanos* took their business elsewhere, unwilling to accept the risks of investment in Latin America when higher profits with greater security could be had elsewhere. Despite the congressional rebuff, Taft and Knox persisted in Nicaragua, and in 1912 an intervention made that country the fourth United States protectorate in the Caribbean. Marines remained in residence until 1933 except for a brief withdrawal during 1925.

The activities of Roosevelt and Taft certainly made the Caribbean an American lake and Latin America a closed preserve of the United States, but the price was dearer than anyone suspected at the time.

"The "colossus of the north" reaped a bitter legacy of Yankeephobia throughout Latin America. It seemed endurable at the time, but it ultimately created enormous difficulties for the United States. Too many Americans failed to recognize that intervention in countries like Nicaragua and the Dominican Republic usually strengthened the hand of local reactionary cliques, always eager to exploit the great majority of their people. Unholy combinations of churchmen, army officers, middle-class capitalists, and great land-owners often secured support from the United States because they seemed to be the only local elements capable of insuring domestic tranquillity. Such calm was what the United States desired; it insured against imagined threats of European intervention in the western hemisphere. Imagined threats they were, because no European power at the time seriously considered a major challenge to the United States in its hemispheric preserve. If unilateral intervention caused rejoicing by the elite of Latin America, it stimulated profound fear and hatred of the United States among oppressed populations everywhere beyond the Rio Grande. The sins of the fathers were visited upon future generations. Americans of later years had cause to rue that careless disregard of human needs and aspirations accompanying T.R. Corollaryism. It is no accident that those countries reduced to protectorate status during the imperial interlude were among the Latin American states most difficult to live with in later years.

The Presidency of Woodrow Wilson seemed to herald a new day in United States-Latin American relations. Shortly after his inauguration in 1913, Wilson specifically repudiated unilateral interventionism and dollar diplomacy at Mobile, promising to replace expediency with principle in future dealings with the hemisphere. Unlike T.R., Wilson was a devotee of anti-imperialism. He hoped to undo the untoward deeds of his two predecessors, and yet, ironically, he presided over some of the most disreputable interventions in our history. Despite his good intent, Wilson was an inveterate social Darwinist, convinced of the superiority of white Anglo-Saxon Protestantism, and assured that he knew better than others what was good for them—especially Latins. His paternalism, which turned into authoritarian behavior when he encountered resistance, militated against a thorough-going reform of Latin American policy.

The vast Mexican complications of 1913–1916 provided a clear example of what flowed from Wilson's moralistic paternalism. After General Victoriano Huerta overthrew Francisco Madero, the father of Mexico's revolution, Wilson announced that he would withhold diplomatic recognition, a dubious departure from the practice of *de facto* recognition pursued by the United States since the time of Jefferson.

Until this hour, the criterion of recognition had been effective power rather than ideology or any other consideration. By November, Wilson had called for the resignation of Huerta and was seeking international support to strengthen his anti-*Huertista* policies. Content for a time to practice "watchful waiting," the President ultimately condoned intervention in April 1914, first at Tampico to efface an alleged insult to the American flag, and then at Vera Cruz to prevent the landing of armaments from Germany which might have shored up Huerta. Wilson was saved from further involvement only by an unsuccessful attempt at mediation by Argentina, Brazil, and Chile, and the ultimate collapse of Huerta.

As if events had not gone far enough, Wilson was barely free of the Huerta business when the picturesque Pancho Villa, a Mexican revolutionary of bandit lineage estranged from the new central government of Venustiano Carranza, killed a number of American engineers in northern Mexico and then raided Columbus, New Mexico, in order to precipitate an American intervention. He hoped an American invasion would discredit his political enemies in Mexico City. Wilson authorized a "punitive expedition" led by General John J. Pershing which spent many months in fruitless pursuit of the *Villistas*. Wilson finally withdrew Pershing and repaired mutilated relations with the Carranza regime, but not until he had proved once again that the road to hell is paved with good intentions.

Wilson could not break out of the Roosevelt-Taft pattern when difficulties arose in Haiti during 1915. A Haitian ruler, Guillaume Sam, took it upon himself to liquidate 167 political enemies. In response the populace rose in mighty wrath and cut him into little pieces. This affair precipitated a visitation by Marines who proceeded to engage in the barbarous Caco War, an attempt to wipe out obstreperous antigovernment elements in Haiti, while the United States placed a puppet president in power and forced him to negotiate the usual customs receivership. Other requirements imposed on Haiti made it the fifth and last American protectorate in the Caribbean. The Marines remained in place until 1934.

Despite his vigorous prosecution of the Mexican and Haitian affairs, Wilson felt an increasing disquietude. Growing realization that much had gone wrong in Latin America probably stimulated his interest in a project assiduously advanced by his intimate friend from Texas, the self-effacing Colonel Edward M. House. He proposed nothing short of a general inter-American treaty based on much the same principles as the Good Neighbor policy of a generation later. The idea of replacing unilateral interventionism with a system of inter-American treaty law to provide collective enforcement of international obligations in the hemisphere had long been current. Only a few years earlier, Elihu Root had moved in this direction by negotiating a security arrangement for Central America based on similar premises. Unfortunately, House's plans did not materialize because of the growing difficulties occasioned by World War I as well as the anti-United States sentiment stimulated in Latin America by Wilson's ill-advised policies. Nevertheless, some precedent for a future *démarche* remained among the ashes of Wilson's hemispheric fiascoes.

However unwise and unnecessary, the guiding concepts of the imperial interlude in Latin America — T.R.'s unilateral interventionism, Taft's dollar diplomacy, and Wilson's moralistic paternalism — seemed reasonably successful at the time, despite a notable reaction against them among the American people on humanitarian grounds. The Caribbean had been secured, and the United States had established an unmistakable hegemony throughout Latin America. Gone were the days when European powers could violate the pronouncement of Monroe with impunity. For better or worse, the future of the hemisphere for a long time to come rested in the hands of the government in Washington. It remained to be seen whether much would come of the impulse toward an inter-American security system to replace the international police power of the United States. In the interim, the legacy of Yankeephobia festered in the hearts and minds of millions across Latin America who seriously doubted that many Marines would get to heaven, much less guard its streets.

*   *   *

If affairs in the Caribbean-Latin American region seemed to proceed satisfactorily during the imperial interlude, few claimed comparable success in the Pacific-East Asian arena. The problem was Japan, opened to western trade only fifty years earlier by the United States. In 1895, Japan made its bow as a Far Eastern power, decisively defeating China in its first modern war. Hopeful of considerable gain at the expense of the decrepit Manchu dynasty, primarily in Korea and Manchuria, the Japanese encountered united opposition from European powers who forced upon Tokyo a settlement somewhat less favorable than had been anticipated. After the Sino-Japanese War, the world witnessed an unseemly scramble for "spheres of influence" in China. Outside powers also sought concessions of the sort that had been extorted from China many times since the Opium War — the right of extraterritoriality, most-favored-nation treatment, etc. Russia strengthened its foothold in the Liaotung peninsula, and the other powers with large interests in China followed suit — Germany in Shantung, Britain in the Yangtze valley, and France in Kwangtung province adjacent to its Indochinese domains.

These events transpired just as the United States entered the politics of East Asia on the wings of the Philippine annexation. The impending partition of China, for that was in prospect, greatly disturbed diplomats in Washington, who feared that the accomplishments of 1898 in the western Pacific might become worthless if China were gobbled up by the imperial powers and closed to American merchants. The British shared these fears. Increasingly alarmed by European difficulties, the British had no wish to become more deeply implicated in East Asian politics, but they hoped to preserve their important commercial establishment in China and elsewhere in the region. Even before 1898, these considerations had led Britain to propose to the United States a cooperative initiative in the Far East in order to forestall further colonial inroads on China. Initially uninterested in these overtures, the acquisition of the Philippines altered Washington's attitude overnight, especially when various American companies began to clamor for action in order to guarantee their hope of windfalls in the China trade.

The outcome of all this was the "open door policy," so handsomely lauded by later generations. Its architect was a new secretary of state, the Anglophile John Hay, just returned from the Court of St. James where he had served as ambassador. On the advice of an experienced American diplomatist named William W. Rockhill who had broad exposure in the Far East, Hay decided to dispatch a circular letter to all concerned powers calling for a general agreement on the future of China. The first open door note, dispatched in September 1899, called for free trade in China. To secure this end, Hay proposed that all powers keep "hands off" existing treaty ports and leased territories; that they insure equal duties for all traders within spheres of influence except in those "free ports" where no tariffs were levied; and that they guarantee equality of treatment for alien nationals trading within spheres of influence.

These proposals encountered noticeable lack of enthusiasm except in the United States and Britain, the two countries with the most favorable competitive positions in the China trade. With the exception of a forthright acceptance from Italy, which could afford it, Hay received highly equivocal responses to his circular. The powers usually replied that they would accept the principles of the open door if others agreed to them, a tactic obviously designed to relegate free trade in China to the diplomatic ashcan. Undaunted by this outcome, Hay decided to bluff. He announced to the world that the powers had accepted the open door note, doing so in a way calculated to preclude

demurrers from those who had actually rebuffed the American proposal. Thus did John Hay gain immortality, but the outcome of his
famous bluff was actually frustration. The open door note was an
admirable statement of principle which any power could ignore at
pleasure—and did. Even Hay shortly thereafter contemplated acquir-
ing a base on the China coast, only to be reminded by Japan that this
procedure would constitute a violation of the open door principle.

Less than a year after Hay's maneuver, an antiforeign manifestation
in China known to later generations as the Boxer rebellion created an
opportunity to achieve what most powers desired—a final partition of
the Middle Kingdom. A siege of the foreign legations in Peking led
Germany to organize a relief expedition. A practical world awaited the
end of Chinese sovereignty. In this tense atmosphere, Secretary Hay
dispatched another circular letter to the powers interested in China,
calling for a general agreement to respect the territorial and administrative integrity of China. The second open door note had as little
practical effect as its predecessor. Fortunately for China the relief
expedition, to which the United States contributed some personnel,
succeeded in lifting the siege in Peking. Tensions rapidly subsided,
and the powers contented themselves with extorting the Boxer indem-
nities from impotent China. If all too many Americans attributed this
outcome to the open door notes, they were entirely mistaken. During
the next two generations the principles of free trade and territorial
integrity for China were continually violated by a number of nations,
among them the United States.

If Asia remained calm for a short time, the quiet ended in 1904,
when a serious quarrel between Japan and Russia concerning their
respective roles in Korea and Manchuria broke into open warfare.
The Japanese opened hostilities with a sneak attack on Port Arthur,
but Americans generally sympathized with them, always ready to
support a supposed underdog. The President shared this feeling,
convinced that Russia was the most dangerous threat to Far Eastern
stability. The outcome of the Russo-Japanese War caused T.R. to
reconsider his earlier attitude. He and many of his countrymen began
to realize that Japan might seriously threaten China in the wake of its
victory over Russia. Early in 1905, T.R. gained an opportunity to
exercise a vast influence on the Russo-Japanese peace settlement, and
he used the chance to inaugurate a new Far Eastern policy.

When the Japanese secretly asked the United States to mediate
between themselves and the Russians, Roosevelt accepted the challenge. Despite its victory, Japan was close to exhaustion; dangerous
domestic upheavals seriously embarrassed Russia. These factors gave
T.R. an opening. After many vicissitudes, he succeeded in arranging

a peace treaty in the unlikely city of Portsmouth, New Hampshire. Japan gained much but not all that it wanted; the upshot was an outburst of anti-American sentiment in the homeland. For his efforts, T.R. later received a Nobel peace prize. The settlement not only restored peace in East Asia but also some semblance of a balance of power. In maintaining the Far Eastern balance T.R. espied the most efficient and least costly method of protecting American interests in the Far East.

If Roosevelt gave continuing lip service to the principles of Hay, he rapidly moved from the open door to a policy of propitiating Japan which entailed certain concessions. The first step in this direction came in 1905, when the affable William Howard Taft visited Tokyo and signed an agreement (the Taft-Katsura memorandum) in which Japan seemed to deny any interest in the Philippine Islands in return for American acquiescence in the annexation of Korea. This *quid pro quo* temporarily relieved both nations of anxieties in those regions of particular concern to each. By this time Roosevelt had begun to realize that the acquisition of the Philippines, so blithely annexed in 1898, had created a difficult diplomatic problem for the Republic. Highly indefensible short of truly extensive military commitments, the islands constantly figured in American calculations regarding Japan.

In 1908, T.R. authorized another secret arrangement with Japan, the Root-Takahira agreement, in which the two countries reiterated their adherence to the open door principles and validated the *status quo* in East Asia. To some it appeared that the President had merely gained another pledge of Japanese restraint in the Philippines in return for his acceptance of recent Japanese penetrations into Manchuria. If Britain welcomed the settlement because it tacitly strengthened the Anglo-Japanese alliance by lessening the likelihood of conflict between two of its closest overseas friends, China was deeply offended. Like the earlier Taft-Katsura memorandum, the Root-Takahira agreement appeared to sacrifice Chinese interests on the altar of Japanese-American *rapprochement*.

For a proponent of the "big stick," T.R. had moved quite circumspectly in East Asia. Unwilling to contemplate a vastly expanded commitment in the region, he worked for a stable Far Eastern balance while currying favor with Tokyo. This approach seemed sound as long as other western nations associated themselves with the United States. Needless to say, Roosevelt was outraged when his hand-picked successor, William Howard Taft, launched a quixotic adventure in Far Eastern dollar diplomacy which threatened to upset the Rough Rider's delicate approach.

The real author of dollar diplomacy was an American diplomat named Willard Straight who had served as consul general in Manchuria during Roosevelt's second term. Increasingly alarmed by Japanese expansion in the area, he conceived the idea of extending official encouragement to private investors who might then be willing to put money into Chinese economic development. This policy would enhance American power in China and serve as a counterweight to Japan. Straight thought of dollar diplomacy as a strategic maneuver to establish the American presence more firmly in Asia rather than as a venture in economic imperialism as such, but it had appeal to those who hoped to turn a quick dollar in China. When Straight returned to Washington in 1909, he sold his project to Secretary of State Knox.

The result was an eminently unsuccessful effort to stimulate American economic penetration of China. Knox first attempted to help China regain control of Manchurian railroads by extending a large private loan to Peking. The only outcome was a strong Russo-Japanese combine against the project. American policy drove these recent enemies into each other's arms, a development which actually injured China. Eternally optimistic, Knox next organized a group of American bankers to participate in an international banking consortium to finance railroad construction in China proper. The outbreak of the Chinese revolution shortly thereafter and various other complications rapidly weakened the resolve of the American banking group headed by J. P. Morgan. When Woodrow Wilson assumed power in 1913, he immediately withdrew support from the consortium, a deed which temporarily ended the effort to substitute the dollar for bullets as a means of shoring up the American position in East Asia. As opposed to dollar diplomacy in Asia as in Latin America, Wilson publicly repudiated its practice and at the same time expressed great sympathy for the Chinese revolution. That outbreak, of course, created opportunities for Japanese aggression, since it undermined the central government.

An even greater incentive to Japanese expansionism was the outbreak of World War I. That conflict completed a tendency manifest for some time—the withdrawal of considerable European power from the region. Encouraged by the temporary inability of Europe to stand in its way and convinced that the United States would not interpose effective opposition, Japan rapidly launched an extensive campaign of aggrandizement. The first step was to honor the Anglo-Japanese alliance and declare war on the Central Powers. Of course, Japan had no intention of making a major effort in Europe; its entry into the war allowed it to move against Germany's holdings in the Pacific-East Asian region. In due course, Japan occupied the German concession around Kiaochow Bay in the Shantung peninsula and also German-held islands north of the equator. Australia and New Zealand occupied those below the equator.

The next step was the issuance of the infamous Twenty-One Demands to the Chinese government in 1915, acceptance of which would have reduced China to protectorate status. Fortunately Japan withdrew most of these demands after a long crisis. For a number of years diplomatic historians attributed to Secretary of State William Jennings Bryan the credit for achieving this end. The Great Commoner's contribution was a note in which he indicated that the United States would not recognize illegal conquests in Asia by Japan, a relatively empty gesture. It was apparent that the United States would go no further. Actually, Japan backed away mostly because of domestic repercussions, Chinese resistance, and British objections.

The episode of the Twenty-One Demands demonstrated that Japan was prepared to take extensive measures in East Asia and the western Pacific whenever opportunities like that of the European war presented themselves. If Tokyo backed away in 1915, the war had only just begun. Its probable intensification would undoubtedly provide further openings later on. The Japanese pretensions greatly alarmed Woodrow Wilson and his advisers, but they could find no effective way of controlling them. In 1916 they supported the Jones Bill providing for eventual Philippine independence, an act reflecting not simply contrition but also a desire to escape growing entanglement in the western Pacific.

Such was the course of American policy in East Asia during the imperial interlude. Shortly after the Spanish war it became clear that support of China was the key to American opportunity and security in the region. After the open door fiasco, T.R. turned to balance-of-power tactics and diplomatic accord with Japan to protect China, a policy Wilson also followed after the temporary deviation of Taft's dollar diplomacy. Much to its dismay, the United States found itself increasingly responsible for Chinese security as other western nations withdrew their power from East Asia just before and during World War I. Developments in East Asia clearly revealed the extent to which European politics influenced events elsewhere in the world. Japan's striking national development had made that nation an important factor in Far Eastern affairs, but the withdrawal of European power made vast aggressions conceivable. For better or worse, the American people were unwilling to accept commitments sufficient to deter Japan. Policymakers in Washington attempted delaying tactics, hoping that time would work to their advantage. As it turned out, time was their enemy. Well before 1917, when the United States entered the European war, the growing complications of empire in the western

Pacific had convinced many Americans that the territorial grab of '98 had been a grievous mistake indeed.

* * *

If policies in Latin America and Asia were revolutionized during the imperial interlude, it appeared that the tradition of disengagement from Europe had been preserved. Politicians still intoned the ancient platitudes of Washington, secure in the illusion that isolation and neutrality would protect the Republic from European discontent in all circumstances. Only one significant exception to the rule of separation marred an otherwise spotless record of abstinence. In 1906, President Roosevelt intervened decisively in the first Moroccan crisis, sending a representative to the Algeciras conference which finally resolved that lengthy dispute.

Two years earlier, Germany had challenged France's imperial monopoly in North Africa. War might have resulted, but eventually the powers came together at the last of those great councils of European powers which kept the peace between 1815 and 1914. In order to strengthen its position at Algeciras, Germany actively courted the United States through its ambassador in Washington, Speck von Sternburg, an old friend of T.R., and mistakenly assumed that it had gained American support. In fact, Roosevelt was vastly suspicious of Germany; he decided to back Franco-British diplomacy at Algeciras, an assignment cleverly carried out by the career diplomatist Henry White. At a crucial moment, T.R. forced a decision which brought the conference to its conclusion and averted war. Roosevelt later boasted that he had "stood [the Kaiser] on his head with great decision." He had indeed.

The unprecedented intervention at Algeciras reflected T.R.'s growing suspicion that American security might now require regular participation in European politics. On his initiative the United States temporarily acted as had England during the preceding century in relation to continental disputes. Serving as an honest broker, the United States had been highly effective in forging a compromise minimally acceptable to all which tended to restore European stability. Roosevelt at least dimly recognized that European calm insured the safety of the Republic, but the American people did not share his insight. The Senate consented to the convention of Algeciras only after voting a reservation stating that the United States had not reversed its traditional policy of nonentanglement. If Americans took notice at all, they probably congratulated themselves when the United States failed to intervene constructively in the European crises of

1911–1914 which finally eventuated in the Great War. As peoples will, they inadvertently committed themselves to an age of violence far more trying than the perils of peacekeeping.

After 1900 the United States missed an historic opportunity to preserve its own security as well as that of others by calling in its power to redress the balance of the old world. Had America followed the precedent set at Algeciras, the future might have taken a far different, and infinitely preferable, course. Humane intervention in the councils of Europe at the outset of the twentieth century would have been a much more useful method of launching America's career as a great power than an ignoble and profitless experiment in empire, but history is crowded with lost opportunities. A decade after Algeciras, Woodrow Wilson clearly comprehended what T.R. had guessed at, but only when it was too late to help preserve an honorable peace.

To the credit of the American people, it must be noted that they impressively supported efforts by every secretary of state from Hay to Bryan to negotiate treaties providing for peaceful mediation and even arbitration of international disputes. They also interested themselves in the Hague peace conferences of 1899 and 1907. Despite a propensity to violence which on occasion forced its way to the surface, as in 1898, the Americans were usually a peace-loving people, and the thought of making legal arrangements to settle international disputes especially intrigued them. The difficulty with this approach was that power realities all too often mean more in international politics than principle. Legal arrangements which lack truly effective means of enforcement are all too often ignored when moments of decision arrive. Woodrow Wilson once said: "The world *runs* on its ideals; only fools believe otherwise." He was quite right. Power exists to serve sound principle. World peace cannot be insured without a consensus on principle reflected in a body of enforceable law. It is equally apparent that unenforceable law will hardly insure the millenium. The growth of an imposing peace movement in the United States during the early years of the twentieth century is testimony to the good will and pacific intent of many Americans, but the failure of that movement to accomplish its goals symbolizes the insufficiency of those mediation and arbitration projects to which it largely dedicated its energies.

* * *

One of the most startling ironies in that extraordinarily ironic era just before World War I was that the United States did not in fact escape a massive range of international entanglements with the great powers. If

American statesmen did not consciously seek out these entanglements and tried assiduously to avoid them, they were an unavoidable outcome of the nation's imperial interlude. Whether they like it or not, great powers cannot in the nature of things avoid international involvement, and the United States did not succeed in repealing this immutable role of world politics. Of those diplomatic relationships which matured during the imperial interlude, two were of the greatest significance for the immediate future. The traditional Anglo-American understanding blossomed into something approaching an alliance, but a severe German-American antagonism also emerged at the same time. British love feasts and German quarrels exercised an impressive influence on American policy not only during the imperial interlude but also after the outbreak of World War I when the United States attempted to preserve its neutrality.

The extraordinary deepening of the established Anglo-American understanding during the imperial interlude was an aspect of Britain's effort to recover its threatened security at the turn of the century. If British ministries sought European connections with France and Russia to balance the growing power of Germany, they cultivated extra-European relations with Japan and the United States to strengthen their security elsewhere. The Anglo-Japanese alliance protected British interests in Asia; the Anglo-American understanding, far less formal but of even greater importance, protected against troubles in the Atlantic basin. It eliminated a potential danger to Britain's control of the seas and a threat to its exposed oceanic flank. The United States gained as well; American statesmen charged a high price for friendship.

The modern expansion of the old Anglo-American tie began at the time of the Venezuelan boundary dispute in 1895 and constantly matured to the outbreak of the Great War. When Olney rudely insisted upon American prerogatives in the western hemisphere, Britain wisely accepted arbitration of the quarrel with Venezuela in order to maintain a working relationship with the United States. At the time of the Spanish-American War Britain preserved a benevolent neutrality, the only European power friendly to the United States during that conflict. The United States, after some hesitation, reciprocated this gesture during the Boer War. These events foreshadowed many further British concessions to the United States.

Some striking examples of this tendency occurred during the first decade of the twentieth century. In 1901 Britain surrendered its right to participate in the construction of a Central American canal by accepting the Hay-Pauncefote treaty. A year later, when the United States came to the defense of Venezuela during the debt controversy,

Britain quickly withdrew its pressure. In 1903 an arbitration settled a long-stanging dispute between Canada and the United States over the location of the Alaskan boundary. (Once again, Canadian interests bowed to the insistent British concern for Anglo-American amity.) Shortly thereafter, Britain withdrew most of its naval strength from the Caribbean in order to reinforce its fleet in the North Sea against German naval expansion, a development removing another potential source of Anglo-American conflict. Renegotiations of the Anglo-Japanese alliance assured that it could not be invoked against the United States. T.R.'s diplomacy at Algeciras impressively demonstrated that American friendship paid useful dividends.

Less dramatic activities contributed to the growth of friendly association. The English-Speaking Union energetically promoted cultural interchange between the two countries. American artists and intellectuals received grand welcomes in London, and many British counterparts found enthusiastic audiences in the United States. Each country carefully accredited sympathetic diplomatic representatives to each other. The Anglophile John Hay was only the first of his breed to serve at the Court of St. James; successors like Whitelaw Reid and Walter Hines Page assiduously pursued his example of cordiality. In return Britain sent to Washington one of its greatest commentators on American life, the astute Lord Bryce, who was exceedingly popular in the United States. Hibernian orators on occasion still bellowed Anglophobic diatribes in great American cities like Boston and Chicago, but something had gone out of the conventional anti-British appeal which could not be recalled.

The parade of Anglo-American adjustments went on and on. In 1911, Britain, Japan, and the United States reached agreement on a North Pacific Sealing Convention. A year later Canada and the United States settled an old dispute over the Newfoundland fishing grounds. Although the two North American neighbors failed to arrange a tariff reciprocity treaty in 1911, the effort demonstrated the continuing vitality of Anglo-American friendship. In 1913, sharp criticism issued from Britain when the United States attempted to levy higher tolls on alien shipping than on American vessels passing through the Panama canal, a violation of the Hay-Pauncefote treaty, but Wilson backed away from this mistake in return for a promise of British assistance against Huerta in Mexico

The Anglo-American friendship prospered because the old nineteenth-century bases of consociation continued to influence the two great English-speaking nations, and because new motivations, derived from America's emergence as a great power and Britain's difficulties with the European continent, imparted additional momentum to the unofficial *entente.* Anglo-American interests continued complementary or noncompetitive, but the situation differed with respect to imperial Germany.

A historic cordiality had characterized the early diplomatic relationship between Germany and the United States, so far as any existed, but the later years of the nineteenth century created strains. As both countries achieved a high degree of national unity, experienced massive industrial revolutions, and entered into the race for overseas empire, they became increasingly suspicious of each other. Wilhelmine Germany's proclivity to autocracy and militarism aroused considerable distaste in the United States, and German critics of democracy frequently scoffed at the American system. These jousts could not in themselves precipitate major diplomatic conflicts, but they exercised a deleterious influence over time because Germany and the United States came into increasing conflict with each other in the Pacific and even in the Caribbean as they pursued competitive imperial designs.

A series of German-American encounters beginning in 1889 gradually deepened mutual suspicion; it reached considerable proportions by 1914. Both countries aspired to the Samoan Islands. They might have come to blows over them if Great Britain had not assisted in establishing a condominium in 1889 which endured for a decade. The islands were then partitioned between the two rivals. During the same period, Americans did not fail to note considerable German interest in both the Hawaiian and Philippine Islands. They were especially irritated by reports, actually unfounded, that a German flotilla had attempted to interfere with Dewey's operations in Manila Bay. The threat of German annexation influenced the decision to acquire the Philippines.

Difficulties multiplied during the imperial interlude. In 1900 Germany spearheaded the effort to convert the Boxer rebellion into a full-scale partition of China, an obvious assault on the open door principles. During the next few years Germany manifested an untoward interest in the Caribbean, enlisting among the nations which exerted pressure on Venezuela and the Dominican Republic. The T. R. Corollary was designed in part to prevent German penetration of the Caribbean. Germany also influenced Denmark's decision not to sell the Danish West Indies to the United States. (They were finally acquired in 1917, when Germany could do nothing to prevent the sale, and renamed the Virgin Islands.) Germany's massive program of naval construction aroused considerable criticism in the United States, and Americans also took umbrage at Germany because of its uncooperative attitude toward the Hague peace conferences of 1899 and 1907. A heavy blow to German-American friendship was the action of

the United States during the Algeciras conference, particularly re-
sented by Germany because President Roosevelt had initially seemed
to favor its interests. When Mexican-American relations deteriorated
in 1913 and after, various German intrigues with sundry revolutionary
figures further poisoned relation on the eve of the Great War. The
Vera Cruz incident stemmed from the imminent arrival of a German
ship carrying arms to Huerta. Throughout these years, American and
German merchants often competed in the same overseas markets, a
rivalry which hardly sweetened exchanges between Washington and
Berlin.

Certainly the antagonism between Germany and the United States
was less well defined than the Anglo-American friendship (which itself
interfered with German-American cordiality), but it was of signal
importance. A natural community of interest dictated Anglo-American accord, but definite conflicts of interest divided Germany and the
United States. Prior developments seriously limited the diplomatic
alternatives open to the United States in determining its course between the two European coalitions during the early years of World
War I. Much earlier than 1914, a series of profoundly influential
political developments had largely prefigured the American relation to
the leading contestants in the Great War. This reality went virtually
unnoticed by most Americans, deluded by official indorsement of
nonentanglement into believing that the nation possessed plenary
freedom of action in its dealings with Europe.

*   *   *

The imperial interlude turned out to be a mixed blessing. Growing
domestic criticism of policies in Latin America and Asia reflected the
fact that it had brought more pain than pleasure. The gains were
ambiguous indeed, especially in the Pacific. The most portentous
legacy of empire was a series of disturbing relationships with several of
the great powers, compensated to an extent by the Anglo-American
association. Tensions with Germany, Japan, and Russia were bound to
play a significant role in future events. The American preoccupation
with its areas of imperial concern, Latin America and East Asia, had
detracted seriously from attention to Europe where the United States
might have made a signal contribution by intervening intelligently to
restore political stability. The price of adherence to the outworn
shibboleths of the Founding Fathers was war—unexampled war of the
most cataclysmic nature—which vastly tarnished American hopes and
dreams during the next half-century.

CHAPTER IV

The Twentieth Century War:
An Introduction

I F THE IMPERIAL interlude launched America on its voyage into world
history, the events of 1914–1918 and after completed the passage.
At just the moment when the Americans prepared to reap the benefits
of their nineteenth-century accomplishments, they found themselves
inextricably tangled in that pattern of plenary violence which has
become the most significant hallmark of world history in our time
—the Twentieth Century War. The hostilities of 1914 began a cycle of
warfare which continued until 1945, and its aftermath still lingers.
The collapse of the European balance after a hundred years of stability inaugurated patterns of world-historical change still far from
complete. Historians still argue endlessly about the origins and causes
of that breakdown, giving particular stress to factors like nationalism,
militarism, imperialism, and industrialization. The century turned into
one of those terrible eras of violence which usually mark the disruption
of the established order and herald the beginning of new departures.

The jumbled history of our times often seems impossible to organize
and interpret; the confusion of so much that was new and different
constantly defeats efforts to unravel the labyrinth of recent events.
And yet, our limited perspective permits at least a few broad general-
izations. Certainly the great conflict of 1914–1918 which began the
Twentieth Century War so shattered Europe, and indeed the entire
western world, that it made unlikely an early escape from vast instability. The very intensity of World War I sowed the seeds of further
conflict. And then, again, the very debility of the West—immensely
weakened by nothing less than an international civil war, if the western world is considered a quasi-political entity—encouraged aggression by nonwestern powers in Asia, particularly Japan until 1945 and
China in more recent years. Finally, the destruction of all the great
European imperial powers allowed nationalist movements in the old
colonial world of Africa and Asia to acquire commanding strength.

51

For almost five hundred years, the West had dominated the rest of the globe. That dominance came to a fiery end in the flames of the Twentieth Century War.

Each principal phase of the Twentieth Century War—the First Conflict of 1914–1918, the Long Armistice from 1919 to 1939, the Second Conflict of 1939–1945, and the troubled Aftermath of recent years—made more apparent the consequence of these developments. Europe was less and less the center of world affairs. If the locus of power shifted for the time being to the great outlying powers of the western world, the United States and Soviet Russia, the recovery of independence in ancient Asian societies such as China, India, and Araby confirmed the redemption of power in regions long victimized by western imperial exploitation. It seemed entirely possible that the revivified eastern societies might ultimately surpass the greatest countries of the western world.

What engendered the pervasive violence of the age? Was it, perhaps, the superannuation of that system of nation-states which had emerged at the dawn of modern history? There were new things under the sun in the twentieth century. Novel complexities wrought by profound intellectual and technological innovations were increasingly difficult to accommodate within the conventional order of power. If this reality was difficult to comprehend, it was because of the prior beatitudes of nation-state organization. That grand tradition seemed too effective to question. Most people thought that the complexities of the new age could be accommodated by adjustment of the international *status quo* rather than its displacement. They all too easily assumed that the nation-state was the final stage of world-political evolution, an ultimate expression of political genius.

From time immemorial, humanity has condemned itself to pandemic violence because it refused to recognize the imperatives of change. The city-state organization of the ancient Mediterranean world had seemed entirely sufficient for all time to those who benefited from its accomplishment, but a long season of warfare ensued when it became obsolescent. The universal empire of the Romans, which replaced the older city-state system, seemed to be an ultimate political accomplishment, but it also succumbed to time, the destroyer of all human pretension, and another term of violence was visited upon civilization. Only the invention of the nation-state system brought Europe out of a thousand years of political stagnation. The achievements of the national idea were so imposing that it is easy to understand why our present commitment to it is so overwhelming. Nevertheless, even before the twentieth century, forces were in motion comparable in their disruptive effect to those which had undermined the ancient Greek and Roman orders of things. As in the past, those who benefited from the ongoing system tended either to defend it *in toto* or to urge reform from within. It was almost impossible to believe that the nation was as replaceable as the cave, the village, or the city as the prime center of political organization and loyalty.

More sensitive spirits thought they discovered a necessity to adopt supranational political organization—sovereign authority beyond the nation—in order to resolve modern international tensions by means short of violence. Of course, supranational polity by no means required the destruction of nations. It meant simply that they must recede in importance. National loyalties would have to be subordinated to a more comprehensive faith, as fealty to the city-state had been subordinated to the imperial ideal of Rome two thousand years before. All too often, prophets of a new political order were dismissed as Utopians. The scoffers failed to weigh the odds against survival within the established order of things. Admittedly, it was one thing to recognize the necessity for change but another to determine effective means of accomplishing it.

The United States was suddenly exposed to a world of change which slowly repudiated the political order within which the newest of the powers had come to maturity. If the foreign policy of the United States before 1914 matured successfully in the congenial atmosphere of the long peace following the Congress of Vienna, the crowning accomplishment of the nation-state system, it ran its later course in the highly inhospitable context of the Twentieth Century War. That war presaged the passing of the old accustomed statecraft. All too often historians extol the wisdom of early American statesmen, particularly the generation of the Founders, and condemn the follies of their successors. This invidious comparison scouts the difficulties of the revolutionary changes which took place during the earlier decades of the twentieth century. It was the fortune of American statesmen from the time of Woodrow Wilson to cope with truly unprecedented waves of profound change. Latter-day change was far more complex than that of the late eighteenth century and certainly far less favorable to American security.

It is easy enough to detail the failings of modern American statecraft, but they were human failings which proceeded from kinder intentions and greater dedication than some of their critics seem to realize. Intellectual integrity commands a detailed criticism of American foreign policy during the Twentieth Century War, but not because those who presided over the destiny of the Republic were always stupid or selfish. They were as confused as everyone else by the arcane outcomes of an unexampled era of change. In the circumstances, the story of American leadership during the half-century just past is a tale of courage and fortitude as well as a catalog of error.

As the Twentieth Century War began its grisly course, the Republic found itself in a fundamentally satiate condition. America had attained its growth; it was comparable in its development to Rome at the time of Caesar Augustus. This condition did not mean that no worlds to conquer remained to the American people, but it did mean that as of about this time they became more concerned with exploiting the national territorial legacy than in expanding it. Few desired further national adventurism in the pattern of 1898. Those who have are naturally inclined to the preservation of the going order. Those in want or concerned about want favor reform or revolution according to the degree of their alienation from the established condition. The burden of affluence dictated a pervasive American tendency to act in support of the international *status quo* — to adopt conserving policy with respect to world affairs.

The imperatives of the age required at least a tremendous alteration within the established order; they probably demanded even more. Many men and women of this century elsewhere in the world believed that the established order was totally inadequate to contend with the complexities of the new age. They argued that only a complete re-tooling would permit the survival of the race. In America, few radicals raised their voices effectively. Basic debate on questions of American foreign policy during this century has taken place largely between reformers who hoped to purify the ongoing international system and those who preferred to support it without change.

Those Americans who urged reform drew inspiration from the historic national tradition of faith in progress. If the United States was sated by success as of 1914, it continued to respond to a markedly progressive ideology — an ideology born during its earliest years and nurtured into principles of democratic society and polity which in its essentials went generally unquestioned by practically all meaningful factions within the relatively narrow range of domestic political controversy. Those clear distinctions which differentiated European radicals and reactionaries, or even liberals and conservatives, were largely absent from the American scene. If the United States possessed a viable conservative tradition, it differed vastly from that of Europe. America was born free, and the great national bounty insured plenty to all those with sufficient energy and imagination to draw upon it, given the felicitous state of international affairs. The domestic political outcome was a pervasive consensus, a liberal or progressive commitment shot through almost the entire polity. With some notable exceptions like Hamilton and Calhoun, those in the American past who called themselves conservatives were usually pale reflections of their liberal enemies.

So it was that despite their affluence—their undeniable presence in the House of Have—the Americans embodied political sympathies and ideas which made them peculiarly sensitive to those who continued in the House of Want. If those who possess never fully understand the meaning of poverty, they can mitigate the eternal conflict of have and have not by embracing a reformist ideology and maintaining a reform temper. Recognition of these requirements inspired that internationalist departure in American foreign policy which found its inception in the mind and heart of Woodrow Wilson during the initial phases of the Twentieth Century War. Wilsonian internationalism has survived into our own time, considerably altered as well as chastened by the tribulations of a violent age. It remains to be seen whether that tradition, however noble, is sufficient unto the day.

The United States entered into the maelstrom of the Twentieth Century War as a satiate-progressive nation, its citizens basically desiring the maintenance of the international *status quo* but receptive to reforms within the going order to benefit peoples less fortunate than themselves. At times, of course, especially when it seemed that all their fine enterprises went unappreciated by others, they gave full rein to their satiety and relapsed into lethargy. If Wilson reflected the progressive instincts of the American people applied to global politics in perhaps their finest form, a generation of successors including the early Franklin D. Roosevelt concerned themselves with national interests to the exclusion of international responsibility. The later Franklin D. Roosevelt revived and built upon the Wilsonian tradition, and his successors generally continued the pattern, deprived of the advantageous circumstances which had allowed evasion of international obligations in the wake of the Wilsonian debacle.

If America's progressive outlook has produced much that is truly admirable, it is open to certain criticisms in its international applications. What is good for Americans is not necessarily good for others. The isolated condition of America in its formative years united with unparalleled national accomplishment during a protected childhood to inculcate in American minds a sense of perfection which was hardly legitimate. It is hard to admit that national commitments which have worked splendidly at home are less than universally applicable. It is of great significance that over time the American people have gradually learned at least parts of this lesson, although frequent backsliding sometimes seems to undo all that has been done to broaden their horizons. It remains to be seen whether the lesson can be fully absorbed in time to help in avoiding still another cataclysm far more destructive than the two violent phases of the Twentieth Century War which have gone before.

Indeed, it remains to be seen whether American ideas of international peace and justice, however noble in conception, are in fact fully applicable to the revolutionized condition of the world today and tomorrow. We see through the glass darkly, but it is the part of wisdom as well as virtue to grasp what is necessary for the well-being of others. As in that mundane world of getting and spending to which we are all eternally condemned, it is well to remember that a larger community of interest transcends all lesser dissensions.

With these considerations in mind, it is time to resume the narrative of American foreign policy, a narrative of its evolution to the present day in the context of unparalleled violence and cruelty—the Twentieth Century War.

CHAPTER V

The First Phase

T HE ORIGINS AND causes of World War I, the first phase of the
Twentieth Century War, are hidden in a quagmire of prelimi-
naries reaching deep into the nineteenth-century past, but it is certain
that the collapse of the European balance opened the door to Armageddon. By 1914 all that was needed to ignite the conflagration was a
spark, and it came at Sarajevo on June 28, 1914. When a group of
Bosnian patriots shot down the Austrian Archduke Francis Ferdinand
and his consort, there followed a chain of events which precipitated
general warfare in little over a month's time. Austria-Hungary soon
issued an ultimatum to Serbia, hoping once and for all to put down
the South Slav agitation behind the assassination at Sarajevo. Russia,
the protector of Serbia, came to that small country's support. Germany
then honored its obligations to Austria-Hungary. When France supported Russia, the fat was in the fire. Britain hesitated, hopeful of
avoiding involvement, but Germany could not wait. Seeking out the
best route to France, the armies of Wilhelm II violated the borders of
Belgium. Britain then declared war. By August 4, 1914, all Europe
was aflame.

The written history of wars is usually dominated by those who win,
and World War I is no exception. The "official" version of its causes,
largely French and British in origin, is that German aggression caused
the outbreak of 1914. A dissenting claque of "revisionist" scholars,
affronted by this simplism, have argued vehemently that Germany had
to take arms against a crushing "encirclement" which threatened the
very survival of the realm. More circumspect analysts usually parcel
out war guilt among all the concerned parties.

Most accounts of origin and causation hardly mention the United
States; it is presumed that the Republic had little or nothing to do with
the prehistory of the war. This is not strictly true. The events of the
imperial interlude influenced the calculations of various European
chanceries in many subtle ways during the chaotic years preceding the
assault on Belgium. In addition, historians often ignore the possibility

that sins of omission often bulk as large as overt acts. The United States might have exercised an extraordinary influence for peace had it discerned the drift of things and entered actively into the affairs of Europe. But "ifs" cannot be taken too seriously, and the United States has largely maintained its reputation as an innocent bystander in 1914.

After the German army burst deep into France and Russia established an eastern front, the war settled down to a long and exhausting struggle. The western battle stalemated along a tremendous line reaching from the North Sea to Switzerland. Millions suffered and died along those dreary trenches during five interminable campaigns, but the front hardly varied at all until the final months of the war. In contrast, a war of movement took place in the East; opposing armies made great leaps forward and precipitate movements to the rear with bewildering rapidity. Unlike the campaign in France, the general trend in the East was toward German-Austrian victory. By 1917, Russia had been all but taken out of the struggle.

Other nations joined the fray from time to time. Like all general wars, the conflict of 1914–1918 had a marked tendency to expand, drawing in all manner of nations for all manner of reasons. Japan entered on the side of its British ally, and Turkey joined the Central Powers. Italy seceded from the Triple Alliance and augmented the exterior coalition in 1915. Rumania and Greece followed Italy, but Bulgaria adhered to the Germans. A series of special treaties, largely secret, interlocked each of the coalitions in a network of diplomatic engagements which vastly complicated the diplomacy of the war and its aftermath.

The horrendous battles waged at either end of the continent soon began to have their effect; they insensibly sapped away the vitality of European civilization. Americans still do not fully appreciate the enormous shock of World War I. As time ran on, the struggle became not only more global but also more total. It turned into what the German military analyst, Colmar von der Goltz, called a war of the nation in arms—a conflict to the death for all the stakes—engaging not only the last energies of fighting men but whole civilian populations as well. The bitterness of the struggle produced a tendency toward political extremes. The leaders of contending nations often moved to the right, casting their lot with a past that was daily being extinguished on the bloody battlefields of the continent. Other desperate men, out of power, became convinced that the old order was totally bankrupt. They contemplated social revolution to do away with all that was ancient and to replace it with an entirely new order. A massive upheaval finally occurred in Tsarist Russia, where the seeds of rebellion had sprouted for many years. If most of Europe fought for traditional objectives, the Russian revolution of 1917 posed a truly radical alternative to established politics.

* * *

The United States surveyed these developments at first with a certain detachment but later with growing alarm. As soon as war began, Woodrow Wilson issued a conventional proclamation of neutrality but coupled with it an unconventional appeal to the people to remain neutral in thought as well as deed. Wilson acted in the spirit of a hundred years and more of national aversion to Europe and Europe's ways. He could hardly guess that the drift of events precluded a permanent neutrality. The United States became the last of the great powers to enter the European war, taking this step in April 1917, but not before its President had conceived an impressive scheme to assure a just and lasting peace during years to come. Wilson's grand design posed a middleground liberal alternative to the European tendencies toward reaction and revolution.

America's intervention was in one dimension a culmination of those historic friendships and antagonisms which had matured during the imperial interlude. The events of 1914–1917 brought into sharp relief the hard realities behind the Anglo-American association and the German-American tension of prewar years. Of greatest import, of course, was the fact that Germany constituted a new threat to the "liberties of Europe," whatever its original intent. This fact was by itself sufficient to induce an anti-German sentiment among Americans. The security of the United States rested on a divided Europe. Ironically, this "realistic" motive for belligerency was not in fact the fundamental inspiration of Woodrow Wilson, although he could not have failed to consider it. What, then, ultimately brought on the American entry—historians like to call it the "reinforcement"—of 1917? The answer resides in two interrelated stories. One deals with the events set in motion by Germany's use of a novel engine of war, the submarine. The other is the unsuccessful effort of Wilson to mediate the war.

If Americans from the first favored the cause of the Allies, they were principally concerned with avoiding involvement, and the President shared this feeling. A near pacifist, Wilson had an outspoken advocate of peace as his secretary of state, the redoubtable William Jennings Bryan, who spent much of his time in the State Department negotiating a series of "cooling off" treaties with no less than thirty nations providing a year's moratorium in disputes while joint commissions inquired into the facts of the situation. Despite his inclination, the President was carried along by forces over which he could exercise only minimal control, chief among which was the question of neutral rights.

The European war rapidly dislocated international trade; in America the consequence was a sharp economic downturn. At the same time, belligerent powers sought credits in the United States to finance the purchase of materials and foodstuffs, required for the war. Bryan quickly imposed restrictions on foreign loans by American bankers, hoping by this device to safeguard American neutrality, but European powers used their own resources to make needed purchases in the United States. International law clearly specified that neutral nations could trade with belligerents in time of war if they avoided traffic in contraband items. It soon became obvious that the war had opened a wide range of markets previously closed to American traders, and it was equally evident that a thriving commerce with the belligerent powers would relieve the recession at home and stimulate a considerable boom.

The fly in the ointment was that the new trade would benefit only the Allies. British sea power controlled the surface seas sufficiently to insure that only a trickle of trade with neutrals would reach the Central Powers across oceans. As in the past, Britain imposed a strict blockade on shipments to its enemies. The chief neutral trader affected by the blockade was the United States. Faced with a difficult decision, Wilson permitted legitimate neutral trading, although it was bound to discriminate against the Central Powers. The new commerce revived the American economy but precipitated dangerous encounters with Germany.

To combat the British blockade, Germany turned to the submarine. In February 1915, Berlin announced a blockade in the waters adjacent to the British Isles and warned neutrals that their vessels were subject to undersea attack without warning if they entered the proscribed zones. The United States objected immediately, standing on traditional interpretations of neutral rights. The law of war on the high seas provided that belligerents could interdict neutral commerce with enemies only after visiting and searching neutral vessels and uncovering contraband materials. The President sent a note to Germany stating that it would be held to a "strict accountability" if any American ships were attacked without the formality of visit and search. The British blockade of the Central Powers hardly met the strict requirements of accepted procedure under international law, but it did not endanger lives or preclude profits. If German policy went unchallenged, these things might occur.

On May 7, 1915, a German submarine torpedoed the British liner *Lusitania,* a noncombatant vessel carrying contraband munitions as well as passengers. Some 1200 people died, including over 120 Americans. This horrible disaster inaugurated a long and dangerous controversy between the United States and Germany. Wilson remained calm, utilizing diplomacy to obtain redress. He demanded that Germany repudiate the practice of unrestricted submarine warfare. A number of notes went to Berlin, insisting on proper observance of established neutral rights. At first Chancellor Bethmann Hollweg attempted obfuscation and delay. He could advance some interesting arguments in behalf of German policy. The submarine was not like conventional vessels of war. It was extremely vulnerable to gunfire from very small weapons which could easily be mounted on merchantmen. It was also vulnerable to the so-called British "mystery ships," well-armed ships disguised as merchantmen sent out to hunt down submarines. Despite the force of these arguments, Bethmann Hollweg finally accepted the American demands, fearful of a declaration of war implicitly threatened by Wilson. After a German submarine sank another British liner, the *Arabic,* causing the deaths of two more Americans, Germany notified Washington that it would observe traditional rules in dealing with liners. The *Arabic* pledge temporarily cleared the air, but in March 1916, another submarine attacked a French channel steamer, the *Sussex,* and sank it without warning. Wilson then threatened to break diplomatic relations, an act eliciting the *Sussex* pledge, in which Germany promised more forthrightly than before to respect international law concerning neutral and noncombatant ships on the high seas.

Wilson had won a great diplomatic contest, but the cost was high. He was now more or less committed to war on Germany if the *Sussex* pledge should be repudiated. The price of settlement was a sacrifice of diplomatic flexibility. America's national honor was now at stake. As long as Germany sustained its commitment, all would be well, but resumption of unrestricted submarine war would almost certainly force an American declaration of war. For the moment, Germany stood by its pledge, but the tide of battle ultimately led to a change of policy.

If the submarine controversy greatly frightened pacifists and other opponents of war who feared that it might ultimately draw the United States into the European struggle, it also alarmed sturdy nationalists like the vigorous ex-President Theodore Roosevelt. He and others participated in an untiring campaign to impose "preparedness" on the country. William Jennings Bryan had opposed the *Lusitania* notes, propounding more cautious initiatives. When the controversy passed he determined to resign, convinced that the President had erred seriously in not accepting his counsel of restraint. Robert Lansing succeeded him at the State Department. He was an experienced international lawyer who entertained advanced pro-Allied sentiments. Soon after, the State Department lifted the ban on private American loans to belligerents, and trade with Britain and its allies expanded at a profitable pace. To deal with the advocates of preparedness, Wilson authorized a limited armaments program. Both the army and the navy benefited by legislation passed in 1916, quieting the clamor of T.R. and his minions.

As these events ran their course, the President had matured a strategy for bringing about a European peace. He and his most intimate counsellor, Colonel Edward M. House, recognized that continuance of the war could only cause further tragedy for the growing list of belligerents and that it would increasingly jeopardize American neutrality. The submarine controversy confirmed this latter judgment. Appalled by the destructive nature of the war and determined to safeguard the interest of the United States, the President's initial effort to find ways and means of intervening constructively in behalf of peace was to send House to Europe as an unofficial emissary in February 1915 in order to make inquiries about the basis of potential negotiations. House soon ascertained that American mediation at the time was out of the question. Neither coalition would entertain thoughts of discussions as long as victory seemed attainable, and high hopes for the campaign of 1915 existed on both sides of the war.

This setback failed to deter Wilson and House; they became more and more interested in American mediation as the terrible casualties of 1915 mounted in the several theaters of war. Wilson was convinced that the causes of the war derived from inveterate European practices conducive to instability. Among these vices he gave special weight to militarism and imperialism, to his mind natural attributes of European error. Like so many of his countrymen, Wilson instinctively partook of that age-old national distinction between decadent Europe and pristine America. Despite his pronounced sympathy for the cause of the Allies, he was early assured that all of Europe had been seriously implicated in the processes leading to the Great War. It might be said that the President founded the "revisionist" interpretation of its origins and causes. If his desperate desire to mediate the conflict stemmed partially from considerations of national interest, reflecting his response to the sated condition of the nation, he also responded to the national sense of mission. He believed that the United States was called to a unique role in world history as propagator of those grand principles which had been so beneficial to the homeland. This sense of mission was a special corollary of America's pervasive progressive tradition, of which Wilson was a prime exponent. He hoped not only to uphold the national interest but to insure the well-being of all other peoples as well.

At some point in his contemplation of the European war, Wilson began to weigh a second general objective to accompany mediation. For many years a good number of Americans had agitated for a general association of nations to preserve world peace. The President became increasingly interested in this concept, and particularly in what he came to call a league of nations. In this potential organization, he espied a way of policing the world in order to frustrate international wrongdoers and also a means of organizing social and economic activities to enhance the general well-being and progress of humanity. The league of nations concept ingeniously reconciled America's satiate condition and its progressive aspirations. If a league would stabilize the going order, it would also encourage constructive reform, giving scope to the interests and aspirations of nations less fortunate than the United States. The project held out special attraction to a man like Wilson, filled as he was with a compulsive desire to accomplish great humanitarian deeds as well as to shield the Republic from danger.

Obviously no league could be created until the recovery of peace. To this end the President once again dispatched Colonel House to Europe late in 1915. As before, he was to determine whether a basis existed for mediation. Also, he was empowered to arrange a deal with Great Britain in order to force German cooperation. This tactic was a legacy of the late discontents over the submarine; at this time Wilson believed that Germany was the chief obstacle to a negotiated peace. The House-Grey memorandum of February 1916, signed by the British foreign secretary and the President's servant, provided that on notification from the Allies, the United States would call for negotiations. If Germany refused, the United States would probably enter the war. Here was a bold plan indeed. Had it been publicized at the time, those of isolationist sentiment would have raised an unprecedented outcry. The exigencies of the great European war had already moved Wilson to diplomatic enterprises far beyond any previously contemplated by an American President—far more advanced than the projects of the energetic Theodore Roosevelt, whose intervention at Algeciras paled by comparison.

As it happened, the House-Grey memorandum was not implemented. The same realities precluding mediation earlier in the war insured against success in 1916. The Allies remained confident of victory. No nation engaged in a conflict as desperate as World War I could voluntarily accept a negotiated peace short of its ultimate war aims as long as total victory still seemed feasible. Growing desire in Britain for a more vigorous prosecution of the war resulted in the replacement of the Asquith ministry by a coalition government headed by the aggressive David Lloyd George. Because Britain never asked the United States to appeal publicly for peace negotiations, the House-Grey machinery never went into operation.

During the summer and fall of 1916, Wilson campaigned for reelection. His victory of 1912 had stemmed from a split in the Republican Party between its Regular and Progressive wings. No such advantage aided him in 1916, but he managed a close victory over Charles Evans Hughes of New York. Wilson had guided a remarkable legislative program through the Congress, one source of his popularity, but the principal slogan of the campaign, "He kept us out of war," also had marked appeal. The result of the election strengthened the President's determination to seek a negotiated peace, despite the bleak prospect. In December 1916, he began his final attempt, sending a note to the belligerent powers requesting them to state their war aims. Wilson would then determine whether they provided an opening for negotiations. This departure greatly annoyed the Allies, but Britain's failure to utilize the House-Grey memorandum, coupled with a relative period of calm in German-American relations, had turned Wilson's feelings temporarily against the western coalition. Early in January 1917, Wilson told House that the United States would not enter the war; it would constitute a "crime against civilization."

Once again Wilson encountered frustration, although his effort culminated in one of the great political orations in American history. None of the replies to the appeal of December were really helpful, but the President decided to make a dramatic public call for a negotiated settlement, an outcome he chose to call "peace without victory." On January 22, 1917 he went before the Congress and laid out his dual approach to world settlement. Asking the belligerents mutually to recede from their more advanced war aims and to accept an early peace conference, he also made an explicit appeal for a league of nations. He could not know that plans were already in motion to insure that his last and greatest attempt at mediation would fail.

On January 9, 1917 the German emperor authorized a resumption of submarine warfare at the beginning of February, a decision prompted by the assumption that Germany could end the war before the United States could bring its power to bear. When the German ambassador in Washington, Count Johann von Bernstorff, delivered notification of this decision, the world anticipated an immediate American declaration of war, but the President delayed his final decision. Profoundly opposed to military involvement, the President had been victimized by two prior developments. He had lost diplomatic flexibility by threatening Germany with dire consequences if it resumed unrestricted submarine warfare. He had also expended great energies in a noble but quixotic attempt to mediate the war, an enterprise doomed to failure as long as either of the opposing coalitions entertained hopes of final victory. Seeking alternatives to full belligerency, Wilson first contemplated armed neutrality, a distinctly pro-Allied step but short of war, although he hesitated to make even this move until word arrived late in February of the Zimmermann note from Germany to Mexico proposing an alliance with that country in return for financial assistance and recovery of territories lost to the United States after the Mexican War. When Wilson asked Congress for permission to arm merchantmen, a faction in the Senate he called "a little group of willful men" blocked the authorization. Wilson then discovered executive power sufficient to order the step.

Despite a desperate desire to remain at peace, Wilson was swept along by developments to which he ultimately had to bow. One obstacle to belligerency was that it meant cooperation with the autocratic Russian government, but this objection was swept away after the overthrow of the Tsar early in March and the establishment of a provisional government. Very soon, word came of German attacks on American shipping, and also of British desperation as financial conditions worsened and the submarine took a dreadful toll of merchant ships. Finally, on April 2, 1917, Wilson went to the Congress and asked for war. The United States, he said, would fight for a just and lasting peace to make the world safe for democracy. "To such a task," he concluded, "we can dedicate our lives and our fortunes, everything that we are and everything that we have, with the pride of those who know that the day has come when America is privileged to spend her blood and her might for the principles that gave her birth and happiness and the peace which she has treasured. God helping her, she can do no other." The speech of April 2nd definitively abandoned the hoary traditions of isolation and neutrality. At that moment, America entered fully into world history. On April 6th, the Congress completed action on the declaration of war.

Why did Wilson opt for belligerency, despite every desire on his part and that of the American people to maintain neutrality? Certainly the cards had been stacked against neutrality from the very beginning. Always before, when Europe had become engaged in general warfare, the western hemisphere had been drawn in. The destruction of the European balance was itself a compelling reason for belligerency. The course of events long before 1914 more or less insured that the United States would ultimately act with Great Britain to restore a stable European balance. In addition, Wilson had to respond to the outcome of the submarine controversy; national honor was at stake.

But in the end, Wilson's decision stemmed most importantly from his profound desire to bring about a world settlement based upon the twin principles of peace without victory and a league of nations. These goals he believed to be not only American but also universal necessities, which must prevail. Having failed to accomplish his end by peaceful means, he finally decided to complete his project by the sword. War was the only means left to him to establish sufficient influence to dominate the postwar peace congress. Thus did Woodrow Wilson embark upon the greatest experiment in national mission undertaken by the United States to his time. The President was impaled on the horns of a truly agonizing dilemma. To turn away from war was to abandon all hope of a just and lasting peace; to accept war was to plunge the United States into what he himself said was "the most terrible and disastrous of all wars, civilization itself seeming to be in the balance." For Woodrow Wilson, "the right [was] more precious than peace," and he launched his crusade for a *pax Americana* on that somber note.

* * *

Wilson pictured the war as a great confrontation between democracy and autocracy, but he remained convinced that all of Europe, not just the particularly odious Central Powers, had contributed to its causation. Having accepted belligerency as the only means of insuring a responsible peace settlement, Wilson turned to the task of guaranteeing that at war's end the United States would possess sufficient power to dictate postwar arrangements to both the victorious and the vanquished of Europe. In his war message Wilson had adumbrated his plans for bending the Central Powers to his will. The United States would contribute sufficient men and materials to achieve victory. He did not say that American force would be applied only in ways to strengthen the President's hand at the peace conference. There he would negotiate more with his associates in victory than with the defeated powers.

To guarantee further that none of the Allies could challenge American leadership in making peace, Wilson specifically set out to avoid diplomatic entanglements of the sort which tied together the other members of the exterior coalition, the network of "secret treaties," in order to maintain the greatest possible freedom of action. The United States would fight hard enough to encompass the defeat of the Central Powers, but it would conduct its diplomacy on an independent basis. The limited nature of the American commitment to the Allies was pointedly reflected in Wilson's reference to the United States as an "associated" rather than an "allied" power.

Many historians persist in the attribution of practically nothing but a pervasive moralism to Wilson the diplomatist. Moralist he certainly was, unmatched in the history of American politics, but he was also a toughminded politician of the most ruthless type who was entirely capable of executing grand political designs in the most "realistic" manner. Those who stress Wilson's moralism too often ignore the methods he utilized to force through the Congress his legislative program, the "new freedom," in 1913–1914 as well as a considerable range of social and economic reforms during 1915–1916. They also ignore his conduct of American foreign policy during 1917–1918. As the United States turned to the prosecution of the war, Wilson applied his political acumen to the task of rendering Europe as subservient to his desire as the Congress. If Wilson was by nature a lion, he was also a competent fox when the situation required cunning.

Wilson moved during 1917 to shore up both Latin American and Far Eastern policy in order to insure against outside interference with the prosecution of the European conflict. Aware that difficulties in the Caribbean and elsewhere in the hemisphere might seriously detract from the American war effort, the President adopted a general policy of conciliation, beginning with *de jure* recognition of the Carranza regime in Mexico. He also encouraged Latin American countries either to declare war or to break diplomatic relations with the Central Powers. No unilateral interventions took place during the duration of the war despite provocation here and there, a restraint helping to curry favor with the other Americas. The war created economic opportunities for many Latin American countries – markets and good prices for Cuba's sugar, Argentina's beef, and Chile's nitrates. United States encouragement of expanded Latin American trade also helped vastly to improve the political climate of the hemisphere. It is not too much to say, although historians have generally not done so, that these undramatic developments marked the beginning of a general turn away from the high-handedness of the imperial interlude. The trend gained strength during the postwar decade and culminated in the Good Neighbor policy of the 1930s.

In East Asia, Japan could contemplate new projects of expansion, since America was deeply involved in the European war. Early in 1917 Japan managed to gain diplomatic support from the Entente powers for its desire to retain the Shantung concession and the German islands it had occupied earlier in the war. Tokyo hoped to extort a comparable agreement from the United States. In November 1917, Secretary Lansing signed an executive agreement with a special emissary from Japan, Count Ishii, which seemed in some ways to compromise the open door. The Lansing-Ishii agreement ritualistically indorsed the principles of Hay, but it also recognized that "territorial propinquity creates special relations between countries," a statement which could have been interpreted as a subtle means of justifying Japanese inroads in China. A secret addendum bound each party not to injure China during the course of the war. If Japan tried to make more of the Lansing-Ishii agreement than intended by the United States, the understanding achieved the minimal objective of American statecraft, which was to restrain Japan until the end of the war.

The year 1917 was hardly a season of triumph for the European Allies. A series of crushing blows placed the Central Powers in a good position to end the war in 1918. Anglo-French offensives on the western front were repulsed with great losses. The submarine made an enormous bag of allied shipping on the high seas. In the fall, an Austro-German offensive at Caporetto caused a precipitate Italian retreat. The final blow was the successful Bolshevik revolution in Russia. Calling for "peace, land, and bread," the Bolsheviks immediately began negotiations for a separate peace. The end of Russian resistance allowed Germany to reinforce its formations in the West with many veteran divisions.

As disaster mounted, Wilson bent every effort to speed the American mobilization. Germany had gambled that the United States would not be able to mobilize before the German army and navy had taken the Allies out of the war. The setbacks of 1917 proved that the United States must undertake an extensive land campaign in Europe to supplement its financial, logistical, and naval assistance. Considerable confusion and inefficiency attended the American mobilization, but it developed at a much faster pace than anyone anticipated. Quite early, Wilson and his military advisers decided to place an independent army in Europe to campaign in its own sector under its own commanders. National pride required separate operations, but the administration also realized that the contributions made by an independent force would strengthen the American position at the peace conference. Here was Clausewitzian *Realpolitik* indeed, from a President supposedly incapable of such calculations.

During 1917 the United States pursued a circumspect policy on war aims. Wilson realized that his objectives were quite different from those of the European Allies, with the exception of Britain. In the early stages of American participation, he preferred to keep silent on his plans for a number of good reasons. For one thing, the crisis of the war was fast approaching—no time to engage in inter-Allied political controversy. In addition, he believed that American bargaining power would be much greater at war's end than in 1917. Many historians have criticized Wilson for not striking a bargain on war aims as a price of American intervention, but Wilson correctly decided that he could get more at a later time than in April 1917. He postponed his demands on the Allies until they were in no position to refuse or minimize them.

The impending German offensives for 1918 finally forced the Allied and Associated Powers to improve inter-Allied cooperation. A great conference at Paris in December 1917 established a large number of inter-Allied agencies to coordinate shipping, munitions, transportation, finance, and the like. In addition, an Inter-Allied Naval Council came into being. All these agencies worked under the general supervision of the principal inter-Allied organ — the Supreme War Council. Set up shortly before the Paris conference, it provided overall political-military direction. The several heads of government were members. The United States participated actively in all these groups and made a major contribution to their success. Their work allowed the western coalition to withstand the heavy German assaults of 1918 and to organize a powerful counteroffensive which forced an early decision.

By the first days of 1918, the western Allies had become heavily dependent upon the American reinforcement, already beginning to have a considerable impact, and Wilson took advantage of this circumstance to start a public development of American war aims. On January 8, 1918 the President went before the Congress to make the most famous of his orations, the Fourteen Points address. Wilson acted unilaterally without prior or later consultation with the Entente powers. He deliberately maintained diplomatic independence while seizing control of coalition diplomacy. The first five points reiterated a number of traditional American objectives including "open covenants openly arrived at," freedom of the seas, elimination of barriers to international trade, disarmament, and self-determination. The next eight dealt with a broad range of territorial questions, measured against the principle of self-determination, in which Wilson frequently expressed views in conflict with the secret treaties. The fourteenth point read: "A general association of nations must be formed under specific covenants for the purpose of affording mutual guarantees of political independence and territorial integrity to great and small nations alike." By the device of the Fourteen Points Wilson made much clearer than before his intention to dictate a peace without victory and to create a league of nations — his dual prerequisites for a just and lasting peace.

As the decisive year of the war ran its course, Wilson occasionally added to the body of American war aims. By October they had been spelled out in considerable detail, although many of them were susceptible to diverse interpretations. In February he announced the "four principles." In July came "four additional principles," and in

September the "five particulars," making a grand total of twenty-seven points. No other nation approached the specificity of the Wilsonian program; detailed American war aims were a matter of public record well before the armistice. The Allies paid surprisingly little attention to these pronouncements. Perhaps they took them as mere propaganda to undermine morale in the Central Powers. Possibly they thought they could handle Wilson later on. They apparently did not realize the deadly seriousness of the American President. He was determined that those young men who sacrificed themselves in France would not die in vain. He viewed his project as one of world-historical significance, an endeavor essential to the preservation and extension of civilization along peaceful and constructive lines.

During 1918 Wilson maintained his policy of making a major contribution to victory in the field while maintaining diplomatic flexibility. The role of the United States in the Supreme War Council illustrated this political-military approach to the war. The President sent a military representative to the seat of the Council at Versailles, the talented General Tasker H. Bliss, but he did not appoint a political deputy to sit in his stead. Colonel House attended the meeting of December 1917, held during the Paris conference, but did not return until the fateful pre-armistice negotiations conducted by the Council in October-November 1918. General Bliss assiduously supported the establishment of a unified command in France which brought General Foch to authority as an inter-Allied generalissimo. He did so because this arrangement promised to speed victory without embarrassing American diplomacy. On the other hand, Bliss actively opposed European efforts to "amalgamate" American troops by small units into the French and British armies, a practice constantly urged by Premier Georges Clemenceau of France and Lloyd George on the ground that it would hasten an effective employment of American man power. These European proposals worked directly against the fixed American determination to create an independent army in France, and therefore Wilson never allowed amalgamation except on a temporary basis when Germany mounted severe attacks during the months of March-July 1918.

The most striking example of America's half-way covenant with the Allies was Wilson's policy toward the Bolshevik revolution. When Lenin took Russia out of the war with the signature of the Brest-Litovsk treaty in March 1918, the Allies renewed earlier propositions of intervention in northern Russia and eastern Siberia in order to reconstitute the eastern front, fearing that the German reinforcement of the western front after the Russian defalcation might allow a German breakthrough. The desire for intervention also reflected a vast fear and hatred of the advanced social revolutionary doctrines advanced by

Lenin and his colleagues. Wilson absolutely opposed all projects of full-scale intervention in Russia and never permitted any of them to take place. In July 1918 he finally condoned inter-Allied landings at Murmansk and Archangel in the north, and at Vladivostok in Siberia, but only to protect war materials accumulated at those ports and to expedite the passage of Czech prisoners of war out of Russia. A covert motive was to place restrictions on Anglo-French and Japanese invasions of the Russian interior.

Wilson had a number of cogent reasons for avoiding full-scale intervention in Russia. He and his advisers never wavered in their advocacy of the "western strategy"—concentration on the theater of war in France. They believed that the war could be won most rapidly at the least expense by massing inter-Allied power along the western front. Why, they argued, divert man power and supplies desperately needed in the principal theater of war to a dangerous adventure in the vast reaches of Russia? They believed that the project lacked military justification because of the very distances of the Russian interior; it seemed impossible in Washington to mount an intervention on a scale sufficient to insure success. Finally, and most important, Wilson and House realized that an armed intervention would violate the principle of self-determination at the very heart of the American postwar territorial plans. The American leaders bowed to no one in their dislike of the Bolsheviks, but they believed that other means of controlling the Bolshevik phenomenon were more appropriate than armed intervention. The Allies, of course, pressed for intervention to achieve other objectives besides military victory over Germany. The United States had no intention of using its power to pursue the imperial projects of Europe.

Germany launched its expected offensive on the western front in March 1918, but after limited success it was finally contained by the Allied armies, largely because of the reinforcement from the United States. American doughboys did not do much of the actual fighting. Instead, they relieved experienced French and British divisions along quiet sectors of the front. These Allied troops then strengthened shaken formations along the more northerly and westerly reaches of the battleline where the heaviest engagements took place. American logistical support of the Anglo-French sectors also contributed heavily to the outcome. By July, Foch was able to mount a counteroffensive which succeeded beyond anyone's expectations. By September it became apparent to Germany that the war was lost. A quick and unexpected end to the struggle was in prospect.

On October 5th, the first peace note arrived in Washington from Germany; it came from a new government headed by Prince Max of Baden, chosen to end the war when General Ludendorff admitted that the German army had reached its last extremities. Austrian notes also came during the same period. The Central Powers negotiated with the United States rather than the Entente precisely because the American war aims were less stringent than those of France, Italy, and Britain. After a clever diplomatic correspondence, Wilson ultimately committed the German government to a negotiated peace based on the twenty-seven points. The President thus at least approximated his earlier aspiration to mediate the war. His exchanges with Berlin greatly annoyed the European Allies, fearful that he might botch the negotiations and also that he might bargain away their wartime aspirations.

Once Germany agreed to his demands, Wilson sought inter-Allied acceptance of his negotiations. To achieve this purpose, he sent Colonel House to the Supreme War Council in Paris. That body showed irritation at various of the Wilsonian points, but at a critical moment House warned his Entente colleagues that their recalcitrance might result in a separate peace between Germany and the United States. This threat was sufficient to win their acceptance of the twenty-seven points with the exception of two reservations. Britain raised objections to freedom of the seas and France insisted on some indemnification. The inter-Allied political accord drafted in Paris was cast in the form of a "pre-armistice agreement" which Wilson then communicated to Germany. The Supreme War Council also reached agreement on the military and naval terms of an armistice. On November 11, 1918 the catastrophic war reached its end.

President Wilson could look back on the preceding nineteen months with great satisfaction. His general plan had worked to perfection. Germany had been cast down in the dust, and both the victorious and vanquished of Europe had been required to accept a negotiated peace on American terms. A truly remarkable achievement, it ranks among the greatest diplomatic accomplishments in United States history. The final stage of the long process lay just ahead. Wilson prepared for an arduous sojourn in Europe in order to complete his grand design for the future of mankind. Some of his advisers, including House, Lansing, and Bliss, thought that the President ought not to attend the peace conference, arguing that he could exercise more influence over its deliberations if he remained at home. But Wilson was determined to participate, believing, quite correctly, that no one else could accomplish as much as he in behalf of his plans for the peace.

*   *   *

Deeply exhausted by the strains of war, Wilson committed a serious political error at its end. Just before the armistice, he suffered an embarrassing repulse in the midterm congressional elections. In order to lend prestige to Democratic political candidates seeking election in 1918, Wilson requested something like a vote of confidence from the people. The people failed to respond. The result was the return of narrow Republican majorities in both Houses of Congress, hardly a favorable portent for the future. The election turned on many issues besides the President's foreign policy; the outcome could not be construed as a repudiation of his international leadership, although bitter opponents like T.R. attempted to place this interpretation on the results. Whatever the meaning of the vote, Wilson went off to Paris without the appearance of national support that negotiators at great peace congresses like to enjoy. Lloyd George and Clemenceau both took care to obtain national mandates before taking themselves to the Paris Peace Conference.

Wilson also erred politically in his selection of the American peace commission. To assist him in Paris, Wilson chose Colonel House, Secretary of State Lansing, General Bliss, and the experienced diplomatist Henry White, the only Republican in the group and a nominal one at that. Wilson's foolish refusal to appoint a leading Republican like Taft or Root and his unwillingness to select a leading congressional figure of either party were gratuitous and unwise acts. They would return to haunt him in the future. For the moment he was confident that the Congress would finally cooperate with him. Never before had the Senate refused consent to a treaty following an American war. In any event, he thought that his public support would be sufficient to coerce Congress into accepting his accomplishments in Paris.

The President also overestimated his general international appeal. When he first arrived in Europe, he made a number of visitations, particularly to Rome and London, which stimulated tumultuous receptions. His advent in Paris was equally encouraging. These experiences seemed to confirm his newly acquired status as the principal world statesman. The cheers would turn into criticisms when Europe finally grasped Wilson's full intentions, but the President at Paris was in a powerful position indeed, strong enough to ride out a considerable reaction against his program across the continent.

Once the conference began work, Wilson proceeded first to negotiate the covenant of the projected league of nations. Aware of considerable opposition to his desire, especially in France, he was determined to obtain agreement on it before any other matters were settled. He also decided to make the covenant an integral part of the treaty of peace with Germany. The heart of the covenant was its article ten, providing for a collective security arrangement. "The Members of the League undertake to respect and preserve as against external aggression the territorial integrity and existing political independence of all Members of the League. In case of any such aggression or in case of any threat or danger of such aggression the Council shall advise upon the means by which this obligation shall be fulfilled." Having forced agreement on an acceptable draft of the covenant, Wilson temporarily returned to the United States to meet his constitutional obligations at the closing of Congress.

Wilson's visit home was hardly as triumphal as he would have liked. Already congressional opposition was brewing, led by one of Wilson's most deadly political enemies, Senator Henry Cabot Lodge of Massachusetts, who would become the chairman of the Senate's Committee on Foreign Relations in the new Congress. At House's suggestion, Wilson arranged a meeting with the Committee to discuss his negotiations in Paris, but the gathering failed to dissolve the distrustful attitude of the legislators. On March 3, 1919, Lodge announced a so-called "round robin" signed by enough Senators to prevent ratification of any peace treaty; it rejected the draft covenant and called for an immediate settlement with Germany separate from the league question. The round robin deeply affronted Wilson, but he realized the importance of conciliating the Senate, and upon his return to Paris he negotiated a number of modifications in the text of the covenant to meet congressional criticism. This development was unfortunate in that it gave France and Britain opportunities to gain concessions on other points in return for revisions of the covenant. Wilson remained adamant against changes in the phraseology of article ten, the most important source of congressional anxiety.

In negotiating the military, territorial, and economic sections of the peace settlement, Wilson was guided by a desire to make magnanimous arrangements, above all seeking to restore some semblance of stability in Europe. In this effort he usually gained British support, at least to the degree permitted by Lloyd George's obligation to honor commitments made during the war to Britain's allies and the Commonwealth nations. France was the chief opponent of American desires. Wilson often found himself defending Germany against rapacious French proposals. Clemenceau, of course, had plenty of justification for his obsession with insuring against any possible resurgence of German power, but France was also interested in obtaining a preeminent position in Europe. The United States and Great Britain had fought the war largely to preclude German domination of the continent: they had no desire to make a peace which gave France continental influence beyond that necessary to guard its security. The French method of achieving continental dominance was, first to impose enormous obligations on Germany including huge reparations and unilateral disarmament, and to seize a powerful strategic position on the Rhine. To subordinate Russia and uproot Bolshevism, Marshal Foch developed an amazing scheme. He hoped to organize a great army of eastern Europeans, supported by American troops, in order to accomplish against the Bolsheviks in 1919 what had been done to Germany in 1918. This fantastic plan was never permitted to mature, but it was striking evidence of French ambitions·on the continent.

Aside from the league, what were the principal accomplishments at Paris? If viewed from the perspective of those who suffered by them, Germany and Russia (the latter not represented at the conference) were the greatest losers. Germany surrendered Alsace-Lorraine to France and accepted the demilitarization of the Rhineland. In the East, it lost territory to the revived state of Poland and to Czechoslovakia. Its Pacific and African holdings went either to Japan or to various Commonwealth nations. In addition, Germany accepted "war guilt," agreed to pay huge reparations to the victors, and undertook to disarm. The Russian territorial loss was perhaps the most devastating single outcome of Paris. A tremendous slice of Russia's western reaches was assigned to a number of new states: Finland, Latvia, Lithuania, Estonia, and Poland. Rumania acquired the province of Bessarabia. The outcome at Paris greatly influenced the course of Russian foreign policy during the long armistice to come and the second phase of the Twentieth Century War two decades later. The behavior of the capitalist powers seemed to confirm Bolshevik assumptions concerning their unregenerate nature.

Other defeated powers also suffered grievously. Turkey surrendered its European territory to Greece except the district including Istanbul, and its old empire in the Middle East was largely mandated to Britain and France (Treaty of Sèvres). Austria and Hungary were separated. Austria lost territory to Italy, Czechoslovakia, and Yugoslavia, and was reduced to a small land-locked power (Treaty of St. Germain). Hungary surrendered land to Rumania (Treaty of Trianon). Bulgaria got off the lightest, transferring some territory to Greece (Treaty of Neuilly).

A number of other arrangements filled out the treaty structure. The mandate system, incorporated in the league structure to administer dependent territories taken from the losers, was a step away from old-fashioned imperialism. Mandatory powers supposed to prepare colonial charges for eventual self-government, but critics claimed that it was merely a device for disguising the old colonialism in new and more respectable garb. The conference side-stepped a number of lesser territorial controversies in Europe by arranging plebiscites in the future. To safeguard the rights of various ethnic groups in eastern Europe whose pleas for national independence

European Territorial Change, 1914-1919

Territory lost
by Germany

Territory lost
by Austria-Hungary

Territory lost
by Russia

SWEDEN

NORWAY

FINLAND

ESTONIA

LATVIA

LITHUANIA

DENMARK

EAST
PRUSSIA

RUSSIA

U.S.S.R.

NETH

GERMANY

BELG

RHINELAND
(occupied)

POLAND

FRANCE

(to France)

CZECHOSLOVAKIA

BESSARABIA
(to Rumania)

SWITZ

AUSTRIA

HUNGARY

(to Italy)

RUMANIA

ITALY

YUGOSLAVIA

EUROPEAN TURKEY
(to Greece)

BULGARIA

(Southern Bulgaria,
to Greece)

ALBANIA

GREECE

TURKEY

could not be granted, protective minorities treaties were imposed upon the countries in which they resided.

Wilson has often been attacked for permitting modifications of the twenty-seven points making quasi-Carthaginian settlements of the Paris treaties. His detractors point to, among other things, the burden of reparations imposed on Germany, numerous violations of self-determination, failure to secure disarmament except of Germany, an inequitable Russian settlement, the political and economic weakness of new states in eastern Europe, and concessions injurious to China gained by Japan. Other observers insist that the most remarkable thing about the treaties was the degree to which they approximated the requirements of the Wilsonian aims.

At least four realities ought to be noted in connection with the President's concessions to the victorious Entente powers. Some of them reflected unavoidable wartime obligations incurred among the Allies. Wilson's desire to insure acceptance of his league gave other countries a chance to extort unwise arrangements of various kinds in return for support of the new international organization. Another concern was the need for rapid decisions. Throughout Europe the specter of violent social revolution had raised itself, not only among the defeated nations but also in some of the victorious countries. Both Germany and Hungary experienced sharp revolutions while the conference met. Both enterprises failed, but they sent a thrill of fear through the delegations at Paris. The haste of the negotiations contributed to their inadequacies. Finally, there was the devastation of the war itself. The shock of the conflict was too severe to permit an easy or rapid recovery. The peace treaty inevitably reflected the disintegration of European politics and culture caused by over four years of unparalleled warfare. Treaties are not negotiated in a vacuum; the Paris settlement was no exception, and it naturally suffered from the general debility of Europe in the wake of the Great War.

Wilson's difficulties with Italy and Japan give some indication of the trying situations with which he had to deal. Italy was determined to acquire control of the Dalmatian city of Fiume, a violation of the principle of self-determination. Wilson believed that it should serve as a port for the new state of Yugoslavia and he resolutely opposed Italian demands. Despite a walkout by the Italian premier, Vittorio Orlando, the President held firm. Japan insisted upon confirming its conquest of German concessions in Shantung. Especially interested in Japanese participation in the league, Wilson bowed when the Japanese delegation threatened to leave the conference unless its desires were met.

Wilson fully recognized the errors and imperfections of the Versailles treaty and the other settlements, but he took comfort in the

thought that as the war receded into the past it would bcome possible
to revise some of the more egregious mistakes through the beneficient
operations of the league, especially certain of the economic provisions
such as the reparations clauses. He left Paris with his league and also
with a number of additional accomplishments which went a long way
toward achieving his second concern—a reconstituted European
balance. The President never repudiated the balance of power despite
certain public statements to the contrary. The principle of collective
security included in article ten was a means of supplementing and
particularly of purifying the balance of power in order to resist its
tendency to break down rather than a replacement of it. The Treaty
of Versailles was signed on June 28, 1919. Leaving other members of
the peace commission behind to complete the negotiation of the
treaties for the other defeated powers, Wilson quit Europe, hopeful
that his labors of reconstruction and purification would secure that
just and lasting peace for which he had worked so long and well.

* * *

Unfortunately for the President, a sea of troubles awaited him in the
United States. A wide range of obstacles insured that the effort to
ratify the treaty would turn into a long and trying struggle. Of these
difficulties, perhaps the most important was a decline in the President's influence at home. Even during the war Wilson had begun to
lose touch with his constituency. He failed to realize that he had not
successfully communicated the content and purpose of his peace plans
to the American people. His tendency to moralistic oratory tended to
obscure the hard political considerations which undcrgirded the peace
treaty. He was asking the people to make a great leap forward in their
practice of world politics. In the end, he asked too much. Wars require
supreme national effort, especially the modern war of the nation in
arms. After such exertions, the people naturally seek relaxation.
Exhaustion makes it difficult to hold them to that pitch of political
responsibility necessary to insure a sound postwar settlement. By late
1919, when the treaty finally came before the Senate, the Americans
were in the midst of a considerable disillusionment. The crusading
spirit of 1917–1918 rapidly evaporated. Wilson's appeal to that spirit
met with something less than approbation when he attempted to
explain and justify his actions at Paris.

Wilson was a tormented man, caught in the grip of certain neurotic
compulsions which had helped him politically in the past but tended to
injure him during the fight for the League of Nations. The experiences of his early life appear to have built into him a severe distaste

for opposition. Earlier in his career, he had gotten into great diffi-culties with those who refused to accept his leadership, particularly while President of Princeton University and Governor of New Jersey. His natural response to political opposition was to run roughshod over it. He often attributed all manner of evil to those who resisted his leadership, finding it difficult to distinguish between difference of opinion and malicious intent. The President's relations with the Re-publican Party in general and with Senator Lodge in particular are excellent examples of this trait. In Paris Wilson controlled his impulses and moved with remarkable circumspection in his dealings with the bitter Clemenceau and the expediential Lloyd George. Worn out by the negotiations, he could not contain himself in his relations with the Senate over the treaty. All this was severely complicated by a near-fatal illness sustained by the President several weeks before the Senate took up the treaty.

Perhaps those two factors, the lack of truly general understanding of the peace settlement and the President's personal failings, counted for most in the defeat of the treaty, but other difficulties also con-tributed to failure. The document aroused considerable apprehension in the Republican Party, hopeful of regaining the Presidency in 1920 after eight years out of power. Many partisans feared that acceptance of the treaty as it stood would insure Democratic rule for another four years. Additional opposition came from various ethnic groups in the United States, particularly those of Irish, Italian, and German back-ground, whose countries of origin had suffered real or imagined indignities at Paris.

The President also encountered concerted opposition from those who disagreed with his concepts of international involvement by the Republic. A significant group of Senators, largely from the Middle and Far West, including the noted Progressives Robert La Follette and Hiram Johnson, still clung to the traditions of isolation and neutrality, fearful that foreign responsibilities would militate against continuing reform at home and persuaded that strategic security could be main-tained best by continuing the practice of nonentanglement. Another group, of which Lodge was representative, accepted the end of the old ways but believed that the proper course of the United States in world affairs was to use its power independently, acting on its own without membership in an institution as untried and restrictive as the league. For different reasons, then, many good men and women of progres-sive inclination and many others of nationalist sentiment opposed the treaty on principle. There was even a small group of advanced inter-nationalists who opposed the treaty and the league because they seemed to them reactionary—a new Holy Alliance. There was some-

thing to be said for all these views. To dismiss those who entertained
them as base scoundrels was surely to err. The perspective of history
suggests that Wilson was wiser than his opponents, but the latter were
certainly privileged to dissent. It is always dangerous to assume that
those who express contrary views are necessarily fools or rascals.

If Wilson had taken many a political scalp during his years in the
White House, he met his match in the venerable Henry Cabot Lodge.
Lodge had many reasons for contesting the treaty. He hated the
imperious Wilson; he was a Republican of Republicans; and he be-
longed to the nationalist school of T.R., convinced that article ten
required an undue sacrifice of sovereignty. The embittered Senator
from Massachusetts was enormously skilled in those legislative arts
required to frustrate the executive branch. At the least hopeful of
securing a considerable revision of the treaty, and possibly intent upon
bringing it down, Lodge practiced all the techniques of delay and
obfuscation peculiar to political minorities. By November 1919, after
offering his own set of reservations to the treaty aimed particularly at
its most unprecedented provision, article ten of the covenant, the
Chairman of the Foreign Relations Committee had the votes he
needed to block consent. Realizing the situation, Wilson's congressional supporters pleaded with him to compromise. Desperately ill, Wilson
remained intransigent. Earlier he had attempted a strenuous speaking
tour of the country to drum up support for the treaty. At its conclusion he suffered a stroke. For weeks he lay next to death's door, completely out of touch with developments and protected from all dis-
turbance by a doting wife and a zealous physician. To the bitter end
he refused to budge from the text of the treaty signed in Paris, convinced that he had already made all the compromises he could allow.

The treaty came to a vote on November 19, 1919. Twice the Senate
refused consent with the Lodge reservations appended. It failed to
vote on the treaty with "mild" reservations far less stringent than those
of Lodge. A vote on the treaty without change failed—thirty-eight for,
fifty-three against. The "strong reservationists" and the "irreconcila-
bles" joined to bury the proponents of little or no change in the treaty
text. The treaty was dead, dead beyond recall, despite a sustained
endeavor in succeeding months to reverse the decision of November.
Another vote took place in the Senate on March 19, 1920, but again
the necessary support could not be found.

The President made a final lonely effort to secure acceptance of the
Versailles Treaty; he attempted to make the election of 1920 a "sol-
emn referendum" on the treaty and the league. Some evidence suggests that Wilson aspired to a third term despite his crippling illness.
In any case, his party turned to Governor James M. Cox of Ohio. He

and his running mate, the Assistant Secretary of the Navy, Franklin D. Roosevelt, made a gallant fight for Wilsonian principles, but the Republican candidate, Senator Warren G. Harding of Ohio, won in a great landslide. During the campaign Harding was elusive on the league question. Some thirty-one eminent Republicans issued a statement in which they indorsed continuing efforts to secure a modified arrangement, one which did not include the disturbing article ten. However, the outcome did not turn on international politics. It reflected the appeal of what Harding called "normalcy," an ungrammatical but popular label for the national desire to be rid of Wilson and all his works. Eight years of crusading, first at home and then abroad, was enough for the American people. So ended one of the most spectacular Presidencies in American history, the age of Wilson. The immediate future was in the hands of entirely different types.

It is impossible to guess at what the future might have been like had the Senate accepted the Treaty of Versailles. Certain it is that the Paris settlements depended on continuing American participation in their implementation, and most particularly on American membership in the League of Nations. The debâcle of 1919 was the first step toward World War II. The postwar settlement was far less than perfect; inherent weaknesses in its structure insured a future fraught with peril. And yet the arrangement was not without considerable merit. The creation of the League of Nations was perhaps the greatest international achievement of its time. If it cannot be argued with certainty that American support of the postwar treaty system would have prevented another violent phase of the Twentieth Century War a generation later, it can be said that the future assuredly would have been different, and it probably would have been better.

*   *   *

World War I deeply affected the destiny of all the world. The exhaustion of the great European powers brought the United States to the very pinnacle of world power; after 1918 it was the single most powerful nation in the world. Europe had been shattered, so much so that gloomy intellectuals often decreed the death of European civilization. In distant Russia, a massive social upheaval had produced the first Communist regime. Lenin and his followers elaborated a concept of radical world revolution as an alternative to Wilson's international liberalism. Even during the war, there began a marked stirring of national consciousness in the colonial world of Africa and Asia. It produced growing agitation for freedom and independence, now conceivable because of European exhaustion. The outcome of the

Great War prefigured the course of the future. Looked at from the perspective of fifty years, the conflict of 1914–1918 appears as a great Pandora's box, loosing on the world a perfect storm of troubles still extant.

After 1919 the rest of the world constantly struggled with the desperate legacy of World War I, but the Americans took a long vacation, broken only by the second violent phase of the Twentieth Century War—a war they might have helped to prevent had they accepted the challenge of international leadership held up to them by Woodrow Wilson. But it was not to be, and the dreary narrative of the Long Armistice bears tragic witness to the wages of irresponsibility.

CHAPTER VI

The Long Armistice

A FTER FIVE OR six years of difficulties in the wake of the peace treaties, the world seemed to recover momentum; it appeared that gloomy predictions of impending disaster issued by intellectuals, artists, and even public men had been premature. Right after World War I Russia and Poland fought a bitter war in eastern Europe. Greece and Turkey followed suit in the eastern Mediterranean. German problems were not resolved; continuing difficulties precipitated a French occupation of the Rhineland in 1923. These untoward events finally resolved themselves; by 1924 or 1925 things seemed to have returned to something like an even keel. The early activity of the League greatly encouraged Europe, and the Locarno accords of 1925 brought Germany back to the councils of the continent. German membership in the League marked a symbolic end to the bitterness of the early postwar years. The relative prosperity and stability of the late Twenties drowned all thought of another great war. If writers like Ernest Hemingway rejected the ongoing society, preferring to live by personal codes rather than public standards in order to endure a world they never made, other folk threw themselves vigorously into the task of rebuilding their lives and fortunes along more conventional lines with considerable success.

And yet, however encouraging the overt trend of things, forces were at work to reverse the hopeful reconstruction of the postwar decade. The most telling problems were economic in character. Never properly resolved, they finally precipitated social and political crises of the gravest magnitude. The war had indeed delivered a tremendous shock to Europe in all respects. The great international collapse of 1929–1930 finally exposed the weakness of the postwar settlement. The structure of international peace rapidly fell apart as the vast economic stagnation of the early Thirties fed the appetite of European totalitarianism, most especially in Germany, where Adolph Hitler rose from the depths to the pinnacle of power and set in motion a national aggrandizement leading ultimately to another general war.

The evanescent reconstruction of Europe seemed to confirm the wisdom of the American decision largely to withdraw from European politics and the international community in general—at least on the cooperative basis envisioned by Woodrow Wilson. The American people were caught up in a "success-exhaustion syndrome." After all, the war had been won, and Yankee intervention had insured victory. In the short run, the triumph of 1918 had brought profound national security in its train. The postwar debility of Europe seemed to guarantee that no dangers to the western hemisphere could emanate from across the sea for a long time to come. The Pacific appeared more likely to become the seat of postwar difficulties.

The people were tired of international involvement. Disillusioned by the outcome of World War I, they sought release from the terrible pressures of responsibility, especially when it appeared that their security would not be threatened by repudiating the Wilsonian scheme of things. If they had been exhausted by the crusade of 1914–1918, they had stored up a considerable interest in turning their energies directly to the satisfaction of personal desires. People wanted a good time, and they often succeeded during the Twenties, that Era of Wonderful Nonsense. They also sought filthy lucre, and in this aspiration, too, many of them succeeded. The war built a pent-up demand for consumer goods which underwrote economic success well into the Twenties. It also opened markets elsewhere in the world, contributing considerably to national prosperity. If the business cycle of the era was far less steady than many now realize, and if a good number of significant economic groups like the farmers never took part in the boom, it was undeniably a "new era," as prophets of the boom psychology liked to call it. In this manner, the recovery of optimism in Europe found its counterpart in the United States.

The success-exhaustion syndrome in America contributed to a general repudiation of international responsibility. The nation by no means reverted entirely to the policies and practices of the nineteenth century, or even of the years just preceding the Great War, but certainly it refused to contemplate anything like the degree of engagement its role as the world's first power imposed upon it. American security was at stake, as well as that of the entire world, but who in the heady Twenties could have predicted the unspeakable outcome of retreat from international duty? If the imperial interlude had ushered the United States into world politics and the World War had brought the nation fully into its complexities, the national mood of frustration at war's end produced a season of tragic error in foreign policy.

As long as prosperity abided, all things seemed to conspire to national security and progress; once again people cultivated the delusion that the world ran best with the United States in general political repose. As it happened, the United States contributed unwittingly to the maturation of those deep-lying forces which eventually undermined reconstruction and precipitated the instability of the Thirties. The onset of the second great violent phase of the Twentieth Century War in 1939 revealed that the world had failed to settle those tensions causing World War I. Instead, that struggle merely intensified them. Had the United States adopted a more responsible course during the 1920s, the outcome might have been much different. The world desperately needed American leadership, but that nation refused the burdens of power—a decision which brought to the American people and to the entire world a portion of tragedy far beyond anything experienced earlier.

* * *

The Republicans who took power in 1921—unkind antagonists called them the "Ohio gang"—realized that a prime source of unrest was the Pacific-East Asian region. There, Japan was restive and China remained weak. Harding and his associates repudiated the internationalist Wilson and all his works, but they sincerely hoped to make a contribution to security in the Pacific and to the great principle of disarmament. The result was the Washington Naval Conference of 1921–1922. It produced a series of treaties which seemed at the time a major contribution to peace and security. Like the United States, Great Britain worried about the Far East, particularly hopeful of escaping the bonds of its Japanese alliance. Secretary of State Charles Evans Hughes, one of the two stars in the rather tawdry crown of Harding's cabinet (Herbert Hoover of the Department of Commerce was the other), saw an opportunity to accomplish a number of diplomatic objectives. One was naval disarmament, a means of reducing defense expenditures, and the other was a general security system for the Pacific.

When the representatives of invited nations convened in Washington, Hughes started off things in unprecedented fashion by making a number of concrete disarmament proposals which at once shocked and intrigued the statesmen of the world. Energetic negotiations produced a "five-power treaty" establishing a ratio of 5 : 5 : 3 : 1.67 : 1.67 for the capital-ship tonnage of the British, American, Japanese, French, and Italian navies. The agreement did not cover lesser craft, but it required several nations to destroy existing vessels, certainly a striking event. Nothing like it had ever been achieved before.

The Pacific settlement came in two other treaties and several related agreements. A "nine-power treaty" pledged the conferees to the traditional open door principles. A fine gesture, it lacked substantive significance because the treaty included no enforcement procedures. A "four-power treaty" between Britain, Japan, France, and the United States established consultative machinery to settle quarrels arising among the signatories in the Pacific. It also required nonfortification of numerous holdings in the Pacific, but failed to include enforcement procedures. Side agreements arranged Japanese withdrawal from the Shantung, the abrogation of the Anglo-Japanese alliance, and American cable rights on the lonely isle of Yap.

Widely heralded at the time and defended since as the best settlement that could have been obtained, the Pacific settlements lacked important elements. The most obvious omission was effective means of insuring that signatory powers adhered to their engagements. Less obvious, but of great significance later, was the fact that the settlement gave international sanction to Japanese gains in East Asia and also enhanced their naval power, especially in waters adjacent to the home islands. The combined Anglo-American fleet would outnumber Japan's by more than three times in capital ships at treaty limits, but Japan had to worry only about the western Pacific, whereas Britain and the United States had worldwide commitments. If men were angels, arrangements like those made at Washington would be entirely commendable. As it was, the Pacific treaty system worked well during the relatively calm Twenties, but when political instability returned to the western world during the next decade, providing another opportunity for Japanese aggression in East Asia, the partial settlement was exposed for what it really was—a jerry-built structure far less contributory to Pacific security in times of crisis than in periods of general international calm.

China failed to gain stability during the Twenties and the United States did relatively little to stimulate improvement. The rise of Chiang Kai-shek during the latter years of the postwar decade seemed to insure new departures in the Middle Kingdom, but domestic gains would be more than offset in the next few years by instability in the western world. In 1924 the United States infuriated the entire Orient by excluding immigration on racial grounds under the National Origins Act, a classic example of the way in which immoral legislation leads to grave consequences. This insult deepened Japanese conviction that the United States would never accept the racial equality of Orientals. Russo-Japanese quarrels over Manchuria boded ill for the future, as did the failure of the United States to maintain its fleet at treaty strength. A naval conference at Geneva in 1927 failed to achieve much, but the disarmament negotiations at London in 1930 extended the principles of Washington by bringing lesser naval craft into the ratio system. These arrangements seemed justified at the time, but they confirmed the weakness of the original treaty by providing no means of enforcement.

If the Pacific remained a cause of some concern, its problems seemed distant to most Americans, who were much more interested in the western hemisphere. The trend away from unilateral intervention in the Caribbean-Latin American region continued during the Twenties, despite provocations that in earlier years would easily have sent the Marines on Caribbean excursions. The events of 1917–1918 had shown that nonintervention did not jeopardize North American interests in the hemisphere. The outcome of the war insured against European adventurism in the Caribbean, depriving the Roosevelt Corollary of its *raison d'être*. Businessmen finally realized that intervention was actually hard on profits, and many Americans criticized it on sound moral and legal grounds. The result was a series of developments which preceded the greater breakthrough of the Thirties.

All the Republican Presidents and secretaries of state during the New Era lent important assistance to the emergence of an inter-American system that could substitute for police actions by the United States. Several conciliation and arbitration treaties came into being, accepted with increasing alacrity by United States delegates to inter-American conferences. In addition, the United States took tentative steps to withdraw from its various protectorates in the Caribbean. Marines left the Dominican Republic permanently in 1924. They also quit Nicaragua temporarily in 1925, but when civil conflict disturbed that unhappy country in 1927, President Calvin Coolidge sent Henry L. Stimson to mediate. He achieved a considerable success, precluding intervention by the United States, but perhaps the best examples of restraint by the United States occurred in its Mexican policy. In 1923 the two nations signed the Bucareli agreements, settling various controversies over title to land and subsoil rights caused by the Mexican constitution of 1917. When additional tensions developed later in the decade, Coolidge sent Dwight Morrow to Mexico as ambassador, and he managed a definite relaxation of tensions caused by the land, oil, and anticlerical policies of President Plutarco Calles.

The noticeable improvement in United States-Latin American relations during the Twenties was a proof that wise restraint paid dividends. If the Good Neighbor policy was not born during the Twenties, it was certainly foreshadowed; what followed later was built on the useful foundations of earlier years. The most striking public act of the era, perhaps, was the issuance of the "Clark memorandum" by the State Department in 1930. If it did not repudiate the T.R. Corollary in so many words, it argued that the original Monroe Doctrine provided no warrant for unilateral intervention, a further sign of impending change in policy. The only remaining step was overt acceptance of nonintervention, and that departure lay in the immediate future.

By various expedients the United States moved in both the Pacific and the western hemisphere to improve on the past, but European policy undermined accomplishment elsewhere during the Twenties. Throughout the Jazz era, the United States studiously avoided political participation in the affairs of Europe. Although it sent "observers" to the seat of the League at Geneva, the country never wavered in its general anti-League policy. Great efforts by protagonists of American participation in the World Court, an adjunct of the Geneva organization, failed to gain sufficient senatorial support. The only multilateral treaty signed by the United States involving Europe during the Republican ascendancy, other than the Washington Pacts, was the Paris Peace Pact. It supposedly outlawed war as an instrument of national policy. When first proposed by the Frenchman Aristide Briand, the principal architect of European harmony at the time, it was actually an effort by France to secure something like a guarantee of American support. At first Secretary of State Frank Kellogg was uninterested — even opposed. When the idea of including many nations in a general treaty came to the fore, Kellogg changed his tune and became an enthusiastic supporter of the pact. When fifteen nations signed the Kellogg-Briand treaty in August 1928, it had been reduced to a fine gesture.

Gestures are often of great importance to international relations; they sometimes precede further negotiations on critical subjects, but it is a mistake to regard them as anything other than beginnings. Otherwise they arouse false expectations. The Kellogg-Briand pact has become a classic example of the futility of unenforceable pledges to assist in keeping the peace when the chips are down. It was honored principally during the Thirties by the practice of waging "undeclared wars" to give spurious color to the claim that it had not been violated. As an indication of good intent, the Paris pact was useful; as a means of preventing wars it was entirely useless.

If the failure of the United States to assume a responsible role in European politics was its principal act of omission during the Twenties, its leading sin of commission lay in the realm of economic policy. Shortly after the war, the United States began to raise its tariff barriers. This policy precluded Europe from earning dollars by selling goods in the United States. The result was what became known in later years as a "dollar gap." Europe needed dollars not only to make needed purchases in the United States but also to repay the "war debts" incurred during the wartime emergency. A complicating element was that the United States became a "creditor nation" during World War I. It was owed more than it owed overseas for the first time in its history. The result was a "favorable balance of trade," in that American exports exceeded imports. A shortage of dollars in Europe with which to buy American goods and to meet war-debts payments led to the use of gold in making international payments to the United States, the reason for the great build-up of that precious metal at Fort Knox.

Every President including Wilson insisted upon European repayment of over $10 billion in war debts, although the pernicious effect of the debts resulted in several efforts to reduce them. The requirement of war-debts repayment was one of the reasons why the victorious powers insisted upon huge reparations from the defeated powers, especially Germany. A clear connection between war debts and reparations developed in the wake of the war. The similarity between the size of reparations payments and war-debts remittances aroused increasing interest among economists. Although the United States never officially accepted the fact of the intimate tie between the two, American negotiators gave their names to European settlements in 1924 (the Dawes plan) and in 1928 (the Young plan) decreasing the burden of reparations on Germany, and a war-debt commission in the United States reduced the obligations of the principal European debtors to America.

Constructive in intent, neither of these approaches went far enough. What was required was a renunciation of war debts by the United States in return for an end to reparations payments in Europe. Had the United States considered war debts as part of their contribution to victory rather than a conventional international loan, the problem could have been disposed of easily. As it was, the war debt-reparations tangle unsettled international finance throughout the Twenties and contributed a great deal to the failure of the international economy to recapture full efficiency. The United States erred seriously in not following policies to enhance the total volume of international trade. It may have gained in the short run from high-tariff policies and rigid loan requirements, but the long-run consequences more than outweighed the temporary benefits. An aggressive search for overseas markets obscured the adverse consequences of economic nationalism for awhile, but in the long pull, difficulties would not be ended.

After about 1924 a curious relationship developed between war debts, reparations, and American private investments in Germany. The American boom provided capitalists with excess funds; they began to sink their dollars into profitable German securities. Capital flowing to Germany moved on to the Allies as reparations. The Allies then returned it to the United States as payments on war-debt accounts. Europe lacked the ability to pay either reparations or war debts, given the general economic dislocation engendered by World War I and the costs of reconstruction at home after the war. The United States could have contributed immeasurably to European recovery by canceling the debts and extending large loans on easy terms, but this concept never gained the slightest currency during the Twenties. What would happen if something interrupted the flow of capital in the war debt-reparations-investment cycle? The answer came after 1929, when the Great Depression forced an abrupt end to American investment in Germany. That country ultimately ceased to pay reparations and the Allies defaulted their debts.

Unsound American policies on tariffs and debts contributed to Europe's underlying economic malaise during the Twenties. To be sure, Europe also pursued unwise policies, but two wrongs do not make a right. Had the United States assumed constructive leadership in the international economy after the war, the terrible strains on the world's business might have been relieved sufficiently either to prevent or mitigate the catastrophe of 1929 and after. The enhanced economic power of the United States conferred upon it not only the ability but also the responsibility to exercise constructive leadership. For its lapse, the United States reaped a bitter harvest during the Thirties.

The world depression began in the United States; it followed the crash of the American securities market in October 1929. If many domestic policies pursued by the business-dominated administrations of the dollar decade helped breed the depression, so did their international economic practices. Production outran demand and triggered a recession in the United States not only because reckless monetary and fiscal procedures dried up the home market but also because equally reckless tariff and debt policies closed out overseas markets. The United States learned too late that prosperity at home depends on international economic cooperation as well as intelligent domestic measures.

* * *

The Americans also divined too late what they might have recognized at war's end, that international prosperity was an essential precondition of general political stability. The Depression opened a veritable chamber of political horrors across both the Atlantic and the Pacific. If the American diplomacy of the Twenties reflected the success-exhaustion syndrome in the domestic body politic, the diplomacy of the Thirties flowed directly from the economic crisis at home and the break-up abroad. A continuing element in foreign policy was the persistent refusal of the United States to mend its irresponsible ways. For reasons different from those of the Twenties, the United States continued to avoid international duties and thereby multiplied the crisis wrought largely by the errors of the previous decade. The recession of 1929 and after turned national energies inward; times of domestic crisis such as depressions usually have this effect. It happened elsewhere as well, particularly in western Europe. Socialist regimes weathered the depression more efficiently than capitalist countries because their governments possessed sufficient power to fight the depression effectively. The autarchic tendencies of the capitalistic democracies produced a failure of international cooperation among them, a circumstance made to order for aggressive totalitarian regimes.

Less than two years after the crash of the American stock exchange, the Depression bred its first great international crisis; Japan resumed its conquests in East Asia. Faced with economic problems at home, a moderate Japanese government fell victim to military adventurism in Manchuria. Once again, western preoccupation with events close to home created opportunities for Japanese aggression. The fragility of democratic institutions in Japan usually became apparent at such moments, and 1931 was no exception. When opportunities for mainland expansion presented themselves, reactionary elements, especially in the army and navy, usually seized power. American statesmen did not appreciate this pattern; they tended to proceed cautiously in Far Eastern crises, hoping by this method to support moderate factions in Japanese politics. However inadvertently, this well-meaning tactic usually strengthened the elements it sought to undermine. On September 18, 1931 an incident on the South Manchurian Railway at Mukden offered a pretext for an occupation of all Manchuria. Straitened China was in no position to resist this blatant violation of the open door principles, once again exposed as useless in adverse circumstances. In January 1932, Japanese troops engaged the Chinese at Shanghai, and another force occupied the province of Jehol. The Manchurian adventure and its offshoots violated numerous international obligations, including the four-power and nine-power treaties, the covenant of the League, and the Kellogg-Briand pact, but these engagements did not deter Japan.

When the League of Nations failed to make a vigorous response, the United States undertook a unilateral effort to force Japanese withdrawal, but it turned into a mere gesture when President Hoover placed strict limits on the "Stimson doctrine" advocated by his secretary of state, Henry L. Stimson. The Secretary announced to the world in January 1932 that the United States would refuse to recognize conquests violative of the open door principles, a new version of Bryan's initiative of 1915. Although the League indorsed the Stimson doctrine, it had little or no effect on the Japanese. Neither the United States nor the international organization was prepared to enforce the statement. It was another expression of support for sound principles, but moral suasion by itself was hardly sufficient to bring Japan in line.

Late in 1932 the League finally condemned Japan as an aggressor, but that nation simply gave its required two year's notice of withdrawal and left Geneva, never to return. In 1934 the Japanese foreign office issued the "Amau statement," a document claiming for Japan a predominant influence in East Asia comparable to that exercised by the United States in the western hemisphere under the Monroe doctrine. Thus began the official elaboration of what ultimately became the concept of the "Greater East Asia Co-Prosperity Sphere." If Japanese expansionists finally withdrew the force at Shanghai and generally found it expedient to remain quiescent for a few years after 1931-1932, the Manchurian initiative had attained great success. A puppet state of Manchukuo provided a vehicle through which Japan dominated the region. The aggression of 1931 was the first in a long train of similar abuses which took place as the Thirties ran their sad course.

In 1936, military extremists again resumed control of the Japanese government after assassins murdered a number of moderate politicians who had recently defeated right-wing candidates in a parliamentary election. This gruesome feat preceded the signature of the Anti-Comintern Pact with Nazi Germany in November 1936, inaugurating the Berlin-Tokyo axis, and the beginning of the "China incident" in July 1937. An episode at the Marco Polo bridge near Peking precipitated undeclared war between China and Japan. The Japanese rapidly occupied most of China's coastal regions. After unsuccessful stands at Peking, Nanking, and Shanghai, Chiang Kai-shek's government withdrew deep into the Chinese interior and established itself at Chungking.

These events finally aroused the United States government. President Franklin D. Roosevelt journeyed to Chicago to send up a trial balloon in the very heart of isolationist territory. The President argued that international lawlessness, like contagious disease, must be subjected to quarantine. He also mentioned the need for "positive endeavors" to deal with aggressors like Japan, probably a euphemism for economic sanctions. The reaction, while often favorable, did not seem to warrant more advanced policies, and Roosevelt was forced to trim his sails, even after Japanese aircraft sank an American gunboat, the *Panay*, on the Yangtze River. In November an attempt to arrange collective international action at a conference held at Brussels came to naught. Japan sabotaged the gathering by the simple device of refusing to appear, and the United States contributed to the failure by refusing to consider Soviet proposals for joint action by the western nations. American businessmen launched a "moral embargo" on shipments of strategic materials to Japan, and the government began limited economic assistance to China, but these measures did not halt the Japanese armies.

By the outbreak of World War II in September 1939, the danger of Japan had alarmed the American people, but an effective deterrent had not been matured. In fact, the Tydings-McDuffie Act of 1934, which guaranteed independence for the Philippines in 1946, was of a piece with its predecessor, the Jones Act, in reflecting a general desire to liquidate American interests in the western Pacific and get out of harm's way. The rise of Hitler's Germany in Europe drew attention away from the Orient. Nationalist China survived only because Chiang wisely adopted a general military strategy of trading space for time, a departure creating a kind of stalemate in the undeclared Sino-Japanese war, with the Chinese retaining much of the interior, although Japan dominated the coastal regions.

If the American people and their leaders hesitated to act effectively against Japan, they were much more responsive to new departures in the western hemisphere. Roosevelt and his secretary of state, Cordell Hull, vigorously elaborated the Good Neighbor policy in Latin America, culminating the repudiation of unilateral intervention and the tendency toward an effective inter-American system. In two inter-American meetings, at Montevideo in 1933 and Buenos Aires in 1936, the United States finally abjured the practice of unilateral intervention. During the same period it continued to liquidate protectorates in the Caribbean, abrogating the Platt amendment for Cuba in 1934 after adopting circumspect policy during a rebellion against the Machado regime. Troops were also withdrawn from Haiti and Nicaragua and improved arrangements were made with Panama. Another contribution to better relations in the hemisphere was the Reciprocal Trade Agreements Act. It allowed the President on his own initiative to negotiate bilateral trade agreements with other nations, reducing tariffs by as much as fifty per cent in return for parallel concessions. Reciprocal trade agreements were signed most frequently with Latin American countries; they made a measurable contribution to the success of the Good Neighbor policy.

The most impressive proof of the changed attitude of the United

States came in 1938, when President Lazaro Cárdenas of Mexico expropriated foreign oil companies who refused to accept demands made on them by striking Mexican laborers. In the days of T. R. and Wilson, this deed would have provoked instant intervention, but in the late Thirties it led to a policy of caution by the United States. The oil companies complained bitterly but ultimately accepted compensation. In this instance the United States adhered strictly to international law. It authorizes expropriation under certain conditions, usually with the proviso that the expropriating nation provide reasonable compensation to property owners affected by the expropriation decree. If F.D.R. followed a sensible policy, it was because his actions accorded with the Good Neighbor policy and because the United States, given the crises then developing in Europe and Asia, hoped to avoid hemispheric troubles.

The final innovation in Latin American policy during the Thirties was the elaboration of collective hemispheric defense. At Buenos Aires in 1936 and then at Lima in 1938, a system of consultation came into being to preclude external dangers to the hemisphere. Behind this development was growing recognition of the degree to which events had gotten out of hand in Eurasia. The Declaration of Lima, committing the American Republics to act together against common dangers, accomplished nothing less than the multilateralization of the Monroe Doctrine. In the future, the principles of Monroe would be enforced by collective hemispheric action rather than by unilateral action from the United States.

The repudiation of unilateral intervention and the multilateralization of the Monroe Doctrine were distinct improvements on the past, but from the perspective of today they seem a little less impressive than at the time. The doctrine of unilateral intervention had to go; it was unsound and unnecessary from its inception. The difficulty was that nonintervention by itself did not insure the futures of most Latin Americans. The great majority found little or no surcease from oppression by local reactionary elites. The policy of hemispheric defense led by degrees to considerable arms assistance for Latin American governments from the United States, an infusion tending to accomplish what intervention had done before, i. e., shore up exploitative regimes. Fulgencio Batista of Cuba was one of the great beneficiaries of the Good Neighbor Policy. So was Rafael Trujillo of the Dominican Republic.

There remained still another problem; the concept of hemisphere defense strengthened the illusion that the United States could ride out great general wars in Eurasia. Isolationists generally supported efforts to improve hemispheric defense; it merely extended what later became known as Fortress America into Fortress Interamericana. Collective security in the hemisphere proceeded on the assumption that it would provide a sufficient defense against involvement in the wars of Europe and Asia, a myth disproven almost as soon as it was born. The idea of collective defense was certainly constructive, but it would make its greatest contribution to national security only if integrated into a larger system of defense taking into consideration the setting at either end of Eurasia as well as the unlikely possibility of incursions in the western hemisphere.

*   *   *

American policy in Asia and Latin America during the Depression matured against the ominous background of another collapse in the European balance. Perhaps the most tragic event of the Long Armistice in Europe was the disintegration of the German Weimar Republic. The struggling governments at Weimar never obtained a really good opportunity to consolidate German democracy. During the Twenties they had to cope with the inroads of the Treaty of Versailles. During the early Thirties they faced the world depression. The combined impact of these blows eventually undermined the regime. Certainly historic as well as contemporary influences worked against the emergence of truly democratic institutions in German government and society after World War I, but had there been a better result from the settlements of 1919 and had there been no depression, the Weimar regime might have accomplished its goals. As it was, Germany succumbed to the totalitarian leadership of the Nazi party and its fanatical leader, Adolph Hitler. A fascist government had flourished in Italy since 1922, and several clerical-fascist governments had come to power in smaller European countries, but only the rise of German totalitarianism with all its bestial features insured that the immediate future would be inordinately influenced by the malfeasances of right-wing dictators in Europe.

In the early years of his regime, Hitler concentrated largely on consolidating his domestic power, but by 1936 he was prepared to begin recovery of territories lost in 1919. His ultimate objective was hegemony in Europe. First violating the disarmament provisions of the Versailles Treaty, Hitler then defied the victors of 1919 by occupying the demilitarized Rhineland in March 1936. The spirit of Locarno fostered during the 1920s was now completely dissipated; France attempted to invoke the guarantees included in the accords of 1925 but found no support elsewhere, and so the German *coup* was allowed to stand. The League was in no position to act. It had failed to control Japanese aggression in Asia. More recently it had collapsed in the face of Italian aggression against Ethiopia. France allowed the brazen Mussolini to aggrandize successfully; it feared an Italo-German *rapprochement* unless it condoned concessions. Britain failed to resist because it feared dangers to its communications through the Mediterranean to colonial holdings in Asia. The inability of the western democracies to form a common front against totalitarian aggression was largely a function of their failure to establish effective cooperation during the decade of prosperity after the Great War, a tendency only exacerbated after 1929 by the domestic economic distractions caused by the world depression. Another significant factor was the growing belief that a strong German state in central Europe erected a desirable buffer against the spread of Bolshevism from Soviet Russia.

As these dangerous events transpired in Europe, the United States looked to its own interests. Almost entirely preoccupied by the struggle against the domestic recession, both the Republican Herbert Hoover and the Democrat Franklin D. Roosevelt did little to influence the decisions of Europe during the depression decade. Hoover, of course, was a declared isolationist. F.D.R. had been a strong Wilsonian, but domestic political exigencies seemed to require abstinence from political entanglements abroad while the New Deal crusaded against the Depression. The consequence was a continuation of the pattern of international irresponsibility inaugurated during the affluent Twenties.

Shortly after the onset of the Depression, Hoover tried to resolve the war debts-reparations problem. In 1931, he declared a year's moratorium of debt payments, although he steadfastly refused to consider cancellation. In June 1932 the European powers met at Lausanne and reduced German reparations to a mere $700 million, hoping that the United States would respond by forgiving the war debts. When Hoover and his successor refused to take this step, the European countries one by one defaulted on payments, all except Finland, whose obligations were minimal. Greatly irritated, Congress passed the Johnson Act in 1934, forbidding private loans to countries in default of war-debt payments, a policy preventing needy European countries from borrowing in the United States to finance economic reconstruction. The American legislation contributed notably to the appeal of the rising totalitarian dictatorships. Thus ended ingloriously one of the most tangled episodes in the history of international finance.

If the war debts-reparations problem had been settled by negotiation, it probably would not have corrected the sad consequence of Hoover's tariff policy. In 1930 Congress passed the Smoot-Hawley tariff, raising schedules precipitately. Other countries naturally retaliated by raising their levies; the result was a further decline in international trade, deflationary in its effect, at a time when all efforts should have been dedicated to expanding its volume. These episodes fully confirmed the United States in its economic nationalism. Washington took little or no effective action to relieve the international economic collapse by intergovernmental cooperation.

Hoover attempted one noteworthy project in international cooperation; he supported a World Economic Conference scheduled for 1933 to reach multilateral agreement, among other things, on comprehensive currency stabilization. When the negotiators foregathered, Hoover had been retired by the American people. Roosevelt gave signs of supporting the stabilization scheme, but he suddenly repudiated the conference and turned to a unilateral policy of devaluing the dollar. The New Deal had continued the general trend toward economic nationalism, thereby lessening the effectiveness of antirecessionary policies. The President has been roundly criticized ever since for this action. Certainly his unilateral devaluation gave only temporary support to the dollar; other currencies followed suit and the initial advantage was soon canceled out.

There are, of course, good grounds for arguing that international currency stabilization would not have accomplished much in 1933. Monetary manipulation was only one of a number of international activities needed; the most critical economic task was to increase consumer purchasing power. The situation did not call for stabilization but for controlled inflation along with measures to encourage investment. The absence of effective international institutions to combat the worldwide recession made the task of recovery that much more difficult. Water brigades cannot put out five-alarm fires. Roosevelt wisely reversed Hoover's tariff policies, but his effort was too little and too late to make a measurable contribution to general economic recovery, much less to the return of political stability in Europe.

A large number of hopeful international projects died aborning in those desperate years. In 1934 a land disarmament conference sponsored by the League and attended by the United States adjourned without accomplishing anything. At the same time Soviet Russia began to urge unity against the fascist dictators, but massive distrust of Stalin and Bolshevism prevented significant accomplishment along this line. After seventeen years of pretending that the Russian revolution had not taken place, the United States finally recognized the Soviet Union in 1933, but the action contributed little to international life. In France, intransigent opposition to all political programs from the Left was summarized in the slogan, "Better Hitler than Blum," a reaction against the socialist leader of a "popular front" movement seeking to unite liberals and radicals of all complexions against the rise of the Right. Distrust of Soviet intent constantly inhibited constructive measures against Nazi Germany during the remainder of the Long Armistice. The Soviet Union joined the League of Nations in 1934, but Germany's departure canceled out the Russian initiative. In 1935, another naval disarmament conference broke up in failure, and the high optimism of 1921–1922 was entirely dissipated. A great armaments race developed at an enormous pace in Europe and elsewhere as nations looked to their own interests.

By 1935, events in Europe had created enough concern in the United States to require some response; it came in the form of congressional reversion to a radical reincarnation of the old neutrality. Three Neutrality Acts in the period 1935–1937 attempted to forestall American involvement in another foreign war as the United States presumably had been drawn into World War I. In 1934 a sensational congressional investigation headed by Senator Gerald P. Nye of North Dakota probed the munitions industry, concentrating particularly on its operations during the period 1914–1917. The result was the untenable thesis that American munitions manufacturers—"merchants of death"—had arranged the American entry into the Great War in order to maximize their profits. An example of the "paranoid style" of politics at its worst, the accusation gained wide currency and contributed immensely to the psychology producing the neutrality legislation. It allowed the President to embargo arms shipments to belligerent powers, to issue a proclamation warning travelers on neutral ships that they did so at their own risk and to ban travel on all ships owned by belligerents, and finally to restrict private loans to belligerents.

The neutrality laws all too often played into the hands of aggressors by penalizing friendly nations who might have benefited from American aid and comfort. When Mussolini attacked Ethiopia, the United States stood by helplessly. During the Spanish Civil War (1936–1939) Congress embargoed arms shipments to Spain, thereby denying help to the loyalist troops and strengthening the insurgent forces under General Francisco Franco who received aid from Italy and Germany. Russian supplies to the Spanish Republic fell far short of what was needed to prevent Franco's victory. Britain and France contributed to the end of democracy in Spain by attempting to isolate the civil conflict so that it would not turn into a general war. Congress relented somewhat from its advanced position only when interest groups complained that absolute embargoes interfered with business as usual. It passed a "cash and carry" proviso allowing belligerents to purchase certain goods in the United States for cash if they transported their purchases in their own vessels. This provision hardly helped land-locked Ethiopia and Republican Spain. F.D.R. did take advantage of loopholes in the legislation to send some help to China, but the amount was too limited to make a decisive contribution to Chiang's resistance.

By 1937, Roosevelt had to recognize the dangers to the Republic inherent in the aggressions of the Rome-Berlin-Tokyo axis, an arrangement completed when Italy adhered to the Anti-Comintern Pact in that year. Ostensibly aimed at Soviet Russia, the loose association of the dictators turned by degrees into a coalition bent on dominating both ends of the Eurasian land mass. The quarantine speech was clear indication of Roosevelt's desire to reorient American policy, but he was hoist by his own petard, his administration having acquiesced in a pattern of neutrality legislation encouraging the public delusion that the United States could escape involvement if another general war broke out in Europe. This circumstance caused the United States for the most part to stand by idly during the critical years from 1937 to 1939 as the crisis in Europe finally erupted into war.

The purposes of Hitler and Mussolini were abundantly clear, but Britain and France chose the path of appeasement. Appeasement was a product of many influences. A mistaken policy from the first, it nevertheless seemed plausible to many in the confusion of the late Thirties. The inability of the great democratic nations to act together led them down the primrose path of least resistance. Internal political conflicts within the several countries, especially France, inhibited joint action against the dictators. An influential contemporary argument for appeasement was the claim that a strong Germany in the heart of Europe would restore the historic central European barrier to Russian expansion, a prospect particularly alarming after the Russian revolution. A final rationale for appeasement was that Germany was merely seeking to recover what was rightfully its own. Hitler himself said so, and this argument played effectively on guilt feelings in Europe, rampant because of the severity of the Versailles Treaty, called a *Diktat* by the Nazis. Behind all this was the memory of the Great War. Europeans were willing to go to great lengths in order to avoid its repetition. Ironically, appeasement contributed a great deal to just such another violent season.

Appeasement worked itself out in three phases during 1938–1939. It was applied by implication when Hitler carried out the *Anschluss,* forced union of Austria and Germany, early in 1938. Hitler's next target was the Sudetenland, a part of Czechoslovakia adjacent to the Third Reich largely populated by German-speaking people. After a long crisis, the powers met at Munich on September 30, 1938, where Prime Minister Neville Chamberlain of Britain and his French counterpart, Edouard Daladier, achieved what they hoped was "peace for our time" by accepting all that Hitler asked of them. Czechoslovakia was required to yield up the Sudetenland. The folly of this concession became apparent in March 1939, when the German army swallowed up the remaining districts of Czechoslovakia—Bohemia and Moravia. Hitler had pledged that the Sudetenland was his last territorial demand, but further aggression against Czechoslovakia revealed his larger intentions. Appeasement was then exposed for what it was, but it continued to influence France and Britain to the very end of the last peaceful summer.

The next obvious step was the conquest of Poland, but the fly in the ointment was Soviet Russia. An invasion of Poland might plunge Germany into war with Poland's French and British allies in the West and Russia in the East, a repetition of the mistake of 1914. Once again Chamberlain and Daladier saved Hitler a peck of trouble. They made only a half-hearted attempt to negotiate a settlement with Russia during the summer of 1939 in order to protect Poland. Stalin naturally suspected that the Anglo-French combine hoped for a Russo-German war to weaken both of their European enemies. In late August the Nazi foreign minister, Joachim von Ribbentrop, flew to Moscow and there negotiated a nonaggression pact with Vyacheslav Molotov. This accomplishment fell like a thunderbolt on the world; the two countries had been sworn enemies. Hitler's Anti-Comintern Pact with Japan and Italy had answered Stalin's attempt to form a united front against the fascist powers. Apologists for Stalin argued later that he accepted the Ribbentrop-Molotov pact only to gain time. His critics alleged that he hoped for a war between the other great European powers in order to create opportunities for later Soviet aggressions.

The outcome of the agreement of August 23rd was the destruction of the Polish state. On September 1st, Germany invaded Poland from the west. Three days later, Britain and France finally turned their backs on appeasement and went to the defense of Poland—the beginning of World War II. Two weeks later, when the German *Blitzkrieg* had practically destroyed Polish resistance, Stalin moved into the country from the east. For his pains, Stalin acquired eastern Poland and also, a little later, was able to make territorial gains at the expense of Finland and to extinguish the sovereignty of the Baltic provinces made independent after World War I—Latvia, Estonia, and Lithuania. Germany acquired the Polish corridor, the free city of Danzig, and the western districts of Poland. In this fashion the two powers who had been penalized most severely in 1919 recovered lost territories in eastern Europe.

The nations of Europe had not expected the United States to enter actively into its affairs during this critical time, and this estimate proved entirely accurate. The course of American policy from the time of the repudiation of Woodrow Wilson offered ample evidence that the United States would refuse to take a stand. If President Roosevelt launched the beginnings of American rearmament in 1938, he failed to secure changes in the neutrality legislation before the war began in Europe. The only American initiative after the conquest of Czechoslovakia was to suggest a ten-year moratorium on attacks against some thirty-one countries by the dictators in Berlin and Rome. As before World War I the United States in 1939 failed to commit its power to effective diplomatic endeavors for peace with honor. It preferred to watch the beginnings of a catastrophic conflict certain to threaten its security as never before during its history.

* * *

The second violent phase of the Twentieth Century War followed directly from the failure to make a satisfactory settlement in the wake of its first phase. Wars always create complications more imposing than those precipitating them; the first phase of the Twentieth Century War provides a classic example of this maxim. Wars also have unintended and unexpected outcomes; World War II offers an equally sufficient example of this truth. Twenty-seven months after the outbreak of World War II, the United States once again was drawn into a great modern war of nations in arms, requiring of it a much greater sacrifice of blood and treasure than the intervention of 1917. The price of irresponsibility was a burden of tragedy far surpassing anything that might have followed from constructive exercise of its imposing power during the Long Armistice. The war of 1939–1945 further undermined the foundations of the established international system. Its outcome made it less likely than before that the established statecraft, even of the most skillful kind, could keep the peace indefinitely.

CHAPTER VII

The Second Phase

THE SECOND VIOLENT phase of the Twentieth Century War further undermined Woodrow Wilson's grand conception – the maintenance of the nation-state system by various international expedients. Above all, Woodrow Wilson was an American nationalist. His plans and purposes were always consistent with the interests and aspirations of America the Beautiful, that satiate-progressive anomaly, although unlike alternative nationalist programs, they held forth great promise to less fortunate nations. From a national point of view, Wilson's diplomatic execution was far more open to criticism than his intent.

Ironically, the Second World War sold the American people as never before on the importance of accepting vast international obligations and responsibilities. They may have learned too late; the proper time to grasp this lesson was 1919 and before. Soldiers often wage war with information gained during the last conflict, ignoring the changes of the interim. Peoples all too frequently compound the military error by attempting to make peace the way it should have been done the last time. World War II vastly transformed and complicated the international setting; its consequences demanded truly innovative statecraft, a species of novelty that few societies could be expected to embrace in the best of circumstances. That is the nature of war; it imposes truly difficult, sometimes insurmountable, tasks upon those who would restore peace with justice.

Once the second conflict began, it was right and appropriate that the United States should take part, if only because the circumstances permitted no other course. The tragedy was that the American people had missed an opportunity to help construct an international order in 1919 and after that might have precluded another great war. As it was, the great Republic helped sow the fields of Mars; in common with other nation-states it reaped a whirlwind of war.

* * *

When Germany attacked Poland in September 1939, the United States adopted traditional neutrality, F.D.R. issued a formal proclamation of neutrality, but he did not reiterate Wilson's plea that the people remain impartial in thought as well as deed. From the outset of the war the American people dominantly favored the antifascist cause, but as in 1914 they desperately sought to avoid involvement. Very soon, events began to chip away at strict neutrality. Roosevelt finally succeeded in modifying the neutrality laws so that Britain could obtain some assistance from the United States. He also spurred rearmament and strengthened the system of hemispheric defense, but always with the hope of remaining at peace. After the conquest of Poland the struggle across the Atlantic settled down to what some called a "phony war" in western Europe, but in early spring of 1940 the German army struck again. Hitler first attacked Scandinavia; Denmark and Norway fell easily before the Nazi *Blitzkrieg*. Then the *Wehrmacht* broke into Belgium and the Netherlands on its way to France. The French army proved incapable of effective resistance. A forlorn British force tried to stem the Nazi tide; it was saved at Dunkirk only by a remarkable combination of luck and fortitude. Before the end of the campaign, Mussolini entered the war. The continent was now generally subservient to Nazi power; besides Britain, only the Soviet Union possessed the capacity to resist German conquest.

In the United States, a great debate ensued between "isolationists" who advocated continuing restraint and "interventionists" who favored assistance short of war to Britain, left to fight on alone against Germany and Italy. The President groped slowly toward a new policy, increasingly convinced of the need to block the dictators but naturally cautious in the face of considerable national division. Hitler's achievements of March to June 1940 opened an opportunity to take important steps. Several stages lie between strict neutrality and full belligerency. The United States was to move through two of these steps, "nonbelligerency" and "undeclared war," before the tragedy of December 7, 1941 forced intervention in World War II.

Nonbelligerency means support short of war to one side in a conflict; by September 1940, President Roosevelt had abandoned straight neutrality for this posture, sustained in his decision by growing public recognition of the extreme danger posed by the Rome-Berlin axis. The most dramatic accomplishment of the early months of nonbelligerency was the "destroyer-for-bases deal." In September, Britain gave the United States leases on a number of naval bases in the western Atlantic in return for fifty "over-age" destroyers (actually they were perfectly seaworthy) to augment its defenses against the German submarine fleet. During the same month, the President secured passage of the first conscription act ever accepted by the American people in time of peace, an important aspect of a general trend toward rearmament. In November, Roosevelt was elected to a third term, another departure from historic precedent. His Republican opponent in 1940, the appealing Wendell Willkie, was an articulate opponent of the New Deal at home, but he was fundamentally in accord with the leading premises of Rooseveltian foreign policy. The election, won by a substantial margin, paved the way for additional assistance to Britain. Early in 1941 the Lend-Lease Act provided a means of extending help to antifascist nations without violating the ban on loans in the neutrality legislation and creating another war-debt problem. Ostensibly, supplies sent to Britain and other nations were lent rather than sold. The United States had become the arsenal of democracy.

The beginning of lend-lease led by stages to the abandonment of nonbelligerency for an even more advanced posture. The flow of supplies across the Atlantic had to pass the German submarine barrier. After interminable delay, the United States fleet finally began to protect convoys proceeding across the northern Atlantic in September 1941, and it speedily became engaged in the shooting war. During 1941 the United States occupied both Greenland and Iceland in order to deny them to the Germans and to provide useful bases for sea and air power.

This departure — undeclared war — followed a new phase in the European conflict. After taking France out of the war, occupying two-thirds of the country, and allotting the rest to a subservient government under Marshal Phillippe Pétain at Vichy, Hitler and Mussolini moved across North Africa toward Egypt and also into the Balkans, threatening British communications to the Middle East and more distant parts of Asia. The armored forces of the Axis powers were contained only a hundred miles short of Alexandria. In the Balkans, Yugoslavia and Greece fell to the dictators after heroic resistance, an accomplishment covering the right flank of a projected assault on the Soviet Union. In 1940, Hitler had attempted to soften Britain for a cross-channel invasion by indiscriminate bombing of civilian centers. The terrible bombing only stiffened the resolve of the British people, and the Royal Air Force managed to blunt the attacks of the German *Luftwaffe* sufficiently to hold Britain in the war.

Frustrated by the loss of the battle of Britain, Hitler's thoughts turned elsewhere, reverting to traditional Germanic dreams of the *Drang nach Osten* — drive to the east. On June 22, 1941 the German army struck across the temporary Russo-German border arranged after the rape of Poland. If the entry of the Soviet Union into the antifascist coalition posed extraordinarily embarrassing ideological problems, the British Prime Minister Winston Churchill expressed the feelings of most in indicating his willingness to league with the devil himself against Hitler. Roosevelt inclined to the same view; he soon arranged to extend lend-lease to the Soviets, assisted in this project by the favorable American response to the gallant defense of the homeland made by the Red Army.

The aid to Russia increased the volume of supplies moving across the North Atlantic; it was another reason to involve the navy more deeply in the undeclared naval war. Roosevelt was less than frank in discussing with the people the conflict in the north Atlantic during the autumn of 1941, and yet it was a logical consequence of America's role as the arsenal of democracy. Certainly a significant step toward full-scale war, it was not in itself insurance of final belligerency. Hitler had good reason to prefer undeclared naval warfare in the Atlantic to outright American intervention, especially after the assault on Russia. The American people still vainly hoped to avoid a repetition of 1917. Roosevelt's caution played into the hands of Germany, but it was a natural reflection of his desire to remain in tune with public sentiment. As it happened, events in Asia brought the period of undeclared war to an early end.

The expansion of the European conflict gave Japan another of those periodic opportunities to aggrandize in East Asia so often accepted in the past. Military extremists, largely in control of the Japanese government since 1936, strained at the bit as the great powers of the western world increasingly committed themselves to the struggle against Hitler. Three expansionist projects presented themselves. Japan could intensify its assault on China; it could attack Siberia, joining its German ally in the war against Russia; or it could move into Southeast Asia and adjacent insular regions. Each alternative posed disadvantages. Chiang Kai-shek had already demonstrated an ability to capitalize on China's great distances, stretching out available Japanese troops to the point of forcing them to stand largely on the defensive in advanced positions. Japan's power resided basically in its naval forces rather than in its land army, but it could not utilize its navy extensively in China. An attack on Siberia was open to the same objection; besides, it was unattractive because the region did not produce the resources most needed in Japan, particularly iron and oil. Southeast Asia was eminently more attractive from this point of view. Its great resources were exactly what Japan needed. The disadvantage was that a strike to the south would certainly arouse intense American opposition. To counterbalance this difficulty, the Japanese fleet could play a leading role in a Southeast Asian campaign. By degrees the Japanese expansionists settled on an invasion of Southeast Asia. Preparations for this assault began in July 1940 with the occupation of northern positions in French Indo-China, only nominally controlled by the weak regime at Vichy.

The United States reacted to this development by restricting the export of strategic goods to Japan, attempting to deter aggression in Southeast Asia by imposing economic sanctions. Roosevelt transferred the Pacific fleet to Pearl Harbor in order to strengthen his diplomacy in the region. The extension of embargoes on exports to Japan took place slowly but surely. Division in the American government slowed its pace. Military advisers believed that severe sanctions would force Japan to abandon its southward movements. Secretary Hull was convinced that a ban on materials like petroleum products would precipitate a war. Roosevelt therefore moved deliberately, hoping to deter Japan without undue provocation. He believed that the war in Europe demanded first priority, an assumption that dictated caution in the Pacific.

During 1940–1941, Japanese diplomacy attempted to secure the Greater East Asia Co-Prosperity Sphere without recourse to war. In September 1940 the Tripartite Pact revived the Rome-Berlin-Tokyo axis, seriously strained by the Russo-German nonaggression treaty of August 1939. Clearly aimed at the United States, it sought to deter the Republic by strengthening totalitarian solidarity. A war against any dictator would require war against all. The next Japanese accomplishment was a neutrality pact with the Soviet Union in April 1941 to insure against Russian interference with expansionist projects in Southeast Asia. After the German aggression on the Soviet Union in June 1941, Japan extended its control across all of French Indo-China. F.D.R. then made the decision he had postponed for so long: he extended the embargo to all strategic materials including oil, the commodity most needed by Japan, and froze all Japanese assets in the United States. A complete economic boycott ensued.

In early July an Imperial Conference in Japan made a firm decision to move across Southeast Asia, but it authorized final diplomatic efforts in the hope that the United States would accept Japanese conquest by means short of war. A group of so-called "moderates," headed by Prince Fumimaro Konoye, proposed that Japan denounce the Tripartite Pact in return for American concessions in China and Indo-China. The "extremist" faction, led by General Hideki Tojo, advocated a massive attack on Southeast Asia at the earliest opportunity, despite the high likelihood of war with the United States. For its part, the United States continued to support the open door principles in its negotiations with Tokyo. In August 1941, Prince Konoye proposed a meeting with Roosevelt in the Pacific to adjust differences. Roosevelt was tempted, but Secretary Hull resisted the project on the sound principle that no basis for agreement had appeared to insure any accomplishment through a summit meeting. All opinion in Washington agreed with the view that every effort should be made to avoid war, but no one could discover feasible means of lessening Japanese-American tension.

In Tokyo, Tojo's faction forced a decision early in September to go to war in late autumn if Konoye failed to negotiate a settlement favorable to Japan through his ambassador in Washington, Admiral Kichisaburo Nomura. The Japanese envoy made the effort, augmented in November by the special emissary Saburu Kurusu, but there were no grounds for negotiation. Tojo seized the Japanese premiership in October after little progress had been reported from Washington. Japan's last offer was a pledge to withdraw from China and Indo-China in time if the United States immediately resumed full commercial intercourse. No one believed that Japan would honor its pledge. Acceptance of the Japanese offer would have constituted a Far Eastern Munich. Hull had to reject the Japanese plan; otherwise forty years of American commitments to China and the open door would have been negotiated away in a trice, exposing Dutch and British possessions to imminent Japanese conquest. Hull drafted a counterproposal, a *modus vivendi* providing for Japanese withdrawal from South Indo-China in return for limited resumption of trade, but other interested countries — Britain, the Netherlands, and especially China — offered little or no encouragement. Hull was left with no alternative but to reiterate traditional American policy. He accomplished this task in a ten-point communication to Tokyo on November 26th, realizing that its contents were completely unacceptable to Japan. Rejection came on December 1st.

War was now unavoidable; both sides had arrived at irreconcilable positions. F.D.R. could have avoided war only by condoning massive retreat in Asia, a step no President conceivably could have taken in the circumstances. All he could do was play for time. If the prior course of American policy from the time of John Hay had been entirely misconceived, as some critics argued, certainly the Republic could not repudiate forty-odd years of commitment to the open door principles without an unbearable loss of prestige and position. Such are the imperatives of "national honor." The Japanese were equally bound by developments at home, committed beyond recall to expansion by fair means or foul. After Japan rebuffed Hull's ten-point proposal, Nomura continued negotiations in Washington as a diplomatic cover while a Japanese carrier fleet moved toward Pearl Harbor. Troop movements in Southeast Asia gave the impression that Japan would strike first against Thailand or the Philippines. On November 27th, a war alert went out from Washington to Pacific posts, including the Hawaiian Islands. On Sunday morning, December 7th, a Japanese air attack achieved complete surprise and inflicted severe damage on naval craft and military personnel based at Pearl Harbor. After that "day of infamy" the United States had no recourse except to accept war with Japan; the Congress so voted on December 8th. A few days later, Germany and Italy honored their obligations under the Tripartite Pact and declared war on the United States. Once again, the collapse of international stability in Eurasia, this time at both of its extremities, had forced the United States to belligerency.

After World War II a group of scholars and publicists accused Roosevelt of seeking to bring the United States into the world conflict by the Pacific backdoor because it had proved impossible to provoke belligerency directly in the Atlantic against the prime enemy. They alleged that the Pearl Harbor attack was the outcome of this scheme; some even cried treason. This interpretation is utterly without foundation, another of those examples of the paranoid style in American politics. The United States was drawn into World War II against the unanimous desire of its leaders because aggressors posed great hegemonial dangers at either end of Eurasia. If successful, the totalitarian powers would have posed unmeasured danger to the Republic, threatening the Atlantic and Pacific defenses of the western hemisphere in the most explicit manner. The Japanese assault on Pearl Harbor proved successful not because of conspiracy or treason but because of inexcusable incompetence in Washington and in the field. American intelligence services, never very efficient, failed to exploit information available to them after they broke the Japanese diplomatic code. Poor staff work in Washington and vast inefficiency in Hawaii account for the surprise. There is not a particle of evidence to support the "backdoor" hypotheses. A conscientious historian must blush to report the existence of such unblemished nonsense.

The Japanese aircraft at Pearl Harbor managed to eliminate five battleships, three destroyers, and other lesser craft, but the attack was far less successful than it seemed at the time. The objective was to prevent the United States from deploying its naval power to interfere with a rapid conquest of Southeast Asia, the Philippines, and the Netherlands East Indies. If the battleship fleet was severely mauled, the attack force did not hit the carrier fleet, out to sea at the time, nor did it destroy either the submarine base or the fuel dumps located at Pearl Harbor. As it turned out, the Pacific war turned largely on control of the air and interdiction of maritime supply—the mission of carriers and submarines. The American fleet quickly recovered effectiveness; within seven months or so it won a series of naval engagements and halted the forward movement of Japan. If the Pearl Harbor attack failed militarily, it was a much more profound error from another point of view. The Hawaiian outrage instantly united the Americans, shocked and angered as never before in their history. Internal controversy between isolationists and interventionists disappeared overnight and the full weight of America's massive power was rapidly mobilized and exerted against the totalitarian aggressors in both Europe and Asia. The Pacific war culminated the sad history of Japanese-American antagonism. It was a direct consequence of instability in the western world.

*   *   *

World War II was very different from World War I; it was at once more global and more total than its predecessor. Many nations were engaged in numerous theaters. They were also deeply implicated. If the first phase of the Twentieth Century War approached something like totality in its final year or so, the second phase was a death struggle from the very beginning. In the nature of things, World War II had to end in something closely approximating complete victory for one side and complete defeat for the other. It was bound to consume much more blood and treasure than World War I, and equally certain to produce an even more difficult and unexpected aftermath.

These elements prevented the belligerent nations from fighting entirely in terms of the famous dictum of Clausewitz, that war is a continuation of politics and should always be fought in terms of political ends. The great German theorist argued persuasively that strategy should always remain subordinate to policy. Woodrow Wilson managed a striking application of Clausewitz' dictum during 1917–1918 precisely because the earlier Armageddon was less global and less total than World War II. The desperate military situation confronting F.D.R. in December 1941 required intense preoccupation with mere survival. The enemy had to be met where he was and engaged in fierce combat. The truly devastating nature of total warfare provided much less area for political maneuver than World War I. The struggle of 1939–1945 developed its own inherent tragedy which human error might compound but not alter. The conduct and consequences of World War I had made it difficult indeed to avoid another conflict. A second war was bound to generate unmatched instability. By 1939 the world was once again on the horns of an insoluble dilemma. Neither peace nor war promised much; tragedy was bound to flow from whatever decisions were made by the nations facing totalitarian aggression.

Those who fought World War II often interpreted it in ideological terms. Ideology is, first, a function of power; it reflects the national condition. Democracy is peculiarly suitable to essentially satisfied and stable societies, just as totalitarianism is often relevant to dissatisfied and unstable societies. Nevertheless, ideology takes on life of its own and becomes an independent force. Men do not fight for bread alone; the sacrifices of combat require higher justification. The antihegemonial coalition inevitably advertised itself as a "peace-loving" bloc set out to insure a just and lasting peace. Its opponents relied on the age-old maxim that victory is the portion of the mighty; superior strength justifies any means to power. Ideological heat is often a dependent variable, which is to say that it is frequently altered in intensity by events, particularly changing power relationships. The course of World War II provides a case in point; the enormous ideological gulf separating Communist Russia from its Anglo-American allies before 1941 was quickly bridged during the joint war against the fascist coalition.

The Grand Alliance temporarily composed its ideological differences sufficiently to insure victory over the hegemonizing powers. Nothing makes friends of former enemies like common dangers. Once danger dissipates, temporary alliances fade as new conflicts of interest revive ideological tension. Politics is rarely a function either of pure ideological conflict or of naked power. It is usually a function of both. The task of those who study politics is to sort out the various interrelated strands of ideology and power. The clarity of analysis inevitably suffers by the effort, but the advantage is a certain maturity denied to those who persist in the lesser arts of more simplistic interpretation.

The elaboration of the Twentieth Century War constantly narrowed the political alternatives open to those who waged it; historians must recognize this immutable trend. Peace constantly mothers political alternatives; warfare aborts them. The web of ideology and power becomes ever more entangling as violence proliferates. All too often across the ironic history of mankind, only exhaustion has allowed the race to unravel that web and begin anew its quixotic progress to permanent peace and justice for all. War gives play to primitive instincts, undermining civility. The unparalleled exercise of violence from 1939 to 1945 was the greatest reproach to civilization within human recall. It seemed unlikely that humanity could survive another recourse to general warfare.

*   *   *

As soon as possible after Pearl Harbor, Winston Churchill hurried to Washington in order to concert plans for the future. His visit inaugurated a regular sequence of wartime consultations between the United

States and Britain. Comparable Anglo-Russian and Russo-American meetings took place less frequently at various diplomatic levels during the war. Bilateral negotiations were capped, of course, by full-cress summit conferences among the Big Three—Roosevelt, Churchill, and Stalin—at Teheran late in 1943 and at Yalta early in 1945. From 1941 until the middle of 1944, inter-Allied exchanges concentrated largely on military decisions. Only after the Grand Alliance approached victory could it turn most of its energies to political discussions concerning the future. For the moment, all attention centered on strategy to turn the tide in the major theaters—western Europe (ETO), eastern Europe, the China-Burma-India region (C-B-I), and the western Pacific. Russia naturally controlled decisions in eastern Europe, and the United States dominated strategy in the western Pacific. Britain initially exercised considerable influence in joint Anglo-American theaters—the C-B-I region and ETO—but the United States gradually assumed a leading role in these areas as British power ebbed away.

Churchill's visit to Washington in late 1941 and early 1942 confirmed two decisions tentatively arrived at even before Pearl Harbor. Early in 1941, secret "ABC conversations" between military representatives of the United States, Britain, and Canada reached the conclusion that in the event of war at both ends of Eurasia, Europe must receive first priority. It was clear that Germany could fight on despite the defeat of Japan, but that Japan could not survive long after the fall of the Third Reich. This fundamental strategic concept governed Anglo-American military decisions throughout the war. In Washington, Roosevelt and Churchill established the Combined Chiefs of Staff to coordinate Anglo-American activity around the world. The conferees also issued the Declaration of the United Nations, pledging twenty-six nations not to negotiate a separate peace with the enemy. The Declaration also endorsed the principles contained in the Atlantic Charter, presented to the world by Roosevelt and Churchill several months earlier in August 1941, after a secret meeting off Newfoundland.

The Atlantic Charter was a general statement of war aims for the Grand Alliance arrived at even before the United States entered the war. It was a rather vague and somewhat adulterated version of Wilson's twenty-seven points. If the Atlantic Charter reflected the common interest of both Britain and America in recovered stability, it glossed over certain differences of view. The United States harbored an interest in a new international security organization to replace the League, whereas Britain placed continuing reliance on balance-of-power arrangements. Churchill hoped to preserve the empire and to defend the interests of the Commonwealth, but Roosevelt was determined to insure that colonialism in Africa and Asia would be liquidated after World War II. Differences of this sort account for various Anglo-American disputes during the war, marring the overall unity derived from supreme desire to destroy the Axis powers.

The Soviet Union adhered to the Atlantic Charter but not because its war aims corresponded with those of the Anglo-American combine. Warped by a general conviction that Communism and western bourgeois democracy were incompatible, and conditioned to hatred and distrust of Britain and the United States by hard years of adversity after World War I, the Russians concerned themselves above all with the task of regaining territories lost in 1919. They hoped to insure postwar security with respect to both Europe and Asia, and no doubt they did all they could to create opportunities for aggrandizement during and after the war. The Russians shared with their American and British allies a common fear of Germany and Japan, although their concern with the Japanese did not result in a declaration of war until the last moments of the Pacific war, several months after the destruction of Nazi Germany. Expediental diplomacy in dealings with bourgeois powers had received the high sanction of the Marxist fathers, who uniformly justified any means to the extinction of capitalism and the achievement of a classless socialist society. Throughout the war, Stalin maintained as much reserve as possible, conducting Soviet strategy and policy on an independent basis whenever he could manage it.

Winston Churchill was an old antagonist of the Bolsheviks—he had urged war against Russia on the Allied and Associated Powers in 1919—but F.D.R. had a different orientation. Churchill felt compelled to cooperate with Stalin in order to insure victory, but the President was hopeful not only of maintaining wartime relations but also of building a basis for continuing association in the wake of the conflict. The collapse of France and the ruination of Germany would leave the Soviet Union supreme on the continent. To F.D.R., this reality meant that the Soviet Union would have to be implicated in the projected postwar security organization. Throughout the war, Roosevelt was haunted by fear that the American people might behave after World War II largely as they had after the first conflict. They might now accept membership in a new collective security agency, but he doubted that they would condone other commitments, for example, a long-term occupation of Europe after the defeat of Germany. These beliefs led the President to the assumption that postwar security and progress would depend on continuing Soviet-American cordiality and cooperation. To accomplish this end, F.D.R. set out on a determined effort to cultivate Soviet confidence, sustained in this project by considerable confidence in his own powers of friendly persuasion. The diplomatic consequence was a tendency at times to avoid confrontation with Russia on the theory that the United States would thereby store up gifts in heaven for the postwar era. Churchill thought much differently; he represented centuries of balance-of-power statecraft in the grand British tradition. Convinced that the Russians would constitute a disturbing influence after the war, Churchill resisted concessions to Stalin beyond the minimum necessary to insure victory.

Much has been written about the consequences of this Anglo-American divergence — perhaps too much. Churchill was never as consistent in his efforts to curb the Russians as his uncritical admirers assert, nor was Roosevelt as unwary as his detractors claim. Churchill was forever a British empire man, concerned primarily with the preservation of the King's domains; he was not one of the great American patriots of the century, nor was he infallible, despite the fact that he was an unusually astute and far-sighted statesman. On the other hand, Roosevelt was no callow dupe of Soviet stratagems. He recognized the depth of Soviet-American conflict, but he hoped to surmount it. Like Churchill a great statesman, F.D.R. was not without human failings, and he too made mistakes.

In the grand perspective of world history, the inherent limitations on action imposed on all the participants in the Grand Alliance appear more influential in determining the course of wartime diplomacy than quirks of personality. The decisions of World War II stemmed more from necessity than individual exoticism or desire. Human error there was, in great plenty as during all wars, but mistakes must be considered in the context of an unusually straitened diplomatic setting. Wartime diplomacy, of course, was not simply the working out of a prescribed destiny, but statesmen conducting the affairs of the Grand Alliance did not enjoy varied options. The choices were limited indeed, a consequence of the war's totality. It is hard to argue that many of the great decisions of the war could have varied to any considerable degree from those actually made, given the information and the problems at hand.

As in the past, the behavior of various national leaders was largely consistent with their conceptions of national interest, conceptions shared by the predominant majority of their countrymen. In most cases, it was all too easy to construe a divergent national interest as in fact the interest of all. The tragedy was that no national interest could encompass the international interest completely, given the incredible complexity and destructiveness of World War II. Viewed from an international perspective, that of the human family, the rights and

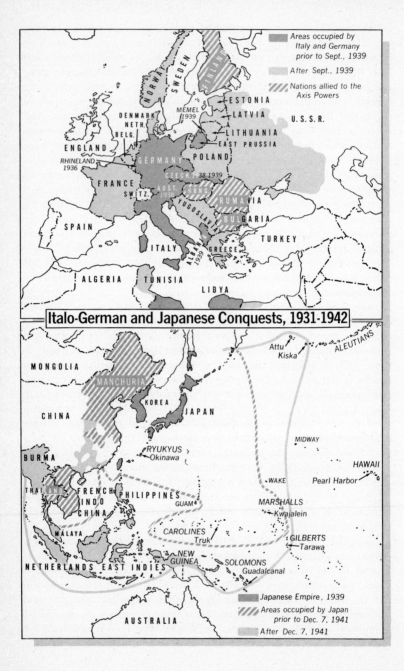

Areas occupied by Italy and Germany prior to Sept., 1939

After Sept., 1939

Nations allied to the Axis Powers

FINLAND

NORWAY

SWEDEN

ESTONIA

DENMARK
MEMEL
1939

LATVIA

NETH.
BELG.

LITHUANIA

EAST PRUSSIA

U.S.S.R.

ENGLAND

RHINELAND
1936

GERMANY

POLAND

FRANCE

CZECH. 38 1939

SWITZ.

AUST.
1938

HUNG.

RUMANIA

YUGOSLAVIA

BULGARIA

SPAIN

ITALY

ALBANIA
1939

GREECE

TURKEY

ALGERIA

TUNISIA

LIBYA

Italo-German and Japanese Conquests, 1931-1942

MONGOLIA

Attu
Kiska

ALEUTIANS

MANCHURIA

KOREA

JAPAN

CHINA

MIDWAY

BURMA

RYUKYUS
Okinawa

HAWAII

THAILAND

FRENCH
INDO
CHINA

PHILIPPINES

GUAM

WAKE

Pearl Harbor

MARSHALLS
Kwajalein

MALAYA

CAROLINES
Truk

GILBERTS
Tarawa

NETHERLANDS EAST INDIES

NEW
GUINEA

SOLOMONS
Guadalcanal

AUSTRALIA

Japanese Empire, 1939

Areas occupied by Japan prior to Dec. 7, 1941

After Dec. 7, 1941

wrongs of the era are far less luminous than those observers would have it whose visions are refracted through nationalist prisms. After all, the Russians were human beings too, although the requirements of ideological conflict impose upon those who wage it a compulsion to view antagonists as beasts, devils, or some other category of dangerous species. Why is it that our enemies always slither through murky darkness brandishing knives, whereas our friends march openly across sunny plains with flags flying and swords sheathed? The fact of Russian sin and error was perfectly apparent, but it must be cast up against a considerable volume of Anglo-American perversity, identifiable only by transcending national perspective.

During the anxious early months of 1942 the Grand Alliance slowly began to stem the onrushing dictators and to contemplate offensive strategies. American forces finally stopped the Japanese short of Australia and India. The turning point in Asia was naval victory, first in the Coral Sea during May and then at Midway Island in June. Landings in the Solomons commenced the long journey to the Japanese home islands. In eastern Europe, the Red Army contained Hitler's powerful armored columns along a vast front short of three key cities — Leningrad, Moscow, and Stalingrad. At the same time, Britain regained the initiative in North Africa. Very soon, the principal preoccupation of planners became the question of what next in Europe.

Stalin clamored unceasingly for a second front in western Europe to relieve some of the tremendous German pressure on his formations, but Britain preferred operations in the Mediterranean, convinced that landings across the English Channel could not be undertaken until Anglo-American strength had been augmented considerably. Churchill called for a sweep in North Africa to be followed by an assault on what he came to call the "soft underbelly of Europe." These proposals stemmed not simply from calculations of Anglo-American capabilities but also the natural British desire to protect its Mediterranean lifeline.

American planners early decided that the proper strategy in Europe was an early cross-channel attack, a conclusion based not only on a desire to lessen pressure on the Red Army but also on the belief that it was the quickest and easiest way to defeat Hitler. General George C. Marshall and his principal aide, a vigorous officer named Dwight D. Eisenhower, correctly assumed that the "soft underbelly of Europe" was largely a myth; the mountainous terrain in the region seemed to them unusually inimical to offensive operations. They could hardly base American planning on the preservation of the British empire. The continuing Anglo-American conflict over the second front in Europe showed once again that a larger community of interest could not obscure a serious division of opinion between London and Washington about the future of colonialism, despite the extreme exigencies of the war.

The upshot of early discussions was a decision to postpone a cross-channel operation in favor of TORCH, an attack on North Africa. The landing force would have to encroach on the African domains of Vichy France. Anglo-American troops invaded the region in November 1942. General Eisenhower struck an unseemly bargain with Admiral Jean Darlan, the Vichyite ruler of North Africa, in order to prevent hostilities with French troops. This arrangement aroused vast criticism from liberals in the United States and mistrust in the Soviet Union. Political purity and wartime necessities do not always mix. After unexpected delays, TORCH finally succeeded in throwing the Germans and the Italians out of Africa. To concert plans for the next phase of the war, Churchill and Roosevelt met at Casablanca in January 1943.

Despite intensified Russo-American insistence on an early cross-channel assault, British views prevailed at Casablanca. The negotiators agreed to an attack on Sicily, maintaining Anglo-American concentration in the Mediterranean. Presumably, an invasion of Italy would be next on the agenda. This decision placed the brunt of the European war during 1943 on the Soviet Union. The Russians reacted vigorously, fearful that their partners in the Grand Alliance desired them to exhaust their strength against German armies in the East in order to lessen their potential influence in continental affairs during the postwar years. If Churchill might have entertained this idea, it was no part of Roosevelt's thinking. To satisfy Stalin and also the Chinese, the President made one of the most dramatic announcements of the war at Casablanca — the doctrine of unconditional surrender.

Much has been written about the presumably baneful effects of this pronouncement; critics have alleged that it gave momentum to Axis propaganda efforts among their own peoples and that the very principle was unsound. These views ignore the principal motive for its release, the necessity of mollifying Stalin and encouraging Chiang. It was always possible that the Russians might sue for a separate peace if they lost confidence in their allies. The doctrine certainly gave Joseph Goebbels and his coadjutors in Nazi propaganda a talking point, but it also lifted spirits throughout the Grand Alliance. Most important, the concept of unconditional surrender publicly acknowledged an undeniable fact — the conflict was already a total war certain to end in something approximating total victory for the winners and total defeat for the losers. The Rooseveltian pronouncement at Casablanca, issued after prior consultations with the British, merely made official what had been generally recognized long before.

The question of a second front in Europe continued to dominate discussion among the Big Three during 1943. Meeting once again in Washington during May, Roosevelt and Churchill finally admitted that a cross-channel attack could not be mounted in that year, a decision causing great anger in Moscow. Instead, they decided to attack Italy. Churchill continued to propose Balkan adventures, but the Americans forced a decision to adopt a tentative date of May 1944 for the cross-channel invasion. Anglo-American planners confirmed the timing for what became known as OVERLORD during consultations in Quebec in August. The United States vigorously resisted new British schemes for diversionary operations in the Mediterranean. The United States was now assuming dominance within the Anglo-American partnership. Churchill's influence, considerable before the United States completed its mobilization, was on the wane. A clear indication of this trend was the first discussion in Quebec of American plans for a postwar security organization.

Shortly after the Quebec conference, the Grand Alliance achieved its first decisive victory, the surrender of Italy. In July, after the invasion of Sicily, Mussolini had been deposed by King Victor Emanuel. Marshal Pietro Badoglio formed a new government. On September 3rd, the day of the first Allied landings on the Italian mainland, Badoglio accepted an armistice. Unfortunately Hitler anticipated this development by occupying much of the Italian peninsula. During September he spirited Mussolini out of the hands of the Badoglio regime and placed him at the head of a puppet government in the north called the Italian Social Republic. Hitler's bold initiative deprived the Anglo-American forces of military advantages seemingly conferred by the Italian surrender, insuring a bitter war in Italy until the final destruction of the Third Reich. The arduous Italian campaigns provided proof that Europe's underbelly was quite firm. The Soviet Union was largely excluded from the negotiations for the Italian surrender and occupation, a precedent it later followed in those regions conquered by the Red Army.

As Anglo-American forces advanced in the Mediterranean, the Russians made great strides against the Germans in eastern Europe, an accomplishment strengthening the bargaining power of Stalin within the Grand Alliance. He was now prepared to engage in direct negotiations with Roosevelt and Churchill. In late October 1943 the foreign ministers of the Grand Alliance gathered in Moscow—Molotov for the Soviet Union, Anthony Eden for Britain, and Cordell Hull for the United States (his only wartime mission of consequence). For the first time, serious discussions of postwar arrangements took place. The foreign ministers agreed to set up a European Advisory Commission to plan surrender and occupation policies for defeated enemies. In addition, Hull achieved his heart's desire, an inter-Allied pledge to create a postwar security agency. Before Hull went to Moscow, Representative J. William Fulbright of Arkansas succeeded in obtaining House acceptance of a resolution approving the "creation of appropriate international machinery" at war's end. Just after the Moscow discussions, the Senate passed a resolution offered by Tom Connolly of Texas calling explicitly for "a general international organization." Hull worked efficiently to avoid the errors of 1919 by securing general congressional support for a new international organization even before its charter had been written. Before the Secretary of State left Moscow he gave assurances that a second front would be opened in Europe during 1944, and he heard from Stalin the comforting response that the Soviet Union would enter the Far Eastern war after the fall of Germany.

The foreign ministers also arranged for the first wartime conference of the Big Three; it took place at Teheran a month later. These discussions were general in nature, but in many ways they prefigured the more publicized exchanges at Yalta later in the war. Stalin was gratified at plans for OVERLORD. He reiterated his intention to attack Japan after victory in Europe. He also agreed to coordinate a Russian offensive on the eastern front with Eisenhower's landings in France. Already Stalin concerned himself with the question of postwar Poland. His plans envisioned a westward shift of that country. He wanted to draw the eastern boundary of Poland close to the old Curzon line, a demarcation between Poland and Russia proposed at the time of the Paris Peace Conference. The western boundary would lie along the Oder and western Neisse Rivers, well into prewar Germany. Stalin also expressed strong interest in recovering possessions in the Far East lost at the end of the Russo-Japanese War. Despite these territorial aspirations, President Roosevelt left Teheran satisfied that he could work amicably with "Uncle Joe" in planning the peace.

After Teheran all energies went into preparations for the cross-channel attack. In June 1944, Eisenhower's great armada moved across the English Channel to Normandy and quickly established a secure bridgehead from which a breakout rapidly materialized. Paris was soon liberated, and General Charles de Gaulle, leader of the Free French movement, assumed control of the French government. At the same time a great Russian drive in the East made striking progress. By early fall, another series of high-level meetings began in order to settle fundamental political questions kept in abeyance during the period of severe military emergency.

*   *   *

If the progress of the European war had exceeded expectations considerably, the American accomplishment in the western Pacific was even more surprising. Relegated to second place in Anglo-American planning at the beginning of the war, the Pacific theater did not receive as much support as ETO, but the remarkable industrial output of the United States allowed planners in Washington to allocate many more men and materials to the Asian conflict than had been anticipated during the earlier stages of the war.

During various Anglo-American conferences in 1943, especially at Casablanca, the negotiators seriously discussed expanded land operations in the China-Burma-India theater. These conversations accorded with President Roosevelt's deep-seated interest in promoting China to great-power status. Despite this desire, the C-B-I theater never grew in importance. For one thing, Chiang Kai-shek could not endure the American General Joseph Stilwell, sent out to serve as the commander in the field. Stilwell reciprocated Chiang's dislike, never missing an opportunity to call the Generalissimo the "peanut." In addition, Britain strongly opposed diversion of strength to the theater, preferring to concentrate on Europe. Most important was the weakness of Chiang's China. The Generalissimo seemed much more concerned about eliminating the Chinese Communists at home than in fighting the Japanese. American diplomats on the scene dispatched depressing accounts of venality and corruption in the governing Kuomintang oligarchy, but no amount of American cajoling altered Chiang's approach to his domestic problems.

Instead of moving against Japan on land through China, the United States proceeded by sea, first crippling the Japanese carrier fleet and then adopting the "island-hopping strategy." After the great naval victories of May to June 1942, the fleet rapidly seized control of the seas and its planes established comparable sway in the air. Under air and sea cover, American troops moved methodically island by island across the long passage to Japan. General Douglas MacArthur assumed supreme command in the Pacific. Having pledged theatrically to return to the Philippines after the defeat of 1942, he preferred a direct route to that goal from Australia through the Solomons and New Guinea. The navy, commanded by Admiral Chester Nimitz, preferred offensive operations along a line of peripheral islands at the eastern edge of the theater through the Marshalls, Gilberts, and Marianas converging on Formosa, assuming that this route would be easier to follow because it was closer to American supply lines and correspondingly further from Japanese bases. The upshot of inter-service difference was a compromise. American forces moved along both routes, but MacArthur's preference for an attack on the Philippines ultimately prevailed, contrary to the navy's desire to bypass them in favor of an assault on Formosa. Successful landings on Luzon in October 1944 placed American forces within striking distance of Japan. Long-range aircraft based on the Marianas began to bomb Japanese cities in November.

F.D.R. persisted long in his effort to make China one of the "four policemen" of the world, despite growing evidence of Chinese weakness and sustained opposition from Britain. The high point in this ill-fated venture was the Cairo conference late in 1943. *En route* to Teheran, Churchill and Roosevelt stopped in Egypt to confer with Generalissimo and Madame Chiang Kai-shek. The Anglo-American combine pledged to strip Japan of its Chinese conquests and also issued a general statement of support for the principle of self-determination in Asia. Churchill was hardly pleased by these arrangements. He managed to block continuing American interest in developing the C-B-I theater. To strengthen the Nationalist regime, Roosevelt sent a series of high-level missions to China in 1944 and 1945, headed by Vice-President Henry A. Wallace, Ambassador Patrick Hurley, and General Albert Wedemeyer, but each attempt came a cropper. No one could arrange an effective coalition between the Nationalists and the Communists or stimulate constructive reform within Chiang's government. Roosevelt finally had to surrender his dream of building China into one of the four great postwar powers, although the Nationalists received one of the four permanent seats in the Security Council of the United Nations.

It is easy to criticize Roosevelt's quixotic attempt to champion Nationalist China, but the President's instincts were sound. The defeat of Japan would eliminate the only great power indigenous to East Asia, leaving a huge power vacuum. Who would occupy that vacuum? F.D.R. hoped that a stable Nationalist regime in China, beholden to the United States, would perform that function. As it happened, Chiang was incapable of leading China out of the wilderness. Instead of the Generalissimo, the saviour of China turned out to be Mao Tse-tung, at the head of a Communist movement completely antagonistic to America. If a great force, largely composed of American troops, had moved against Japan across China, the future of China might have been different, but such a campaign was impossible, given the "Europe first" strategy and the debility of the Nationalists.

* * *

By September 1944 the diplomacy of the World War II had entered its second and final phase. Victory was now assured: triumphal armies were about to encompass the final destruction of Germany and Japan. In these circumstances, pressing political questions came to the fore; a series of inter-Allied negotiations dealt with them in rapid-fire order as the war rushed to its close in both Europe and Asia.

The most critical European question was the future of Germany. At the second Quebec conference in September 1944, Roosevelt and Churchill initialed the abortive Morgenthau plan, a policy developed by the Secretary of the Treasury, Henry Morgenthau, Jr., proposing to divide and ruin Germany by imposing brutal reparations, distributing much of its territory to neighboring states, and stripping it of industrial capability. Conceived at the height of the European conflict when news of the bestial extermination of European Jewry was reaching the outside world, the Morgenthau plan reflected the intense hatred of Nazism which dominated practically all segments of opinion within the Grand Alliance. Its advocates held that it would improve the prospects for postwar collaboration with the Soviet Union by insuring against an undue revival of German power, a source of great Russian concern. As time passed, other counsels prevailed. Secretary of War Henry L. Stimson and Secretary Hull strongly opposed the Morgenthau plan, recognizing that defeated Germany would have to make a meaningful contribution to postwar stability and economic reconstruction in Europe. The policies ultimately settled for Germany were certainly severe, but they bore little resemblance to the evanescent Morgenthau plan.

As Britain's power declined during the later phases of the war, Winston Churchill observed a growing body of evidence indicating that Soviet Russia would exercise a preponderant influence in continental politics after the conclusion of hostilities. Fearful for the postwar balance of power and especially concerned about Britain's future position in the Balkans and the Middle East, the British prime minister went by himself to Moscow in October 1944, and there struck a fateful bargain with Stalin. (Roosevelt was then engaged in campaigning for a fourth term and could not take part in another Big Three meeting until his re-election was assured.) In Moscow, Stalin initialed a paper on which Churchill had written that after the war Britain would exercise prime influence in Greece, the Russians would predominate in Rumania and Bulgaria, and the two powers would share influence in Hungary and Yugoslavia. Both parties understood that Russia would gain territory at the expense of Rumania, especially Bessarabia and Bukovina. This remarkable bargain reflected political-military realities in the Balkan region at the time. Russian troops were flooding throughout eastern Europe.

The most difficult eastern question was the future of Poland. During the early stages of the war, a conservative Polish government-in-exile had established itself in London. When Russian troops moved into Poland, Stalin sponsored a rival left-wing government at Lublin. In August and September 1944 the Red Army hesitated at the gates of Warsaw while the German garrison systematically stamped out an uprising of the Polish underground in that city, a tragedy playing directly into the hands of the Lublin government. What Stalin wanted was Anglo-American acceptance of his proposed borders for postwar Poland—the Curzon line at the east and the Oder-Neisse line at the west—along with a "friendly" Polish regime. At the beginning, this meant a coalition of the London and Lublin governments dominated by the latter element. Stanislaw Mikolajczyk, the head of the government-in-exile, doggedly refused to accept these arrangements, despite bullying from both Churchill and Stalin. Roosevelt shared Churchill's belief that concessions had to be made to Russia, although both hoped to preserve as much Polish freedom as possible in the circumstances. No settlement had been reached at the beginning of 1945, but Russia recognized the Lublin government in January. The presence of the Red Army on Polish soil made unlikely any last-minute reprieve for the London Poles.

If Churchill was preoccupied with eastern Europe and the Balkans during the later months of 1944, the United States government concerned itself particularly with a series of negotiations making plans for important postwar organizations. The preliminary proposal for the United Nations was drafted at Dumbarton Oaks in Washington from August to October 1944. Many difficult questions were disposed of before a final conference met at San Francisco in April 1945 to reach final agreement on the Charter of the United Nations, although disputes over membership and the great-power veto remained unsettled. In September, another conference gathered at Bretton Woods, New Hampshire, and produced plans for a world bank to make loans to needy countries after the war and an international monetary fund to maintain stable currencies. General support for these institutions reflected a profound international desire to avoid postwar economic problems comparable to those which arose after World War I.

All was now in readiness for a general discussion of international questions. The outcome was the most publicized, and certainly the most controversial, of the wartime conferences. Early in February 1945, Roosevelt and Churchill traveled to the resort town of Yalta in the Crimea. Churchill felt considerable foreboding as he entered into the negotiations. Roosevelt was desperately tired, although in full possession of his faculties. The decisions reached at Yalta had all been foreshadowed by earlier developments. Despite later criticism, it is difficult to conceive of much different outcomes. The course of the battle dictated most of the settlements. Other factors influencing the negotiations were the American desire to insure Russian participation in the final assault on Japan and the hope of securing Russian cooperation in constructive international activities after the end of the war.

By February 1945 the Red Army was in full control of Poland, and possession is nine points of the law. After considerable wrangling, Churchill and Roosevelt were compelled to accept a settlement that doomed the London Poles. They agreed to make the Curzon line the eastern boundary of Poland. Stalin pressed for the Oder-Neisse boundary between Poland and Germany, but Churchill and Roosevelt authorized only the transfer of some east German territory to Poland. They agreed to accept the Lublin government with the proviso that it be reorganized to represent the London Poles and that "free and unfettered elections" be held in the future to choose a free government. In time, Russia subverted the entire settlement. Poland was gradually communized and Stalin created the Oder-Neisse boundary with East Germany by fiat.

The German settlement also reflected the course of the battle. Russian and Anglo-American forces were about to converge on the ancient centers of German power. The Yalta negotiators planned a four-power occupation by the Soviet Union, Britain, France, and the United States. Reparations would be exacted. It was understood that a figure of $20 billion would serve as a point of departure for future discussion, with the assumption that half of the sum finally decided upon would go to the Russians. Berlin, lying within the Russian zone, was to undergo four-power occupation. No right of access was guaranteed to the western powers, an oversight that created enormous difficulties later on. These arrangements were certainly severe, but they were a far cry from the Morgenthau plan. As the war reached its conclusion, the United States gradually accepted the British view that European security after the war required the rehabilitation of both Germany and France. The Yalta agreement on Germany reflected this awareness.

The line of demarcation between the Russian zone of Germany and the western zones was drawn on the basis of military estimates. The location reflected the best guess as to where the converging armies of the Grand Alliance would come together. General Eisenhower in effect drew the line somewhat west of where it might have been. His insistence on advancing along a broad front was safe and sound strategy, but it meant that the Russian and Anglo-American armies would probably encounter each other further west than might have been the case had the supreme commander authorized deep penetrations by powerful armored columns aimed at the great central European cities of Berlin, Prague, and Vienna. Such probes would have created deep salients, always difficult to defend. Armored commanders such as the American Patton and the British Montgomery believed that their forces were equal to the task, but it is hard to question General Eisenhower's prudence at the time. His decision had a fateful outcome, a prime example of the way strategy dictates policy in time of total war.

The decisions about the Far East reached at Yalta became the most criticized acts of the conference. Since the Soviet Union was still at peace with Japan, secrecy had to be maintained, a factor seriously beclouding the arrangements. The Soviet Union was promised the return of southern Sakhalin lost in 1905, the cession of the Kurile Islands, and recovered influence in Outer Mongolia, Manchuria, and Korea. In return, Stalin officially agreed to enter the Pacific war two or three months after the German surrender and also to negotiate "a pact of friendship and alliance" with China defining future relations between the two countries.

All this must be considered in the context of the times. Hopes for the postwar world were pinned on the maintenance of Russian cooperation with the United States, Britain, and China. It seemed obvious that the Soviet Union could accomplish by unilateral endeavors in the Far East most of what it obtained by agreement. In addition, the United States attached supreme importance to the pledge of Russian assistance against Japan. Intelligence estimates at the time predicted a bitter battle for the Japanese homeland which might require several more years of war and exact a million additional American casualties. The atomic bomb had not as yet been perfected or tested. No one could be certain that it would prove out. As it happened, the intelligence reports available to Roosevelt at Yalta were fallacious; Japan was actually close to exhaustion. The bomb was developed about six months later. Nevertheless, no decision in February 1945 could have been taken on the assumption that the bomb would work and bring Japanese resistance to an end without the necessity of Russian intervention to save many American lives. Given the information and assumptions of the moment, it is difficult to imagine a settlement along markedly different lines. All too often, the Yalta negotiations are considered in terms of China's later history, but it is indisputable that the Communist triumph of 1949 was not a function of the accord in 1945.

A final agreement of great importance at Yalta engendered profound relief and hope. Russia promised to participate in the San Francisco conference scheduled for April to draft the United Nations charter. In preparation for this negotiation, Roosevelt secured Stalin's acceptance of a workable solution to the problem of the great-power veto. They agreed that it would be exercised when voting on substantive issues but not on procedural questions. Invitations to San Francisco were to be extended to signers of the Declaration of the United Nations and to countries declaring war on the Axis powers by March 1, 1945. The Yalta arrangements virtually assured the creation of an international security organization, an historic accomplishment often ignored by critics of the conference.

Franklin D. Roosevelt passed away only a few weeks after returning to the United States, but his successor, Harry S. Truman, decided immediately to continue with plans for the San Francisco conference. Meeting from April 25 to June 26, 1945, statesmen from fifty nations arrived at a charter acceptable to all. Some additions to the Dumbarton Oaks proposals developed at San Francisco, including the principle of trusteeship to replace the old mandate system. The voting arrangement settled at Yalta created considerable controversy. Molotov refused to accept the plain meaning of the Yalta accord, but he eventually came around after Harry Hopkins made an appeal to Stalin in Moscow. Like its predecessor, the League of Nations, the United Nations could not hope to accomplish its central peacekeeping mission in the absence of great-power unanimity, but it could always work in other areas through its various nonpolitical instrumentalities. Secretary Hull's careful preparation of Congress insured an early and almost unanimous consent to the Charter of the United Nations. The vote of July 28, 1945 favored it by 89–2 after rapid hearings and debate.

The acceptance of the United Nations symbolized the remarkable distance traveled by the American people during more than three years of global conflict. Isolation was a thing of the past. No matter how difficult the future course of world politics, there would be no turning back after World War II. The irony of it all was that the world was far less amenable to the soothing ministrations of an international security agency supported by the United States after 1945 than after 1918. It remained to be seen whether a remedy which might have succeeded handsomely after World War I would achieve success after the second phase of the Twentieth Century War.

Security and Containment Since 1945

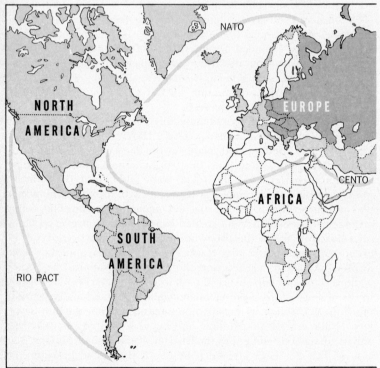

NATO 1949
United States
Canada
United Kingdom
Iceland
Norway
West Germany
Netherlands

Denmark
Belgium
Luxembourg
Italy
Portugal
France
Greece
Turkey

RIO PACT 1947	(OAS 1948)	CENTO 1959
United States	Guatemala	United Kingdom
Honduras	Ecuador	Turkey
Panama	Brazil	Iran
El Salvador	Paraguay	Pakistan
Venezuela	Peru	(United States has
Dominican Rep.	Bolivia	executive
Haiti	Mexico	agreements with
Argentina	Costa Rica	Pakistan, Iran,
Uruguay	Chile	Turkey)
Nicaragua	Cuba (expelled,	
Colombia	1962)	

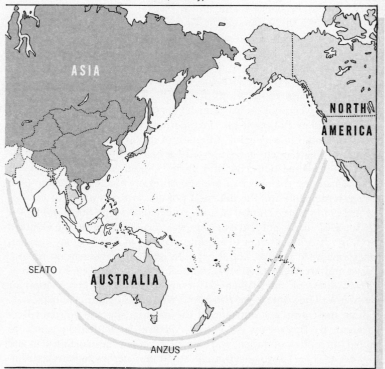

BILATERAL PACTS OF U.S.
Philippines 1951
Japan 1951
South Korea 1954
Taiwan 1954
(Also with three CENTO
countries, 1959; Pakistan,
Iran, Turkey)

ASIA

NORTH
AMERICA

SEATO

AUSTRALIA

ANZUS

SEATO 1954	ANZUS 1951	COMMUNIST BLOC OF NATIONS	
United States	United States	U.S.S.R.	Czechoslovakia
United Kingdom	Australia,	Mongolia	Hungary
France	New Zealand	China	Rumania
Pakistan		North Korea	Bulgaria
New Zealand		North Vietnam	Albania
Australia		Poland	Cuba
Philippines		East Germany	Yugoslavia
Thailand			

While the San Francisco conference deliberated, Nazi Germany finally collapsed. Beset from the east and the west, Hitler to the end refused surrender. Not until his suicide in a Berlin bunker was it possible to arrange an armistice. The capitulation at Rheims on May 7, 1945 brought down in the dust the once-proud Third Reich, but it inaugurated a long-sustained time of troubles in Europe. Postwar tensions stemmed in large part from the depredations of a regime unmatched in bestiality during all the tragic history of mankind.

In July 1945 the leaders of the Grand Alliance met for the last time during World War II at Potsdam, Germany, to make firm arrangements for postwar Europe and to concert Far Eastern policy. Clement Attlee, whose Labor Party defeated Churchill's Conservatives in a general election, sat for Britain. The interim since Yalta had been marked by growing indications that the Soviet Union had no intention of honoring certain of its prior commitments. Despite Churchill's urging, neither Roosevelt nor Truman was willing to authorize retaliation in kind, but a general stiffening of attitude became apparent at Potsdam. The United States pressed for comprehensive settlements of all European questions, but the Soviet Union demurred on several crucial matters. A Council of Foreign Ministers was established to plan peace settlements for the defeated powers, and a number of controversial issues were referred to it for future discussion. Stalin did seek a Polish settlement, but this question was also delegated to the Council. So was a Russian attempt to acquire territory in Africa. Some German questions were settled. The Big Three reached agreement on reparations, and an Allied Control Commission was established in Berlin as the medium of inter-Allied cooperation during the occupation of Germany. The conference also authorized trials of war criminals.

The most dramatic outcome of the meeting was the Potsdam Declaration. By this means the Grand Alliance demanded the unconditional surrender of Japan, warning of complete destruction if it did not occur. The Tokyo government, still dominated by military extremists, immediately rejected this ultimatum, insuring the use of the atomic bomb against Japanese cities. President Truman learned of the first successful test of a nuclear device just before he traveled to Potsdam. He chose to inform Stalin casually of its existence, but the Russian leader did not seem particularly impressed. The decision to employ the bomb against civilian centers was not made impulsively; it had been discussed at length by a secret government committee. Some urged a demonstration of the weapon to prove its destructive potential and facilitate a Japanese surrender. This proposal was rejected on the ground that it might misfire. The President authorized the attack on Hiroshima in the belief that he had no alternative. Otherwise, it

seemed clear that many Americans would die in the Pacific before
Japan capitulated.

The first atomic bomb fell on Hiroshima on August 6th; a day or so
later the Soviet Union attacked Japan. When the Japanese government maintained its intransigence, a second bomb was employed
against Nagasaki. Despite the horrible toll exacted by the bombs, the
military faction persisted in its desire to continue the war, but Emperor Hirohito settled matters by ordering surrender, provided that
his crown was preserved. The United States accepted this slight deviation from the principle of unconditional surrender. An armistice arranged on August 14th was confirmed at an impressive surrender conducted by General MacArthur in Tokyo Bay on September 2nd. The
terrible war had reached its end but only after some 34,000,000 casualties, untold billions of property damage, and unmatched human misery.

* * *

The return of peace did not bring the new day hoped and planned for
by many during the war. Almost six years of total warfare had left the
world in vast disarray, to a much greater degree even than after World
War I. The war of 1939-1945 completed a series of trends inaugurated
in 1914-1918. Two great superpowers dominated the world in the wake
of World War II, the Soviet Union and the United States. All other
great powers suffered temporary or permanent eclipse. Great vacuums
of power existed at both ends of the Eurasian land mass, insuring serious political instability in those regions for an indefinite period to
come. The war had awakened colonial peoples everywhere; it created
an unparalleled opportunity for them to regain independence. All the
old colonial empires were doomed after 1945. Anticolonial leaders
blossomed everywhere to guide movements of national emancipation
and regeneration.

Over the heads of all brooded the enormous mushroom cloud
produced by the atomic bomb, a massive symbol of potential doom for
the entire human family. Never before had peace brought troubles to
compare with those of September 1945 and after. But then, never
before had the peoples of the world engaged in such plenary warfare.
The price of victory was a legacy of international instability far beyond
anything ever before bequeathed to humanity in the wake of general
warfare. It was clear that the world could not endure another harvest
of death, certain as it was that nuclear conflict would wreak destruction far beyond anything experienced even during the most destructive of wars just past. Despite this awareness, no one could be sure in
1945 that the Twentieth Century War had reached its conclusion.

CHAPTER VIII

The Aftermath

W HEN THE WAR reached its end, few Americans desired a whole-sale retreat from international responsibilities comparable to that of 1919 and after. The striking support for the United Nations was sufficient proof of this change in national attitude. And yet, despite willingness to assume peacetime burdens far beyond any ever before contemplated by the Republic, there was hope for some surcease of responsibility. The desperate war had been preceded by the long recession of the 1930s, making some sixteen years of continuing crisis. With prosperity and peace in prospect, the fighting men who came home and the families who welcomed them had a certain claim on an armistice from tension. They hoped that the United Nations could largely resolve international questions, supported by a sufficient degree of Soviet-American cooperation. This promise had been held out during the war by the President and many other prophets of a new day. The inauguration of the new world organization in October 1945 seemed to confirm the wartime vision.

But it was not to be. The world could not hope to recover its balance quickly, torn asunder as it was by thirty years and more of violence. There was bound to be a long aftermath, a dangerous period of adjustment. Even before the victory, numerous signs and portents suggested that the United States and the Soviet Union would reach an early parting of the ways. Their interests clashed seriously, especially in Europe and to a great degree in Asia as well. The bipolarity of power becoming rapidly evident after 1945 made the two super-nations peculiarly sensitive to the massive vacuums of power present at either end of Eurasia—the warred-over districts. The basic concern of the United States remained, as before, to reconstruct a stable balance in Europe and East Asia conducive to American security and progress. For its part, the Soviet Union hoped as a minimum to insure that the vacuums were occupied by "friendly" countries. At most, Stalin hoped to fill them with Russian power. Although Soviet-American rivalry was rooted in different conceptions of future developments in

Europe and Asia closely related to divergent notions of national interest, the contest stressed ideological disputation as well. The United States envisioned a new flowering of democracy across the oceans, whereas the Soviet Union anticipated a vast expansion of "true" socialism. The American tradition of national mission thus collided with Marxist theories of world revolution.

These conflicts produced the Cold War. Neither peace nor war in any conventional sense, the years of the Cold War were fraught with enormous anxiety, made all the greater by nuclear weaponry, at first monopolized by the United States but soon acquired by the Soviet Union. At bottom the Cold War was a short-run phenomenon wrought by the immediate consequences of World War II. Less than a decade after its beginning, it had passed its zenith, slowed by the dissolution of those vacuums of power providing its reason for being. It did not wane rapidly, but after 1953 or so new problems insistently obtruded themselves upon both Russia and America. These difficulties ultimately began to forge a community of interest between the two huge nations, despite historical and ideological differences which at times seemed to preclude any possibility of peaceful coexistence.

Both countries experienced the shock of adjusting to the recovery of energies taking place in Europe and Asia within a few years after 1945. A decade after the war it was apparent that the simple bipolarity of the early postwar years was already diffused. Western Europe, dependent in the immediate wake of the war on American aid and comfort, had vastly recovered. Eastern Europe, subjected to Soviet hegemony during and shortly after World War II, was also beginning to reassert its independence. At the same time, both Russia and America began to experience the difficulties posed by the rise of a successful social revolutionary regime in China. As always, nothing makes friends of former enemies like common dangers. The Cold War mood lingered, sustained far beyond its useful life. If it proved remarkably hardy, insistent historical forces gradually eroded its substance, and twenty years after World War II it was possible to believe that something like workable (if hardly cordial) relations could be established in a relatively short time.

The Cold War was a supremely dangerous but largely evanescent phenomenon specifically related to the outcome of World War II, but another postwar phenomenon, the emergence of the nonwestern world, was a product of the overall course of the Twentieth Century War. This development was in its earliest stages as the Cold War approached its end. The destruction of the great imperial powers during the Twentieth Century War imparted enormous impetus to anticolonial movements in Africa and Asia. Proud peoples long held in subjection to Europe strove magnificently to restore their ancient independence and to accomplish vast social changes. Overwhelmed by a great "revolution in rising expectations," the hope of independence and progress, the peoples of the old colonial world moved rapidly to consolidate their recaptured freedom and to build modern economies. Beyond political and economic reform was a vision of social and spiritual well-being shaped not only by ancient traditions but by extensive contact with the western world.

The rise of the ex-colonial world seemed likely to rank with the Twentieth Century War as one of the great historic themes of world history during the twentieth century. Beside it, the Cold War began to assume its proper dimensions. In its early stages, the recovery of power in the ex-colonial world became intertwined with the Cold War, not by choice but by necessity. As time passed the two strands began to separate, but a complete disentangling would take some years to accomplish. Is it surprising then, that both the Russians and the Americans too often failed to distinguish between the Cold War and the rise of the new nations? Some score of years after World War II they still entertained vast misconceptions about the nature and direction of developments in Africa, Asia, and also Latin America.

In a certain sense, Latin America was also a part of the old colonial world. If it had broken away from Spain and Portugal at the beginning of the nineteenth century, much of it, particularly the Caribbean regions, had been subjected in many ways to quasi-colonial status by the United States during the earlier years of the twentieth century. Ostensibly part of the western world, Latin America had failed to develop as successfully as North America. Throughout the region, a rebirth of hope comparable to that sweeping across Africa and Asia stirred social revolutionary aspirations. If Britain and France encountered serious difficulties with their colonies in Africa and Asia immediately after the war, the United States began to experience troubles a bit later in Latin America looking suspiciously like those of their European friends.

Taken together, the interrelated experiences of the Cold War and the emergence of new nations posed unparalleled challenges to international statecraft. They stimulated innovations in world politics never before conceived of in the wildest imaginings of the most inventive intellects. The shock of these departures was enormously unsettling to the western world, accustomed as it was to leadership along lines of its own devising. The old system of world politics, weighed in the balance and found wanting during the Twentieth Century War, began to look increasingly superannuated as the Cold War (in its way a final exercise in old-fashioned international procedure) gave place to the novelties of a vast new international polarization – the confrontation of the western world and the ex-colonial world.

* * *

If the Cold War had its official inception in 1947, it was preceded by a long decline in Soviet-American cooperation. Both nations took action calculated to alienate the other. As soon as possible after the war, Russia confirmed its power in eastern Europe and the Balkans. Many ancient countries in those regions became Soviet satellites. Poland, Bulgaria, Hungary, Rumania, the Soviet zone of occupied Germany, and finally even Czechoslovakia fell to the hammer and sickle. Of the Balkan countries, only Greece escaped communization. In Yugoslavia a died-in-the-wool Communist, Marshal Tito, seized power, but he refused to accept Russian domination.

By degrees cooperation in occupied Germany fell apart. The policies of the Soviet Union reflected the traditional Russian fear of a strong German state. Despite insistent urgings by the United States, Stalin refused to make a German peace treaty. He systematically thwarted economic integration of the Russian and western zones of occupation. By early 1947 the world realized that Germany would remain divided for a long time to come. It was equally apparent that Britain could not exercise sufficient power in western Europe to preserve the region against Russian expansion. Stalin finally agreed to peace treaties for all the defeated powers except Germany and Austria, but the German settlement was by far the most important of the lot.

The Soviet Union gave indication of independent desires in other parts of the world as well. It rapidly extended its authority to those areas opened to it in the Far East by the Yalta agreement. A temporary line across Korea at the thirty-eighth parallel hardened into a firm boundary between distinct Korean governments. In the Middle East, Stalin at first refused to leave areas of Iran occupied during the war. The United Nations achieved its first success in helping to arrange a Russian withdrawal, but the episode contributed to a mounting sense of foreboding. The extensive activity of Communist parties in western Europe and elsewhere suggested that subversion of established governments by unconstitutional means remained an important aspect of Soviet foreign policy.

One of the greatest tragedies of the immediate postwar era was the failure of the nations to agree upon a plan for international control of atomic energy. In 1946 the United States proposed at the U.N. to relinquish its atomic secrets and ultimately its stockpile of nuclear weapons if the great powers agreed to an extensive system of inspection and waived their veto power in matters of enforcement. Once again, the Russians proved unwilling to accept an American proposal. They refused to consider any settlement until the United States agreed to liquidate its nuclear arsenal, something American leaders were not prepared to undertake. The failure of the U.N. to reach an accord on nuclear controls was the most severe blow the peace-keeping agency endured during its early years. It had been founded on the assumption of great-power unanimity. Without consensus among the Big Five, its peace-keeping capabilities were strictly limited. The U.N. made many useful contributions, but it could not become the principal safeguard of international security and progress as long as the great powers refused to cooperate closely in its various instrumentalities, especially the Security Council.

After the war, Britain had attempted to provide much-needed aid and comfort to Greece and Turkey. Both exposed to potential Soviet aggression, these countries controlled the eastern Mediterranean, long vital to British security. By early 1947, severe economic difficulties at home compelled the Labor government of Clement Attlee to end its support of Greece. This development forced the hand of the United States. In March, President Truman announced the doctrine which became known by his name. He asked Congress to provide $400 million in financial assistance to Greece and Turkey because "it must be the policy of the United States to support free peoples who are resisting attempted subjugation by armed authorities or outside pressures." In May, Congress agreed to provide the funds, and the Cold War officially began. The Truman Doctrine was a clear indication of American willingness to support Europe against further Communist advances. The vast economic dislocation in the aftermath of war had been mitigated to some extent by the United Nations Relief and Rehabilitation Administration and bilateral support, particularly to Britain and occupied Germany, but the dimensions of European economic and social malaise called for much greater efforts.

The Truman Doctrine was the first round of what became known as the containment policy. Cast in classic form by George Kennan, a career diplomatist well versed in Russian affairs, the concept of containment assumed that the Soviet Union would threaten international peace and security for a long time to come and that the United States would be required to give assistance at critical junctures to block Russian expansion. In practice, containment came to mean extensive economic assistance to threatened nations coupled with regional military alliances in order to deter the Soviet Union.

Shortly after the United States extended assistance to Greece and Turkey, Secretary of State George C. Marshall announced an unprecedented proposal to send massive financial support to all of Europe if it could concert a workable plan of action. His invitation included the Soviet Union and its satellites, but Stalin refused to allow participation by any nation within the Soviet bloc. The European Recovery Program, better known as the Marshall Plan, became fact in April 1948. Rapidly organized but extraordinarily well conceived, it wrought almost unbelievable economic miracles in western Europe. Skillful mobilization of bipartisan support for ERP insured its passage by the Eightieth Congress, notoriously opposed to the domestic policies of the Truman administration but willing to respond to the international challenge.

It became clear during the next few months that the security of western Europe required additional measures. In March and April 1948, the Soviet Union began to interfere with access to Berlin, reacting against the trend toward unification of the western zones into a single economic and political unit. By June the Berlin blockade was complete. To counteract it the United States inaugurated an airlift and managed to supply the western sectors of the city for many months until Stalin finally relented. He had not succeeded in undermining Anglo-American determination. The West German Republic came into being early in 1949. If the Russians backed down, they refused to formalize the right of access to Berlin or to negotiate a German settlement, and these problems regularly returned to cause serious difficulties in later years.

The last important aspect of containment in Europe was the creation of the North Atlantic Treaty Organization. NATO was a collective defense arrangement. Its twelve original members pledged themselves to assist any member subjected to attack. It provided a vehicle for developing multilateral military, naval, and air defense to protect the entire Atlantic community. General Eisenhower agreed to serve as the first NATO commander, an important factor in establishing its prestige and popularity. In October 1949, Congress passed the first of many laws authorizing military assistance to its allies. After the Korean War, military assistance bulked ever larger as an arm of American foreign policy.

By 1950, western Europe was well on the road to recovery; the temporary danger of communization had passed. The continent, of course, remained divided along the line of the iron curtain. Where Russian armies had conquered during the late war, Communist influence was pervasive. Where Anglo-American armies had triumphed, the United States accomplished its desires. The power vacuum existing in Europe after the war had been largely occupied by infusions of Russian strength in the East and American strength into the West.

During the 1950s, both countries would encounter increasing difficulty in maintaining their positions as client countries rapidly reasserted themselves.

*   *   *

Both the United States and the Soviet Union improved the immediate postwar years in the Far East by stabilizing their influence in regions they had conquered or occupied during the war. The Japanese islands located in the mid-Pacific came under a United Nations trusteeship administered by the United States. The Philippines finally acquired independence in 1946. Most important, the United States undertook a unilateral occupation of Japan and Okinawa under the proconsulship of General of the Armies Douglas MacArthur, refusing a Soviet proposal of joint occupation. MacArthur's headquarters in Japan presided over a remarkable program of domestic change, including land reform and disarmament. The United States occupied Korea below the thirty-eighth parallel, but largely withdrew its forces from other locations. The Soviet Union quickly asserted its claims to Sakhalin and the Kuriles, and its power rapidly flowed into Outer Mongolia, Manchuria, and Korea above the thirty-eighth parallel. Efforts to arrange free elections in order to unify Korea broke down as a result of Russian intransigence, and separate regimes appeared in that country, much as in Germany.

Elsewhere in East Asia, lands conquered by the Japanese were reclaimed by national governments such as in China and Thailand or were temporarily recovered by their colonial masters. France returned to Indo-China, the Netherlands attempted to reassert its control of the Dutch East Indies, and Britain reclaimed authority in Malaya. All the western imperial powers experienced insurmountable difficulties with nationalist movements during the early postwar years. Indonesia, guided by Achmed Sukarno, achieved independence from the Netherlands very quickly, and Britain granted independence to India, Pakistan, Burma, and Ceylon, the beginnings of a vast anticolonial trend in South and Southeast Asia. France alone refused to part with its colonies, and a long struggle for Indo-Chinese independence began shortly after the conclusion of World War II.

The China tangle continued to unsettle East Asian affairs as Roosevelt's hopes for Nationalist China went whistling down the wind. Despite an energetic effort by General George C. Marshall to effect a coalition between Chiang and the Communist dissident, Mao Tsetung, as well as to encourage internal reform in the impossible labyrinth of Kuomintang venality, the Chinese situation deteriorated with lightning speed. American economic assistance failed to correct a pattern of Communist expansion across China from Mao's bases in the northwestern provinces. The Soviet Union allowed the Chinese Communists to lay hands on Japanese arms stockpiled in the north, but the weakness of the Nationalist regime was the principal ally of Communist victory. Later it became apparent that nothing short of armed intervention in China by the United States could have preserved the Nationalists, a policy the American people were not prepared to authorize while involved in the European crisis. The Sino-Soviet agreement of 1945 required by the Yalta understandings seemed to work with some degree of efficiency. Russia did not intervene extensively in China proper, confining most of its activity to its own territories and spheres of influence. Like the United States, it was tied down by the Cold War in Europe.

In the absence of a considerable Russian or American presence in China, internal factors largely determined the shocking outcome of the civil war between the Nationalists and the Communists. In 1949, Chiang was forced to flee the mainland. He established himself and the remnants of his following on the island of Formosa, hoping someday to return triumphantly to the mainland. The victory of radical social revolutionary leadership in China presaged a number of other violent rebellions against colonial or counterrevolutionary regimes in Asia, giving a tremendous psychological lift to comparable movements elsewhere. In the western world dismay induced negative policy. The United States refused to recognize the People's Republic of China proclaimed by Mao in October 1949. It also refused to consider U.N. membership for the new government.

The collapse of Nationalist China greatly alarmed the people of the United States. Lulled into false assumptions about the efficacy of Chiang's regime and increasingly disturbed by Communist pretensions elsewhere in the world, they found it difficult to comprehend what had happened. Efforts to explain the debâcle by President Truman and his new secretary of state, Dean Acheson, encountered considerable doubt and suspicion. The Communist victory gave impetus to a domestic interlude of red-baiting, largely stimulated by congressional agitation. It reached its peak during the Korean War and did not subside until after that struggle reached its end. The red-baiters developed the ridiculous thesis that treason from within the United States government had fostered Mao's victory in China. Legislators like J. Parnell Thomas of New Jersey, Richard Nixon of California, and especially Senator Joseph McCarthy of Wisconsin rose to national prominence by exploiting the theme of "twenty years of treason" in various ways. McCarthy never substantiated a single one of literally hundreds of accusations. He and his associates muddied the waters at a time when careful analysis and planning were desperately needed. If the Red Scare was of relatively short duration, it hindered American policymakers considerably during a particularly critical period. The Red Scare confirmed a growing American tendency to construe every international question as an aspect of the Cold War, a dangerous delusion constantly injurious to American foreign policy in years to come, especially when the Cold War passed its peak after 1953 and began to recede in significance.

On June 25, 1950, armed forces from North Korea suddenly invaded South Korea. As the assault rapidly developed deep below the thirty-eighth parallel, Communist China massed troops on the mainland adjacent to Formosa, presumably to liquidate the irritating Chiang. No firm proof is yet available concerning the exact origins of what was in effect a war against the United Nations. The U.N. had established the Republic of Korea in the south after the Soviet refusal to permit unification on any terms other than its own. Some believe that the North Korean leader, Kim IL Sung, acted on his own initiative. Others attribute the aggression to Chinese provocation. It seems most likely that Stalin whetted the appetite of Kim IL Sung, hoping by a Korean success to recover Soviet prestige lost in Europe and to expand the sway of "friendly" regimes in Asia. If so, he underestimated the willingness of President Truman to accept this direct challenge to the Pacific *status quo*. Perhaps Stalin had been encouraged by the tendency of General MacArthur to place Korea and Formosa beyond the American defense perimeter in the western Pacific. Following MacArthur's lead, Dean Acheson defined that perimeter as lying along a line formed by the Philippines, the Ryukyus, Japan, and Alaska in a statement made in January 1950.

Truman's capacity for decision was never more in evidence than in June 1950. When it became apparent that North Korea had mounted a full-scale offensive designed to conquer all of the peninsula, he ordered MacArthur to support South Korea and the Seventh Fleet to prevent hostilities between the two Chinas. On June 27th, the United States obtained from the Security Council of the U.N. a resolution authorizing defense of South Korea against aggression. Fortunately, Russia was then boycotting the Security Council and did not interpose its veto. The police action was on. At the beginning the Korean War was conceived and executed by the United States in terms of limited objectives. Its purpose was generally to restore the *status quo* of June 25, 1950. Serious difficulties arose when criticism of its limited character developed in the United States.

After several months of defeat, the U.N. forces found themselves confined to the southern tip of the Korean peninsula at Pusan, but reinforcements arrived in time to permit a brilliant amphibious attack on the west coast of Korea near Inchon. The landing force broke cross-country to Seoul and threatened to cut off the North Korean army below the thirty-eighth parallel. The result was a precipitate retreat by the enemy. South Korea was rid of the aggressor force by October.

The question now became whether to press the U.N. offensive north of the thirty-eighth parallel. MacArthur wanted to proceed, convinced that he could conclude the campaign before Christmas. His intelligence reports denied the likelihood of Chinese intervention, although it had been threatened by Peking. After the administration gave permission and a rather ambiguous U.N. authority had been secured, MacArthur ordered an assault beyond the thirty-eighth parallel. It was a fateful decision, one that thoughtful Americans have since had cause to regret. At first the operation achieved great success, but as U.N. forces approached the Yalu River, dividing North Korea and Manchuria, they encountered Chinese troops in great force, contrary to the expectation of their commander. By New Year's Day, the augmented army of North Korea had penetrated below the thirty-eighth parallel and recaptured Seoul. This setback confirmed widespread suspicion in the United States and throughout the U.N. that it had been unwise to move beyond the limited objectives announced at the start of the police action.

MacArthur reacted differently; he wished to expand his own effort, especially intent upon obtaining permission to use air power against "privileged sanctuaries" of the enemy across the Yalu. President Truman prudently adhered to the concept of a limited war for limited objectives, accepting the counsel of General Omar Bradley who correctly asserted that an expanded conflict with China would result in the wrong war, at the wrong time, at the wrong place, with the wrong enemy. When MacArthur publicly criticized the decision, he was warned to desist, but he persisted in his rank insubordination. In April 1951, Truman reluctantly removed his recalcitrant General from the U.N. command. MacArthur then staged a dramatic return to America and argued his case before the American public, notably in a famous oration before the Congress ending with the plaintive note that "Old soldiers never die; they just fade away." Much to his surprise, MacArthur did indeed fade away. The inherent wisdom of limited warfare in Korea ultimately undid the General, despite a series of remarkable public demonstrations of affection for the old victor of the Pacific war.

In a short while, the Korean front stabilized roughly along the thirty-eighth parallel. In June 1951 the Soviet Union suggested that the war might be ended by negotiations, and the U.N. authorized its new commander, General Matthew Ridgway, to seek an armistice. For two long years, American and North Korean negotiators met regularly in an effort to end the struggle. Meanwhile a bitter war of attrition continued along a relatively stable front. The talks deadlocked on disputes over the location of the truce line and repatriation of prisoners of war. This frustrating situation lent strength to the Republican Party's effort in the United States to regain the Presidency after twenty years in the wilderness. Split into conservative and moderate factions, the Republicans finally opted for the moderate aspirant to their Presidential ticket, the beloved General Dwight D. Eisenhower, who resigned his command of the NATO forces and returned to the United States to wage a successful campaign for the nomination over Senator Robert A. Taft of Ohio, the conservative Republican favorite, and an equally successful electoral campaign over Governor Adlai E. Stevenson of Illinois, the Democratic nominee. The General's most impressive campaign statement was a promise, if elected, to visit Korea. This announcement stimulated great hopes of bringing the war to an early end. After inspecting the Korean front in late 1952, Eisenhower decided to continue Truman's search for an armistice, but he heightened pressure on North Korea by intimating that he might utilize nuclear weapons if the peace negotiations did not come to a conclusion.

In June 1953 a truce was arranged in Korea establishing a line between the contending forces roughly along the thirty-eighth parallel. It also set up a prisoner exchange. America sustained approximately 140,000 casualties by the end of the war, a terrible toll indeed for a "police action," although North Korea and China suffered many times that number. Far too many of them came after MacArthur launched his ill-fated attack to the north in 1950. The conservative Syngman Rhee, President of South Korea, violently opposed the settlement; he preferred complete reunification of Korea on his own terms. Eisenhower and his secretary of state, John Foster Dulles, overrode his objections. A firm anti-Communist, Rhee was of equally firm authoritarian inclinations, a constant embarrassment to the United States and the United Nations. His regime in South Korea was hardly a model of progressive democracy, a condition reproduced in Formosa by Chiang. The reactionary policies of these two dictators consistently gave the lie to American propaganda concerning the benefits that would accrue to nations who joined the anti-Communist front. Many countries, including some of America's staunchest friends, wondered whether the defense of the "free world" against Communist expansion justified aid and comfort to authoritarian regimes like those in South Korea and Formosa.

The outcome of the Korean War confirmed the wisdom of Truman's limited strategy, also followed by Eisenhower. If the Korean problem had not been completely resolved, the line had been held against a truly severe challenge. As in Europe, the policy of containment had worked effectively. The principles of the United Nations had been upheld without precipitating a third world war. Despite the success, the American people never really accepted the Korean War. After the experience of unconditional surrender in 1945, they found it hard to comprehend the nature and purpose of limited warfare. On the other hand, many incautious "experts" later advocated limited warfare in situations, unlike that of Korea, when it was an unwise and inappropriate policy. Limited warfare was a useful stratagem in certain circumstances, but it could not replace sound diplomacy as a primary means of resolving international tensions. Even limited war has a tendency to breed more war, a trend to be avoided whenever possible. In an atmosphere of severe tension, even the slightest use of force can multiply into widespread conflict. The threat of utilizing nuclear weapons made during the Korean War only underlined more clearly the necessity of avoiding any possible occasion for their use, especially after the Soviet Union developed its nuclear capability.

The Korean War produced a complicated net of entangling alliances in the western Pacific in order to preclude Communist expansion in the region. An important step in this direction was the negotiation of a peace treaty with Japan, despite the unwillingness of the Russians to participate. Their belligerency in the last stages of the Pacific war entitled them to a seat at the peace conference, but the United States decided to proceed without them, much as the Russians ignored America in settling with regions under their control. A surprisingly nonpunitive settlement was reached with Japan in September 1951. A bilateral treaty of defense signed at the same time allowed the United States to retain bases on Japanese soil, a necessity because the peace treaty outlawed Japanese rearmament. Even before the Japanese settlement, the United States entered into a collective defense pact with Australia and New Zealand, the ANZUS treaty, to strengthen security in the southwestern Pacific. Other bilateral pacts incorporated the Philippines (1951) and the Republic of Korea (1953) into the growing Pacific security system.

If these alliances enhanced American military security, they tended to incline the nation to military aid as against economic and technical assistance to the new nations of Asia. They often shored up conservative and even reactionary regimes, frustrating the revolution in rising expectations to a notable degree in several important countries. When the threat of Soviet meddling declined in the Far East, military assistance became largely unnecessary. The satisfaction of social revolutionary appetites assumed primary importance, but the Eisenhower administration was slow to recognize this reality, shifting its concern about aggression from the Soviet Union to Communist China as the Peking regime established itself as the most popular and stable Chinese government in modern history.

* * *

The year 1953 marked a distinct alteration in the intensity of Soviet-American rivalry. Stalin died in March 1953, and a "collective leadership" succeeded him, directed initially by Georgi Malenkov. Domestic difficulties within the Soviet Union probably contributed to the onset of the so-called "Thaw" in the Cold War, but the primary reason for lessening tensions was the gradual elimination of the power vacuums at either end of Eurasia remaining after World War II. Like the people of Russia, Americans yearned for a respite from international crisis, and the Republican administration of President Eisenhower tried to meet this demand. The business orientation of the new government—Eisenhower's first cabinet was jokingly referred to as "eight millionaires and a plumber"—indicated an intense concern with domestic prosperity and a corresponding lack of interest in a great range of pressing international problems. Eisenhower's secretary of state, the vastly experienced John Foster Dulles, seemed unusually qualified for his position, and the amiable Chief Executive constantly accepted his judgment on world politics. As it happened, Dulles was far less successful than had been anticipated, a result not only of novel international problems arising during his tenure but also because of a certain rigidity of mind and temperament that some thought was "Wilsonism turned sour."

After 1953 the Cold War seemed to oscillate, but the overall trend was toward relaxation of Russo-American relations. Competitive but peaceful coexistence became the objective of each country in its relations with the other. Regular crises disturbed this pattern, especially when the social revolutionary movement in Africa, Asia, and Latin America achieved a full head of steam, but conflicts in the conventional theaters of the Cold War recurred less and less frequently. Vast internal changes within the Soviet Union seemed to presage a turn away from the old Bolshevik past, especially after a de-Stalinization campaign gained momentum under the emergent Nikita S. Khrushchev. If these developments hardly proved that Russia was on the road to democracy like that of the United States, it suggested that a much greater degree of reasonableness might be expected in Soviet-American exchanges. Russia and America increasingly discerned common or parallel problems. No challenge was more likely to force recognition of similar concern than the rise of Communist China. At first hailed in Russia as a great triumph in the struggle for world revolution, the Chinese leaders soon insisted on an independent and even competitive variety of national Communism. This trend created growing doubts and fears in Russia, the ancient home of the "yellow peril" concept. Established and affluent powers by comparison with most other nations, the Soviet Union and the United States rapidly grew in understanding of the shared danger posed by the possibility of nuclear war. Although concrete moves toward disarmament were few and far between, a continuing series of negotiations demonstrated a long-run desire in both countries to achieve a satisfactory degree of arms control.

The pattern of Soviet-American *détente* began in 1954 when the two countries agreed to attend a conference at Geneva to settle the crisis in Indo-China. France had divided the region into three governments within the French Union — Cambodia, Laos, and Vietnam — but in the latter country national resistance forces administered humiliating defeat to French forces. The Geneva accords of 1954 divided Vietnam temporarily along the seventeenth parallel. National elections were to produce a general government for the entire country. A radical regime under the nationalist hero Ho Chi-minh established itself at Hanoi in the north. In the south, the United States became the patron of a government at Saigon finally controlled by Ngo Dinh Diem. The national elections scheduled for 1956 never materialized. The United States supported Diem in his refusal to authorize them because it became clear that Ho Chi-minh would receive an easy majority if the ballots were ever cast. This resolution of the Indo-Chinese crisis, however unsatisfactory, was a first step in temporarily lessening world tensions.

Despite the ominous sound of facile slogans like "massive retaliation," "rolling back the Iron Curtain," and "agonizing reappraisal" frequently voiced by that energetic practitioner of brinksmanship, John Foster Dulles, President Eisenhower was deeply interested in achieving world peace. A strong indication of this desire came in 1953 when he proposed the atoms-for-peace program at the U.N. This scheme for sharing nuclear knowledge and materials for peaceful purposes at first encountered Russian resistance, but in 1956 an international agency was finally established to administer the program. Domestic political circumstances increasingly favored an American initiative for peace. The President successfully weathered an attack on executive prerogatives in the making of foreign policy, the so-called "Bricker amendment." After spectacular television hearings in 1954 exposed his methods, Senator McCarthy rapidly lost his influence, another gain for the administration. By 1955, hope had risen that the Soviet Union might be prepared to help bring about a general relaxation of international tensions. An indication of good intent was the successful negotiation of an Austrian peace treaty.

The result was a gathering at Geneva of the principal world leaders—Eisenhower, Marshal Bulganin and Khrushchev for the Soviet Union, Anthony Eden of Great Britain, and Edgar Faure of France. It was the first such meeting since Potsdam in 1945. Secretary Dulles was skeptical of success, believing that councils of heads of government should be preceded by firm indications of useful accomplishment. Realizing that the prime international questions were nuclear arms control and a German settlement, he hoped for prior understandings on these issues. Despite their absence, Eisenhower went to the summit. The conversations at Geneva took place in an atmosphere of unusual cordiality, but they failed to resolve many important questions. Russian proposals on Germany proved completely unacceptable, and Eisenhower failed to obtain a nuclear arms settlement, despite his dramatic "open skies" plan envisioning inspection by air.

If the reestablishment of contact at Geneva was a marked gain, nothing of substance came in terms of prime issues, and the hopeful "spirit of Geneva" ended in disillusionment. The trend from 1953 to 1955 had been encouraging, but the events of 1956 seemed to destroy all that had been accomplished during the "Thaw." Two unrelated developments, disturbances in eastern Europe and the Middle East, suddenly flowed together to produce a great international crisis in October.

As early as 1953, signs of discontent in the satellite countries of eastern Europe had begun to appear. National aspirations rather than undue opposition either to totalitarianism or socialism caused increasing restiveness over Russian preponderance. This trend encouraged the American dream of "liberating the captive peoples of eastern Europe" and "rolling back the Iron Curtain." If Dulles lent some support to these ideas, he soon ceased to discuss them publicly. The idea of "liberation" was bound to complicate efforts to reduce Cold War tensions. Early in 1956, partially to deal with growing difficulty in eastern Europe, Khrushchev launched his remarkable program of de-Stalinization with a speech to the Twentieth Congress of the Communist Party, thoroughly documenting Stalin's cruelty and injustice. In the satellite countries, Khrushchev's initiative brought back to power a number of nationalist leaders who had been purged by hard-line Stalinist regimes. Much to the dismay of Khrushchev, de-Stalinization encouraged eastern Europe in the idea that the opportunity was ripe to assert a degree of independence from Soviet dictation.

In June 1956 a series of riots in Poland exposed the unpopularity of the Moscow-dominated government. The outcome was the rise of Wladislaw Gomulka, a resurrected anti-Stalinist of good Marxist background who managed by circumspect politics to establish himself at the head of a more popular regime. The Polish uprising was not aimed against Communism; it reflected historic anti-Russian feelings in Poland. Gomulka had no intention of making a break with Moscow comparable to that of Tito; he hoped to develop a more nationalistic brand of Communism than his predecessors.

Another outburst of resentment in volatile Hungary erupted in a much more severe revolution during October 1956. An old anti-Stalinist, Imre Nagy, led a rising against the regime in Budapest and temporarily forced Russian troops to withdraw from that city. As in Poland, the revolution was primarily nationalist in character, although bourgeois elements lent heavy support to it. Nagy might have scored a success in Hungary comparable to that of Gomulka if he had been as circumspect as his Polish counterpart. A sudden Israeli-Egyptian war in the Middle East gave Khrushchev an opportunity to intervene decisively in Hungarian affairs without fear of meaningful western opposition.

The Middle Eastern crisis culminated a long train of events which had their roots in Arab-Jewish animosity. In 1947, Britain referred the problem of Palestine's future to the U.N. The extermination of six million Jews during World War II had revitalized the Zionist project to create a "national home" in Palestine for the Jews, but British relations with the Arabs, who opposed immigration into Palestine, had greatly interfered with the project. The U.N. decided to partition Palestine, but the Arab leaders rejected this plan. Britain withdrew its forces in May 1948, an act precipitating the formation of a Jewish state—Israel—and a short war in which the Israelis defeated the combined opposition of their Arab antagonists. The United States from the first had shown great sympathy to Israel, recognizing the new state within hours of its establishment. An American, Dr. Ralph Bunche, headed a United Nations team which managed to arrange an uneasy truce between the Jews and the Arabs. Ever since, Arab-Israeli tension has caused insecurity in the Middle East.

In 1954, Colonel Gamal Abdel Nasser seized control of a revolution against the corrupt Egyptian monarchy and immediately launched a policy of internal change stressing agrarian reform and industrialization. Nasser's foreign policy centered on Arab unity under Egyptian leadership. To create a basis for unifying the quarrelsome Arab states, he assumed control of the effort against Israel. In 1955 the Egyptian leader was much annoyed by the formation of a collective security arrangement for the so-called "northern tier" of Arab countries, aimed at the Soviet Union. The Middle Eastern Treaty Organization included Iraq, Iran, Turkey, and Pakistan, along with Great Britain. The United States did not join, but Dulles was an assiduous sponsor and supporter of the agreement. Nasser's response was to organize a competitive group of states including Syria, Saudi Arabia, and Yemen. Another consequence of METO was Nasser's acceptance of arms assistance from the Communist bloc. The United States feared that Nasser might use his newly acquired weapons against Israel.

In order to divert Nasser from war, the United States hit upon the plan of financing the Aswan high dam on the Nile River, a project to enlarge arable acreage in Egypt and to provide electrical power. Britain, the United States, and the World Bank reached an agreement to finance the Aswan Dam. It would take many years and huge sums of money to complete. These plans fell apart when Secretary Dulles suddenly withdrew American support from the project, reacting against Nasser's pro-Soviet policies. Not one to endure an insult of this proportion without retaliation, Nasser responded by seizing and nationalizing the Suez Canal from which Britain had earlier withdrawn its armed forces. This bold initiative precipitated a frenzied interlude of negotiations through which Dulles hoped to correct a situation for which he was largely to blame. The Secretary hoped to establish some sort of international control over Suez, refusing to believe that Nasser could operate the canal successfully and hoping to pacify outraged sentiment in Britain and France. The French hated Nasser because of his support for nationalist movements in North Africa, particularly in Algeria, where an insurrection against French rule not unlike that in Indo-China had broken out during 1954.

Disgusted by American bumbling, Britain and France secretly decided to chastise Nasser. Plotting with Israel, they arranged a surprise attack on Egypt. Late in October, while the Hungarian revolution was taking place and the United States was absorbed in its Presidential election, the three countries struck at Nasser and achieved a short-lived victory in a brief campaign. The adventure exposed marked division within the NATO alliance, and it immobilized the West in relation to Hungary. Khrushchev rapidly augmented Soviet troops in that country and used force to topple the Nagy regime. Janos Kadar was placed in power, and he rapidly restored Hungary to Communist orthodoxy.

If the Suez adventure allowed Khrushchev to recover his prestige in eastern Europe, it eventuated also in diplomatic triumph for Nasser. He lost the war but won the peace. The United States refused to condone the Anglo-French-Israeli aggression. When the Suez matter came before the Security Council of the United Nations, the United States joined with the Soviet Union and the Afro-Asian nations to censure the aggressors. Ultimately the occupation forces were withdrawn and Nasser gained permanent control of Suez. Secretary Dulles had no choice except to condemn the actions of Britain, France, and Israel.

Attempting to re-establish American prestige in the Middle East, Dulles championed the "Eisenhower Doctrine" in 1957. It offered economic and military assistance to Middle Eastern nations threatened by external aggression. Although aid to Jordan and Lebanon prevented Nasser from absorbing those weak countries in 1957–1958, he strengthened himself by establishing the United Arab Republic in 1958, originally a fusion of Egypt and Syria. Iraq, Egypt's principal rival for leadership in the Arab world, temporarily associated itself with Nasser after a bloody *coup* in July 1958, but the Iraqis soon reverted to their traditional anti-Egyptian policy. Dulles' final Middle Eastern initiative was to reorganize METO into the Central Treaty Organization (CENTO), including the United States in its membership, but his various efforts failed to insure lasting stability in the region. In June 1967, Nasser once again precipitated a Middle Eastern crisis, but the remarkably efficient armed forces of Israel humiliated the armies of Egypt, Jordan, and Syria in a mere six days. The Communist bloc, treating Israel as an "outpost of western imperialism," lent support to the Arabs, but Soviet efforts at the U.N. to condemn the Israelis as aggressors came to naught.

The crisis in Hungary and Egypt confirmed trends developing slowly in previous years; both Russia and America realized more clearly that their power was on the decline in Europe. The NATO alliance had begun to lose cohesion as the danger of Russian aggression faded and western Europe regained its economic and political health. The subservience of the satellite countries to Russian authority had been seriously challenged by Poland and Hungary, and in the future the Soviet Union would have to accept a slow but meaningful assertion of independence along the lines of "national Communism" in eastern Europe.

One consequence of the crisis of 1956 was a searching re-examination of the concept of containment. The respected George Kennan, who drafted the classic statement of containment theory in 1947, advanced an alternative after the Suez crisis, recognizing changes taking place during the preceding decade. His proposal became known as "disengagement"—the idea of establishing a neutral zone in central Europe to relieve tensions and to permit negotiation of problems

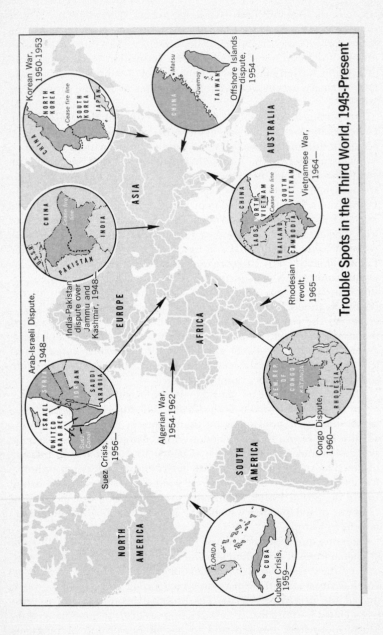

Trouble Spots in the Third World, 1945-Present

like that of German unification. A comparable solution was urged by the Polish foreign minister, Adam Rapacki. Unreconstructed practitioners of containment, notably Dean Acheson, remained insistent on the old approach, and the Eisenhower administration generally held firm against major innovations in policy.

The advent of earth satellites after the successful launch of Sputnik I in 1957 stimulated a new departure in the armaments race, the development of ballistic missiles to deliver nuclear warheads. Fears of a "missile gap" contributed to a continuing military emphasis in American policy, working against the more pacific alternative of extending economic and technical assistance to needy countries around the world. Eisenhower's policy of "fiscal responsibility" in budgetary matters conflicted with the international role and obligations of the United States. He tried to compensate for the cost of the "space race" and foreign assistance by expanding the nuclear deterrent—"more bang for a buck"—a policy that might have left no alternative but the use of nuclear weapons in the event of war.

Additional European complications arose in 1958 when General Charles de Gaulle regained power in France and liquidated the North African war by ultimately granting independence to Algeria. The Fourth Republic went down. A new constitution strengthened the executive authority and the pre-eminence of the proud old General. De Gaulle shortly elaborated a policy of diplomatic independence from the United States and the NATO alliance, a further indication of European recovery from World War II. If de Gaulle's policy reflected a long-time grudge against Britain and America dating from World War II and his dream of restoring French *grandeur,* it was also an indication that Europe in general was prepared to reassert a more independent role in world politics.

The last years of Eisenhower's administration were filled with disappointments for the old warrior; the course of events reflected the growing diplomatic isolation of the United States, committed to policies showing distinct signs of wear. Old friends, such as Britain and France, became cool and sometimes even angry. The greatest setback was the failure of a promising enterprise in summitry. In late 1958, Khrushchev had revived European tensions by calling for a German settlement no later than May 1959. He threatened to make a separate peace with East Germany if his demands were not met. The United States reluctantly agreed to a meeting of foreign ministers during May. No settlement was reached, but the Soviet deadline passed without incident. Pressure continued to build for a summit meeting, and a marked relaxation of Soviet-American tension occurred when Chairman Khrushchev, now dominant in Russia, visited the United

States in September 1959. President Eisenhower planned to return the visit during 1960. In the interim, the two leaders were to meet at the summit.

Summitry has useful functions in certain circumstances; it can contribute to relaxed feelings and provide a vehicle for public acceptance of new international policies. It can also be pernicious unless preceded by a relatively firm understanding to agree. The meeting scheduled for Paris in May 1960 turned into a fiasco precisely because no prior accord could be reached on the critical issues it was to consider—the same old questions of arms control and German reunification. Khrushchev apparently realized that the meeting was doomed. To avoid embarrassment, he utilized the U-2 incident as an excuse to torpedo the meeting. Just before the summit conference, an American reconnaissance plane was shot down deep inside Russia while taking aerial photographs of Russian installations. After initial denials, Eisenhower accepted responsibility for the espionage flight and justified it on grounds of national security. A touching demonstration of honesty, it was also a violation of normal international etiquette. Soon after arriving in Paris, Khrushchev demanded an apology, despite Eisenhower's suspension of further U-2 flights over Soviet territory. The conference then broke up in utter disarray. By this device Khrushchev escaped blame for what he knew would be useless negotiations.

In 1960 the American people turned away from the policies of the Eisenhower years, refusing to elect as their President the man chosen by the retiring Chief Executive as his heir. Events both at home and abroad had finally stirred a sense of undefined unease in the electorate. Vice-President Richard Nixon lost the closest election in the history of the Republic to Senator John F. Kennedy of Massachusetts, the youthful nominee of the Democratic Party. The victor constantly stressed the need for new energy in American foreign policy, although he did not specify his intentions in great detail. Nixon had to defend the record of the Eisenhower administration, a troubled assignment.

Although the new President had considerable difficulty obtaining congressional assent to the domestic aspects of the New Frontier, he was more successful in foreign affairs where he could exercise executive initiative. To strengthen the bargaining power of the United States and to provide broader military capability, Kennedy altered American military policy, placing stress on the creation of "balanced forces" capable of waging limited "brushfire" wars as well as nuclear conflicts. He also vastly expanded the American space program to equal and surpass the striking achievements of the Soviet Union in this area. Like Eisenhower, Kennedy was a man of unusually pacific intent. His sponsorship of the Peace Corps, a program sending Americans to developing countries on missions of economic and social assistance, was an intelligent and humane departure comparable to his predecessor's interest in developing the peaceful uses of nuclear energy.

Kennedy's approach to the Cold War reflected a growing desire to reach accommodation with the Soviet Union, although a number of serious crises occurred during his Presidency. In June 1961 he met Khrushchev for two days of conversations in Vienna, hopeful of making progress toward a German settlement and arms control. Khrushchev's unbending demeanor in Vienna preceded another crisis over Berlin. When the Russian leader once again threatened to negotiate a unilateral settlement with East Germany, the President mobilized a large number of reserve units to demonstrate his determination. Khrushchev then permitted the east Germans to construct the Berlin wall, sealing off the entire eastern zone of the city from its western sectors. The Berlin crisis of 1961 gradually eased, but the pressure for an ultimate settlement of the German question continued to trouble Soviet-American relations. Khrushchev also defied world opinion by resuming nuclear tests in the atmosphere, ending a voluntary moratorium on such activities dating from 1958. This deed emphasized once more the necessity of reaching accord on arms control. Delay insured that additional nations would acquire nuclear armaments, a development certain to enhance the danger of war.

A prime source of tension with the Soviet Union was the Cuban revolution of Fidel Castro. In April 1961, Kennedy supported an abortive anti-Castro expedition which met ignominious defeat at the Bay of Pigs. In October 1962, American intelligence detected a number of Russian missile sites under construction in Cuba. There ensued the most dangerous encounter in the history of the Cold War. Khrushchev's challenge to the Monroe Doctrine was at once audacious and ill-advised; Kennedy's response was to order a "quarantine" on ships moving to Cuban ports, a euphemism for a blockade. For several days the world hovered close to war, but fortunately cool heads prevailed. Khrushchev finally agreed to remove the missiles from Cuba in return for an end to the "quarantine" and an American policy of hands off Castro. The Cuban leader refused to permit inspection of the missile sites, an act which seemed to release the United States from its pledge to avoid another invasion of Cuba, but thereafter the situation eased considerably.

The Cuban missile crisis preceded another "thaw" in Soviet-American relations and produced a new start toward arms control. Greatly chastened by the near approach of war over Cuba, Khrushchev reverted to his interest in establishing peaceful coexistence with the non-Communist bloc of nations. The outcome was the limited test-ban treaty of 1963. This agreement ended nuclear testing in the atmosphere and in the seas, but allowed underground tests. The treaty was no substitute for extensive controls on the production of nuclear weapons or the means of delivering them, but it was a basis from which further negotiations might depart. Neither France nor the Chinese People's Republic adhered to the treaty, but over a hundred other nations appended their signatures. Unlike the Kellogg-Briand Pact of the Twenties, also relatively unenforceable against violators, the test-ban treaty was never depicted as a panacea for all the world's ills. A modest first step, it performed a considerable service for peace.

Despite continuing controversy over events in the ex-colonial world, Soviet-American tension continued to moderate, especially after the downfall of Khrushchev and his replacement by a regime reminiscent of the "collective leadership" taking power after the death of Stalin. European tensions seemed ever less dangerous as problems mounted elsewhere in the world. If confrontations like that of the Cuban missile crisis were supremely dangerous, its settlement short of serious violence confirmed the view that the classic Cold War was on the way out. Problems in the traditional Cold War theaters — Europe and East Asia — rapidly gave way to difficulties in other places, mostly in Southeast Asia and Africa, of a different diplomatic genre than earlier controversies. Both the United States and the Soviet Union increasingly found themselves on the defensive in Europe. General de Gaulle launched a frontal attack on NATO, exposing that arrangement for what it had become, a largely obsolete arrangement in need of considerable adjustment in order to retain its usefulness. In eastern Europe a comparable reaction took place against the Warsaw pact, the Soviet counterpart of NATO. If eastern European countries seemed bound to remain Communist, they were equally likely to pursue markedly independent policies.

Under its new leaders, Russia contemplated the prospect of closer relations with western Europe as a means of limiting American influence on the continent, a tactic hardly likely to threaten the security of other nations. Resumption of cultural and economic exchanges between Cold War antagonists presaged an improving diplomatic climate, although the pattern of ups and downs characteristic of the Cold War since 1953 seemed likely to endure for an indefinite term. It seemed more and more likely that if there was to be another violent phase of the Twentieth Century War, it would stem from extra-European developments. Events in Latin America, Asia, and Africa more and more dominated the evolution of world politics as World War II receded into the past.

* * *

At the end of World War II, the future looked bright for United States-Latin American relations. The war brought to fulfillment the Good Neighbor ideal and the policy of hemisphere defense. Despite the favorable outlook of 1945, the aftermath of war bred considerable tension. For one thing, the United States looked mostly to those Eurasian regions where the Cold War had its principal impact. Latin America received relatively less attention in Washington because of America's greatly expanded commitments in Europe and Asia. A more important source of difficulty in the long run was increasing social revolutionary agitation throughout the other Americas. If the repudiation of interventionism and the multilateralization of the Monroe Doctrine had vastly improved intergovernmental relations in the hemisphere, it had worked against the interests and aspirations of lesser folk. Dictators like Batista in Cuba actually strengthened their power under the aegis of the Good Neighbor. The war stimulated vast hopes for the future in Latin America as it did in the colonial regions across the oceans. Leaders of emancipation from authoritarian regimes naturally depicted their countries as quasi-colonial outposts of the United States and hated regimes as agents of Yankee imperialism, sometimes with considerable justice. The consequence was a resurgence of Yankeephobia like that of the T. R. era; it became a regular component of social revolutionary politics in Latin America.

Largely insensitive to these developments, the United States moved to perfect the inter-American system in the wake of the war. A conference at Rio de Janeiro in 1947 established the principle even more firmly that an attack on any American state was an attack on all, to be met with collective measures. The Inter-American Treaty of Reciprocal Assistance signed at Rio established procedures to implement this commitment. A year later at Bogotá, another conference created the Organization of American States, a regional agreement within the meaning of Article 51 of the U.N. Charter, in order to foster continuing cooperation across the hemisphere. These hopeful actions obscured for the moment the growing resentment in Latin America at the refusal of the United States to include it among the beneficiaries of extensive foreign assistance. Economic dislocations created considerable difficulty in the region, but the United States either ignored or contributed to those problems. Pleas for help from the south went largely unheeded; relatively unimportant assistance contributed through Point Four and various lending agencies of the United States government did little to minimize the new Yankeephobia.

The hemisphere was supposedly immune from the Cold War, but it ultimately complicated inter-American relations. Social revolutionary movements in the western hemisphere, like those elsewhere in the world, showed considerable interest in the Soviet model for national development. Russian agents, later joined by counterparts from China and elsewhere in the Communist bloc, sought to infiltrate protest movements in Latin America. Local Communist parties appealed to the populace as movements for national regeneration opposed to United States imperialism. The colossus of the north showed increasing sensitivity to this development, especially after that doughty cold warrior, John Foster Dulles, took charge of the State Department. In 1954, annoyed by Communist activities within the left-wing regime of Jacobo Arbenz in Guatemala, Dulles secured an inter-American agreement to invoke sanctions against Communist-dominated regimes at a conference held in Caracas. Shortly thereafter, the Central Intelligence Agency lent independent support to an armed rebellion in Guatemala which succeeded in overthrowing Arbenz. This disguised reversion to unilateral interventionism frightened many in Latin America. It was interpreted not simply as an anti-Communist measure but as a challenge to social revolution. American toleration of the notorious Trujillo regime in the Dominican Republic and the Pérez Jimenez regime in Venezuela were only the most notable examples of United States willingness to collaborate with ruthless authoritarian governments in the hemisphere. This tendency exposed once again the vital flaw in the policy of noninterventionism—its inability to get beyond governments to the people themselves.

Continuing Latin-American requests for economic assistance went largely unheeded until 1958, when Vice-President Richard Nixon was sent on a "good-will tour" of the region. Much to the surprise and dismay of the entire country, Nixon encountered angry mass demonstrations wherever he went. In Caracas a mob actually threatened his life. Although some patriots chose to interpret this episode as an insult to the nation, wiser advice (including that of Nixon himself) suggested changes in United States policy. The President's brother, Milton S. Eisenhower, had become an important counselor on Latin-American affairs, and he added his voice to those who proposed a cool attitude toward dictatorships of the Trujillo type and supported a program of expanded economic assistance.

In 1959 the hemisphere experienced its most significant social revolutionary *coup* when Fidel Castro succeeded in overthrowing Fulgencio Batista of Cuba, for so long a recipient of United States support and a particularly odious example of Latin-American reaction. At first the United States attempted to cooperate with Castro's government, but the radical tendency of that regime, which included expropriation of United States companies, hardened attitudes in Washington. Castro increasingly communized his government, but the Eisenhower administration suffered a setback when attempts to invoke the Caracas agreement against Castro came to naught. The United States gradually invoked economic sanctions against Cuba and finally broke diplomatic relations in January 1961, just before the inauguration of John F. Kennedy. The course of events in Cuba reflected the failure of the United States to recognize the differences between indigenous social revolutions and what it persisted in calling "the subversive activities of the international Communist movement." More sympathetic response to social revolutionary impulses would certainly decrease the likelihood of Communist infiltration and control, but this lesson was hard to learn. It is entirely conceivable that the Cuban revolution would have followed a much different pattern if the United States had reacted differently.

Social revolution in Latin America, as elsewhere in the world, was dominantly a nationalist phenomenon, a means of revitalizing the sovereignty and power of given countries. Social revolutionary governments almost always embrace authoritarian politics and socialist economics. They become authoritarian because strong central government is the only way to combat both internal and external challenges to the revolution. They adopt socialism because that system seems the most logical means of accomplishing the primary domestic goal—rapid economic development. In Latin America, social revolutionary regimes espoused Yankeephobia precisely because of its broad political appeal. Harsh responses to social revolutionary success, like the reaction against Castro, only heightened the political utility of anti-United States diatribes and policies. Estrangement from the United States naturally caused Castro to look elsewhere for assistance, which Moscow was only too happy to supply. Despite a pervasive distaste for authoritarian-socialist regimes, the Republic would have to learn to live with them or face proliferating crises in the hemisphere.

However reluctantly, the Eisenhower administration took the first steps toward meeting the challenge of social revolution in the Americas; these beginnings were broadly expanded by President Kennedy. In September 1960 the "Act of Bogotá" inaugurated a program of assistance called Operation Pan America, designed to penetrate beyond governments into the daily lives of ordinary people in Latin America. In March 1961, Kennedy vastly expanded the scope of this program by launching the Alliance for Progress. It was an ambitious and enlightened attempt to correct the flaw in the Good Neighbor Policy, its tendency to stifle popular aspirations. Assistance of this nature would work against disorder in the hemisphere while preventing the rise of more regimes like that of Castro. The Alliance for Progress envisioned the expenditure of some $80 billion during the decade of the Sixties, $20 billion to be provided by the United States, so that Kennedy's challenge might be met. The hemisphere, he said, had the task of showing that "man's unsatisfied aspiration for economic progress and social justice can be achieved by free men working within a framework of democratic institutions." In 1961 a conference at Punta del Este, Uruguay, developed plans for the Alliance, and Congress made initial appropriations of funds to begin operations.

Much to the disappointment of many throughout the hemisphere, the Alliance for Progress did not immediately exercise a large influence. A number of tragic setbacks to social progress occurred during the next few years in Latin America; military *coups* such as those in Brazil and Argentina frustrated efforts to banish the reactionary politics of the past. In addition, it proved difficult to implement the promises of Punta del Este. Neither the people nor the Congress of the United States seemed truly interested in accepting the expense needed to insure the success of the Alliance. The death of President Kennedy in 1963 was a further blow to its elaboration. Kennedy had done much to undermine his Latin-American policy by condoning the participation of the Central Intelligence Agency in the abortive invasion of Cuba by anti-Castroite elements in April 1961. His striking success during the Cuban missile crisis hardly allayed Latin-American suspicion that the Organization of American States was a vehicle of hemispheric action only at the convenience of the United States. Kennedy acted first and then consulted the OAS, which gave rather reluctant support to his policies. The unanimous vote by the OAS in favor of the Cuban quarantine was a consequence of Kennedy's *fait accompli* rather than fervor. Kennedy ultimately achieved unsurpassed personal popularity in Latin America, a tribute to his understanding and compassion for the Americas, but anti-United States sentiment continued to grow.

President Lyndon B. Johnson did little to reverse the adverse trend. During his administration the Alliance for Progress continued to lag. Growing Mexican-American cooperation hardly compensated for mounting antagonism elsewhere. Johnson's tendency to cooperate with Latin American military regimes was all too reminiscent of the Eisenhower years. One of the most ironic outcomes of recent times was that much of the unrest in Latin America emanated from those countries held in protectorate status before the Thirties. Johnson's greatest mistake was to launch an armed intervention in true T.R. style, Marines and all, against the Dominican Republic, when the democratic regime of President Juan Bosch, supplanting the tyrant

Trujillo's government, supposedly fell under Communist influence. Once again the OAS was called into the affair only after the United States took action. Many Latin Americans continued to wonder whether that organization was a truly independent force in hemispheric relations or merely a creature of United States policy. Increasingly preoccupied by problems in Asia and Africa, President Johnson seemed unwilling to shoulder the full burden of the critical hemispheric situation.

* * *

The Latin American policy of the United States exposed the difficulties of coping with social revolution in Africa and Asia. In its long-range implications, the sweep of social revolution was a far more significant legacy of twentieth-century violence than the Cold War, potentially productive either of great good or unmatched evil. Social revolution constituted a particularly difficult problem for sated America, accustomed to thinking of change in gradual constitutional terms within the established order of things. Perhaps the hope that social revolution could be accomplished under democratic auspices was an illusion. The absence of any notable degree of democratic institutionalization anywhere in the social revolutionary world except in the former British colonies suggested that authoritarian-socialist regimes of radical persuasion were far more likely sponsors of vast social change than democratic-capitalist governments of moderate bent.

Increasingly, the hope was that economic and social regeneration might lead to a flowering of democracy. Certainly, successful social revolutions like those of Turkey and Mexico suggested that this development could take place, although with agonizing slowness and many setbacks along the way. The experience with Castro seemed to indicate the importance of maintaining communications with social revolutionary governments at all costs, enduring the slings and arrows of expropriation and comparable incitations with stoic reserve. The United States had something to offer that was desperately needed in all social revolutionary countries, economic assistance in the form of investment capital and technological knowledge. Help of this nature could be used to moderate more extreme measures by social revolutionary governments. The tendency to view Latin American social revolutions as simply occasions for Communist penetration of the hemisphere often obscured the boundless human suffering at the root of revolutionary activity. In the absence of sympathy from the United States, social revolutions naturally sought assistance elsewhere. The logical place was Moscow, and Peking waited in the wings.

Throughout Latin America, Africa, and Asia, a strong desire to avoid involvement in the Cold War was everywhere manifest. The consequence, especially within the growing Afro-Asian bloc of nations, was to adopt independent policies strongly reminiscent of those followed by the United States in its early years. The instinct of leaders like Nehru of India, Sukarno of Indonesia, and Nasser of Egypt was to avoid undue involvement in international affairs—to adopt an uncommitted policy frequently called "neutralism." One of the most ironic outcomes of recent years is the opprobrium attaching to this term in the United States, not so long ago the very epitome of isolation and neutrality. Social revolutionary leaders all recognized the importance of general peace to the success of domestic reform. They wanted aid rather than alliances from both great western protagonists of the Cold War, the two nations most able to offer it.

Americans found it difficult to comprehend the seemingly irrational policies of the neutralist bloc. They were explicable only if one realized that Nehru and other neutralist leaders continually strove to seize and hold the balance of power between the contending Cold War factions. Alignment with either the Americans or the Russians would lessen their ability to obtain economic assistance from both sides, and it would also decrease their power to maintain a general peace by balancing the rival factions. The act of holding the balance led the uncommitted nations toward the anti-Communist bloc when it underwent adversity, and away from it when the Communist nations sustained setbacks. This independent course was in the national interest of those countries who practiced it. All too often, Americans who argued that the national interest was the only safe guide for the United States failed to allow similar beliefs to neutralist countries in search of social and economic regeneration. The practice of neutralism was one of the most important contributions to the maintenance of the uneasy general peace that endured for twenty years and more after the conclusion of World War II, punctuated as it was by a myriad of small wars.

* * *

If Soviet-American relations improved after the end of the confrontation in Europe and East Asia, the growth of Communist power in mainland China constantly stirred trouble in South and Southeast Asia as well as in nearby insular countries. Throughout this huge region, as in Indonesia and India, social revolutionary movements frequently came to power. In other places, conservative governments established themselves, especially where the United States exercised primary influence, as in Formosa, Thailand, and South Vietnam. The social revolutionary regimes were much more concerned with progress at home than with external dangers, but the United States gave precedence to the real or presumed ambitions of the Chinese People's Republic. Nothing proved more difficult for the United States than to reconcile its strong anti-Communist policies with the task of working with social revolution in Asia.

In 1953 and 1954, Mao Tse-tung attempted to seize the islands of Quemoy and Matsu lying off the Chinese coast held by Chiang, and also showed interest in the Pescadores some ninety miles out to sea. The Formosa government was determined to retain control of them, claiming that they were essential to the defense of Formosa, and the United States supported its erstwhile ally. Late in 1954, Dulles negotiated a bilateral treaty of defense with Formosa comparable to earlier treaties with Japan, South Korea, and the Philippines. Early in 1955 the Congress authorized President Eisenhower to defend the offshore islands from Communist attack. These departures probably caused Peking to relax temporarily its pressure in the Formosan strait.

Signs of growing Communist pressure in Southeast Asia once again allowed Secretary Dulles to indulge his penchant for alliances. In September 1954 he hurriedly put together the Southeast Asia Treaty Organization, heralding it as an Asiatic counterpart of NATO. SEATO was a relatively loose consultative pact rather than a binding system of collective defense, and it failed to include most of the more important countries of Southeast Asia. India, Indonesia, Burma, and Ceylon all refused membership. Only two signatories, the Philippines and Thailand, were located in the area, and they were American wards. The other members were Australia, New Zealand, Pakistan, Britain, France, and the United States. SEATO never functioned as Dulles had predicted. Its weakness was apparent during every one of a large number of crises in Southeast Asia during later years.

Despite abundant evidence that Chiang Kai-shek was hardly an exponent of all-out democracy, the United States maintained its assiduous support of Formosa. When Communist China resumed its pressure on the offshore islands in 1958, Eisenhower once again stood by the aging Generalissimo, although the Nationalist leader was finally required to foreswear plans for invading the mainland. Critics of Dulles wondered whether the offshore islands were really an integral part of Formosa's defenses. They also questioned whether support of Chiang was worth the risk of nuclear warfare, especially since his regime was distrusted throughout the social revolutionary world. Assuming a serious military threat from Communist China, Dulles preferred to support a conservative government long the recipient of heavy backing from right-wing political elements in the United States.

Senator William F. Knowland of California became known as "the Senator from Formosa," but he was only the noisiest of many vocal supporters of Chiang who advocated retreat from Europe but intervention in Asia. The futility of refusing diplomatic recognition to the Chinese People's Republic was everyday more apparent, but diehard pressure groups blocked this step and also U.N. membership for the Peking government.

How dangerous was Communist China? Peking obviously had its hands full at home. Despite heavy participation in the Korean War and the seizure of Tibet, the Chinese Communists were deeply preoccupied with herculean domestic tasks. They committed enormous energies to the task of industrializing China and improving its agriculture. Despite serious setbacks, particularly the unsuccessful attempt to collectivize farms, the regime developed considerable domestic support. If refugees flowed out of China into Hongkong in great numbers, it was apparent that China had at long last gained an effective government. Communism had come to stay. Peking actively pursued nuclear research, and by the middle Sixties had made considerable progress, although it did not immediately develop modern means of delivering nuclear weapons. Despite enormous man power, China was by no means a great military nation—surely no match for the United States. It lacked two necessary components, a strong navy and air force, and its nuclear capability would require a good number of years to develop. When tensions with Moscow created a great Sino-Soviet rift in the late Fifties, Russian aid programs dwindled to a bare minimum, definitely injuring China's military potential. If Communist China was certain to become a great military power at some time in the future, it was much more a "paper tiger" than the United States during the Sixties. Its attacks on India were limited in nature, designed to make minimal territorial gains along the Sino-Indian border. However portentous for the future, they did not presage any immediate invasion of the Indian subcontinent. The severe domestic disturbances associated with the "cultural revolution" of Mao Tse-tung further restricted the offensive potential of the Communist regime.

China could not contemplate direct armed aggression in Southeast Asia, to which it looked with great longing, but it could lend aid and comfort to anticolonial political movements which might enter the Communist camp at some future point. The result was "wars of national liberation." The Chinese Communists were extreme devotees of guerilla warfare, a practice particularly relevant to resistance movements operating in difficult terrain without an extensive supply of modern weapons. Limited assistance to guerilla movements in adjacent Southeast Asian countries like Laos and South Vietnam would insure serious domestic tumult. It might create political opportunities in the future. After the middle Fifties, Peking became a fervent supporter of "national liberation fronts" waging civil war against moderate or counterrevolutionary governments in the emergent states of Southeast Asia. The United States found it difficult to react intelligently to this political tactic, a circumstance working against sound policies in relation to the Southeast Asian region.

After World War II Japan became perhaps the most reliable of America's allies in the western Pacific. Tutored to recovered independence during an extended occupation, Japan rapidly regained its economic capabilities and resumed its activity as an important international trader. Hopeful of returning to the China market, the Japanese encountered stiff opposition from Washington. Tokyo also courted the anger of Secretary Dulles and his successors by flirting with neutralism, a logical policy for an unarmed state. In 1960, the United States renegotiated its bilateral treaty of 1951 with Japan, making many concessions to its new friend. If Japan gained considerably from this step, domestic opponents who thought the new treaty might lead to war demonstrated furiously against it and threatened to prevent its ratification. President Eisenhower scheduled a visit to Japan for June 1960, but the Japanese government felt compelled to withdraw its invitation after serious rioting broke out, a pathetic humiliation for the retiring Chief Executive. Despite intense difficulties, the treaty finally achieved ratification, although the government negotiating it fell immediately thereafter. These events suggested that Japan would be increasingly unwilling to accept American proposals regarding East and Southeast Asia. Japan continued to interest itself in revised policies toward Communist China, but usually encountered gentle but firm rebuffs in Washington. Kennedy's ambassador to Tokyo, Edwin O. Reischauer, was a respected American authority on Japan. Fluent in Japanese, he contributed greatly to the maintenance of cordial relations after 1961, but continuing agitation in Japan against the government's pro-American policies gave plenty of indication that difficulties lay ahead.

Kennedy's first Asian test came in Laos, one of the independent countries forged from French Indo-China. A moderate neutralist regime had taken power, only to be challenged by conservative opponents on the right and a largely Communist resistance movement on the left called the Pathet Lao. By 1958 a coalition government had been arranged, but soon its leftist members were purged. The Pathet Lao then launched guerilla warfare, receiving assistance from neighboring North Vietnam. By 1961, Laos had assumed the proportions of a major international crisis. The right-wing regime patronized by the United States seemed close to disaster. One aspect of the Laotian crisis was the exposure of SEATO for what it was, a pretentious but useless arrangement. President Eisenhower had popularized the so-called "domino theory," holding that the fall of any Southeast Asian state to Communism would topple all the rest. Supposedly, a Laotian collapse would open the gate to Peking. This theory ignored the patent fact that Communist or quasi-Communist resistance movements achieved significant success only where social revolutions were obstructed, frequently by the United States. Earlier "wars of national liberation" had been frustrated in the Philippines and Malaya by combining sound military operations and responsible social reform. This combination was more difficult to achieve in regions previously exploited by the French, where far less capacity for self-government had been inculcated in the people.

Kennedy resolved the Laotian mess temporarily through another international conference meeting at Geneva during 1961–1962. He agreed to a coalition government representing the three principal factions in Laos—leftist, conservative, and middle-ground—the last group of neutralist persuasion. Since the Geneva accords of June 1962, a precarious regime headed by Prince Souvanna Phouma has managed to maintain itself at Vientiane, but the possibility of further difficulty complicated United States policy in the region. One consequence of the Laotian compromise was a decision to base America's defenses against further Communist aggression in Southeast Asia on South Vietnam. Ngo Dinh Diem had initially preserved a degree of success in that country, buoyed up by extensive American assistance, but after 1960 his policies stimulated an expanding civil war against the Saigon government by the Viet Cong, the armed force of a dissident faction calling itself the National Liberation Front.

The civil war in South Vietnam constantly grew in magnitude as Diem proved incapable of unifying the country. President Kennedy slowly augmented American forces in Vietnam, hoping by a program of expanded assistance to end the civil conflict. Just before the President was shot down in Dallas, Diem was assassinated in Saigon, and a succession of unpopular military governments came and went in that unhappy city. It became evident that the Viet Cong, controlling most of the Vietnamese countryside, was likely to achieve victory in the absence of even more American assistance. President Johnson accordingly proceeded by degrees to "escalate" the war. Premature assurances of quick victory by Secretary of Defense Robert McNamara proved incorrect. By 1967 over 400,000 American troops had been committed in Vietnam. Victory seemed far distant despite signs that the Viet Cong had suffered greatly from American attacks. As the American effort grew in Vietnam, so did the involvement of military units from North Vietnam, supported by both Russia and China. The Russians showed little stomach for the Vietnamese conflict, but Moscow's prestige was definitely put to the test. Mao and his cohorts expanded their criticism of Soviet "revisionism," especially the tendency of Moscow to seek peaceful coexistence with the non-Communist world. The Chinese made of Vietnam a test of fealty to advanced principles of world revolution, from which the Russians had receded slowly despite lip service to conventional Marxist theory.

President Johnson coupled his escalation of the war with a constant emphasis on its limited nature and his desire to reach a negotiated settlement. At the same time he held forth the vision of a "new deal" for Southeast Asia, a massive program of assistance to meet the region's insistent demands for economic and social progress. Much to the chagrin of many Americans, Southeast Asia itself was often critical of American policies. Those who knew the region best remained of the belief that the principal cause of the Vietnamese conflict was the unwillingness of Diem and his successors to countenance a major social revolution. The ruling clique in Saigon had inherited the old French interests in the region. Desirous of maintaining power, they naturally resisted social revolutionary impulses finding expression in the Viet Cong movement. That indigenous protest became more and more a creature of the North Vietnamese and Chinese governments as it was forced to accept increasing support from its neighbors.

The war in Vietnam became increasingly unpalatable in the United States as casualties mounted into the thousands. Critics of administration policy pointed out the inconsistency of supporting a counterrevolutionary regime in Saigon, obviously unloved even by those loyal to it, while at the same time making glowing promises of aid and comfort to the social revolution. What would it profit either South Vietnam or the United States if the conflict made a desert and called it peace? The Viet Cong, North Vietnam, and Communist China all made as a condition for negotiations sought by Washington the withdrawal of all American forces in South Vietnam. This hard line reflected their confidence that events would ultimately work in their behalf. On the other hand, the United States did not seem able to exert sufficient pressure on the Saigon regime to quell constant intimations that the ultimate objective of South Vietnam was forced reunification of the entire country under its own auspices. One of the military dictators, Marshal Ky, seemed bent on precipitating hostilities with Communist China.

The American program of rehabilitation in "pacified" districts of

South Vietnam proceeded at a slow pace. It seemed obvious that domestic development and the war could not proceed hand in hand. Hope for mediation by the U.N. seemed unlikely to materialize as long as the great powers remained divided on the question. Attempts to reconvene the Geneva conference foundered on the rock of Russian objections. Delay was injurious; the United States found itself diplomatically isolated as its usual supporters one by one voiced opposition to the struggle in Vietnam. Even Britain's Labor government grew increasingly restive as the United States attacked major North Vietnamese cities from the air.

The administration in Washington persisted in its claim that the war was being waged to preclude further Communist expansion in Southeast Asia. Clearly the potential threat of direct armed aggression by Communist China might become real at some point in the future, but at present the Peking regime could intervene only indirectly. It lacked the military capability to follow any other policy. Of course, an invasion of North Vietnam, like the invasion of North Korea years before, would probably provoke defensive Chinese operations. American statesmen stubbornly refused to recognize that the Vietnamese war was in its inception primarily a civil war, and that it had assumed other characteristics only after the American intervention. Communist aid to the Viet Cong grew to significant proportions in response to the American escalation. Assistance to the Viet Cong was never more than a mere fraction of American assistance to Saigon, although it went a long way because of the guerilla tactics utilized by elusive jungle-fighters against South Vietnamese and American forces.

Had American policy been different from the beginning, the struggle in Vietnam might have taken a much more favorable course. The war proved once again, although official Washington seemed unable to accept the obvious, that the prime political factor in Southeast Asia was nationalist social revolution rather than Communist penetration. Failure to recognize this reality was what presented the Communists in the region with their political opportunities. Supporters of the President's policy in Vietnam often accused dissenters of "appeasement," ignoring the fact that the situation in Southeast Asia was completely unlike that of Europe in 1938. China in no sense posed dangers comparable to the threat of the Third Reich; threatened nations in Europe at the time of Chamberlain and Daladier were not in the throes of social revolution; and no one then possessed nuclear weapons.

Some advanced opponents of the war, outspoken but few in number, agitated for complete withdrawal of American forces, whereas others at the opposite end of the political spectrum advocated an all-out military solution. Sensible moderates preferred a policy of maintaining an effective military presence in Southeast Asia consisting largely of air and sea power based on available insular locations, a sufficient deterrent to Chinese aggression, but they stressed the importance of working with the social revolution. The problem was to provide a means of checking potential Chinese expansionism without engaging in military episodes like the war in South Vietnam, unnecessary as containment measures and subversive of social change. As the war intensified, the likelihood of arriving at this solution constantly diminished. As always, warfare narrowed the political alternatives open to those engaging in it.

The peoples of Southeast Asia were no more interested in subordination to China or the United States than they had been in the domination of the old colonial powers. As in Latin America, nationalism was the most potent political commitment. The principal danger was that American policy might drive social revolutionary politicians at the head of popular nationalist movements into the arms of the Chinese Communists, as in the case of the Viet Cong. Secretary of State Dean Rusk seemed to understand these things (it was hardly an imposing intellectual feat), but he generally supported policies which had their inception in the Pentagon rather than in Foggy Bottom. The growing predominance of military men and military thinking in United States policy reminded many of President Eisenhower's warning against undue influence by a burgeoning military-technological elite, attuned mostly to its narrow interests and rarely sensitive to the complexities of nationalist social revolution. President Johnson's inexperience in foreign affairs and his apparent lack of talent in this realm was further cause for concern among moderates who inclined to the views expressed by intelligent observers like George Kennan, Senator Robert F. Kennedy of New York, Walter Lippmann, and Senator J. William Fulbright of Arkansas, men who could hardly be accused of starry-eyed idealism. They urged that the administration avoid further escalation of the war while constantly seeking a diplomatic solution, recognizing the inherent difficulties in the situation caused by years of mistaken initiatives. They placed special emphasis on the fact that the United States could not expect to dominate the region as it once had dominated the Caribbean. All that could be hoped for was that careful aid and comfort might make constructive contributions to its security. One thing seemed certain amidst the mounting uncertainties of the time. Even if the Vietnamese war came to an early end, the vast problems of Southeast Asia would endure for a long time.

*   *   *

After 1960, problems in Africa began to compete with those in Latin America and Southeast Asia for the attention of the United States.

Americans did not welcome this intrusion, involved as they were in many other places. Africa had long been a European preserve, and Americans showed a strong inclination to leave African decisions to those with detailed knowledge of that continent. They found it difficult to transcend the national bent to think of Africa as an exotic and even fearful place inhabited mostly by apes, cannibals, and the tsetse fly. Travelers, missionaries, and moving pictures had so confirmed this image that it was difficult to recognize great changes in the face of Africa. The old conception of the Dark Continent had been psychologically soothing to white America, steeped in centuries of guilt feelings about black Afro-Americans stemming from criminal treatment of them both before and after their supposed emancipation at the time of the Civil War. For most people, the easiest antidote to African problems was not to think about them, but events deprived the country of this luxury.

Difficulties with Nasser and French North Africa had troubled the Eisenhower administration, but problems in Africa below the Sahara came to the fore during Kennedy's years in the White House. As in other parts of the ex-colonial world, vast troubles stemmed from the failure of the old imperialists to prepare the region for self-government. Even the British colonies experienced marked political turbulence after gaining independence. The obvious solution to political stability within the new African countries seemed to be military control, but military regimes frequently proved unresponsive to social revolutionary aspirations. Interference with the revolution of rising expectations, in Africa as elsewhere, was bound to cause serious tension. The situation was not helped by the tendency of both sides in the Cold War to make an ideological battleground out of Africa. The region was perhaps the most dedicated neutralist area of all, its internal problems even more difficult than those of Latin America and Asia. No region was more in need of sympathetic assistance from other countries, but none received less than Africa.

The greatest African crisis occurred in the Congo. Belgium left the region hurriedly in 1961 without having done much to prepare the way for independence. Anti-European riots broke out very soon after the Congo government of Patrice Lumumba took power. Lumumba obtained U.N. assistance in the form of a police force, but the situation became more complex when the richest Congolese province, the Katanga, attempted to secede from the central government located at Leopoldville. Moise Tshombe, the strong man of Elizabethville, led the Katanga revolt. The use of U.N. troops against Tshombe's secessionists aroused considerable criticism in the United States, but most of it came from disgruntled right-wing elements who believed that the repudiation of colonialism had been a grievous error. Senator Thomas F. Dodd of Connecticut typified this group, becoming known as "the Senator from Katanga." President Kennedy fortunately persevered in his support of the U.N. action, and Tshombe ultimately ended his resistance. A few years later, he recovered sufficient influence to head the central Congolese government for a short time. If some semblance of order had been restored, the Congo remained a source of likely difficulty in the future. The police action was only the beginning of what had to become a long-sustained program of assistance, if the country were to develop along peaceful and constructive lines.

Another endemic problem in Africa was insistence on white supremacy in those parts of Africa still ruled by Europeans. No nation was more difficult in this respect than South Africa, the home of *Apartheid*, or separation of the races, despite the fact that the whites were only a small minority of the population. No amount of U.N. pressure broke the intransigence of South Africa, despite growing international disgust and black African protest. The South Africans encouraged Rhodesia in its espousal of similar practices. A U.N. resolution led to an economic boycott of Rhodesia after it defied the parent British government, demonstrating worldwide disapprobation of segregation in Africa. A large number of new African states had entered the U.N., a sign of that continent's future potential in world politics, although most of the new countries were far from stable for the moment. It seemed obvious that African questions and African desires would play an important role in world politics at no very distant time. In the interim, the problem of African military *coups* loomed ever larger as important countries such as Ghana and Nigeria experienced army revolts. The United States still lacked a general understanding of African developments and a policy relevant to the region. Some gloomy observers wondered whether the nation was not repeating the errors made earlier in Southeast Asia.

* * *

By 1967 the pattern of world politics seemed incredibly variegated, and all signs and portents indicated even greater complexity in the future. It seemed clear that the Cold War was in its latter stages. Ideological tensions still troubled relations between the two greatest powers, but the course of postwar world politics bred a growing community of interest between them. The recovery of energy in Europe required both Russia and America to surrender much of their previous authority in the councils of Europe. The rise of Communist China seemed dangerous to both nations, although in the long run the

Peking regime seemed likely to cause more trouble for the Soviet Union than the United States. The Chinese were at the doorstep of Russia, and they were competitors for ideological leadership within the Communist bloc of nations. Peoples recognized these realities much less rapidly than their leaders, but the declining Soviet-American tensions of the Sixties had begun to affect public attitudes.

If the Cold War receded in importance, the rise of the new nations in Asia and Africa as well as unrest in Latin America posed a whole new range of problems for the western world which seemed increasingly to dwarf the controversies of the immediate post-World War II years. The Cold War began to look like something of a pink tea party compared with the difficulties of adjusting to a whole new efflorescence of power in the ex-colonial world. Accustomed to the range of considerations dominating their thinking during the Cold War, Americans found it hard to empathize with the new nations, who manifested an annoying tendency to think for themselves while all the time expecting massive aid from the United States. It remained to be seen whether the intellectual and physical effort required of the American people would be forthcoming in sufficient measure. If beyond today there loomed the strong likelihood of Soviet-American *rapprochement,* an effective response to the interests and aspirations of the new nations seemed much more difficult to predict.

Epilogue: Beyond Today

IN THIS CENTURY, America the Beautiful became what it always aspired to become, the richest and most powerful of nations, but the achievement failed to produce all the blessings expected of it. At home we Americans are now engaged in abolishing poverty. Certainly we have the capacity to accomplish this goal, and we are working hard and well at the task. The rub has come abroad; there we have too often failed miserably. Once we dreamed of solving the problem of discontents elsewhere in the world simply by ignoring them, but the myth of isolation died during the Twentieth Century War. We are citizens of the world as well as of the United States, and must participate extensively in the world's business beyond our favored shores. Membership in the human family imposes many trials upon us, but we ought always to realize that world citizenship brings opportunity as well as danger in its train.

Where do we go from here? Historians seldom ask questions of this sort, and they answer them even less frequently. Devotees of Clio almost universally abhor the task of dealing with the future. Preferring to "muddle through," they remain convinced, if others are not, that they have little or nothing to contribute to the solution of tomorrow's problems. Eternally contemplating the making of the future, they infrequently contribute to it. This restraint has a certain charm in a world unduly preoccupied with power. It relieves Clio of burdens others seem quite eager to bear. Clearly, then, historians who violate the general folkways of their guild ought to be viewed with a certain reserve. What follows is not only tentative, but also suspect. It is offered not to settle, but rather to sustain, a discussion that cannot be ignored, even among those who find their principal solace and competence in the contemplation of things past.

The troubled history of the United States and the Twentieth Century War teaches certain lessons. One is that the world cannot hope to avoid another season of mass destruction, a third violent phase in the Twentieth Century War, unless it makes marked changes in its methods of resolving international tensions. Always before, the race has turned to violence when no other solution remained to it. If heretofore it stopped short of total devastation, it perhaps was only because it lacked the capability to destroy itself. We human beings so exhausted ourselves that we lived to fight another day. It is a commonplace today to observe that the globe remains constant in size, but that the killing power of weapons has multiplied many times. At some point the world cannot survive its engines of war. Obviously, the advent of nuclear weapons brings us much closer to the end point.

A related lesson is that the present system of nation-states is pathetically obsolescent and that it must be replaced at no very distant time. Our problems are not simply a consequence of unsound procedure within the going order. The going order is itself unsound. Always before, the solution to political obsolescence of this nature has been found in an advance to a more comprehensive form of organization. Is it possible to contemplate fundamental changes of this nature in our own time? We do not lack pundits who inform us that no viable form of organization exists beyond the nation-state. They argue that violence is an inherent and ineradicable aspect of human affairs and that we must continue to live with it. Have they forgotten that the enterprise of civilization is based on a constant search for means of controlling violence through enforceable law? If the so-called "realists"—those improvident romantics who ignore incontrovertible evidence that the world simply cannot go on as before—are allowed to determine the course of policy, then we had all better say our prayers. The nation-state system is no longer sufficient to guarantee anyone's future. We cannot contain conflict effectively within it.

Just what is it that we must undertake? In the broadest terms what we seek is supranational political organization. If it is still impossible to specify in detail what forms such organization should assume, we may speculate profitably on what might be done to prepare the way for this insight. Certain pressing tasks can be performed immediately. There is reasonable expectation that their completion will gain time in which to define the shape of future world organization. The accomplishment of these tasks would in itself begin that difficult task of definition. One is to create an effective system of arms control leading ultimately to general disarmament. The other is to provide massive economic assistance to the ex-colonial societies of Africa and Asia and to Latin America on a hitherto undreamed of scale.

For twenty years negotiations to achieve some degree of arms control have dragged on with few notable accomplishments. Only the shortest of first steps has been taken, the test-ban treaty of 1963, ignored by France and China, although the nations in 1967 concluded a treaty banning the use of nuclear weapons in outer space and made considerable progress on an agreement to inhibit the proliferation of nuclear armament. What accounts for this depressing record? No effective steps toward arms control can be expected unless there is a prior relaxation of political tensions. No nation can be reasonably expected to disarm extensively in the face of insecurities like those of the present day. The opening in the clouds is the tortuous but notable decline in the intensity of Russo-American antagonism.

Much has been written about the historical and ideological gulfs dividing America and Russia, but far less about the ties that increasingly bind the two peoples. Even the bitterest of enemies often unite in the face of common dangers. Both countries face the task of adjusting to the rise of Chinese Communism, the reassertion of European power, and the recovery of energy in the ex-colonial world. A new and common history is being made for the two outlying powers of the western world. As Russia approaches affluence, its ideological commitments are bound to assume forms much more compatible with our own than used to be the case. The beginnings of this phenomenon are now fully apparent; the burden of past experience blinds us to present reality. Old wounds heal slowly, but they also heal surely if wisdom nurses the patients. The times call for every possible effort to nurture Soviet-American understanding, just as the circumstances of the immediate postwar world required a rapid resumption of friendly relations with Germany and Japan. It could confer on both countries benefits comparable to those flowing from the historic Anglo-American understanding. Above all, it could permit the negotiation of effective arms-control agreements leading someday to general disarmament. The only possible means of moving toward arms control is to speed a reduction in Soviet-American tensions. What will be thought of us later if we do not make this effort now, difficult as it may appear?

We live in a world of hard choices; the circle constantly narrows. The time for decision is now. It will profit us nothing if, by continuing our present ways, we postpone another general war for ten, twenty, or thirty years. The imperative task is to insure against the recurrence of general warfare at any time. If the world should again be visited by conflict involving nations on a scale at all comparable to the first and second phases of the Twentieth Century War, it would mean inconceivable death and destruction. Some would possibly survive such a war, but who can contemplate this prospect without unsurpassed terror?

Even if Russia and America achieved a *rapprochement* sufficient to permit cooperation on arms control, it seems unlikely that the Chinese Communists would join in the arrangements. Perhaps France would also abstain. A conceivable solution to this problem is to vest nuclear power in an independent supranational agency supported by both

Russia and America as a deterrent to the power of nonparticipating nations, gaining time to bring all nations eventually into the agreement. To vest such power in a joint agency would be to take an unprecedented step away from national sovereignty, but this step is the price of peace, perhaps even of survival. If in 1967 it seems impossible to conceive of anything like this course of events, it is quite easy to deduce the probable consequences of nuclear proliferation in the absence of arms control.

A few years ago Professor Neil Chamberlain wrote a vastly intelligent little book entitled *The West in a World Without War*. He began by assuming that arms control and general disarmament would eventually take place. (If it did not, there would be no future worth mentioning.) Thereafter, world politics would turn on a whole new principle: competition between the western world and the nonwestern world. The political influence of the West would decline greatly with the loss of its nuclear power. The ancient distinction between the House of Have and the House of Want would then operate on a global scale. In the absence of rapid economic development in the ex-colonial world, the probability was great that political tensions would appear on an unmatched scale. How could this outcome, likely to breed general warfare, be prevented? The answer, wrote Chamberlain, was massive economic assistance to the developing world—assistance on a much greater scale than had ever been contemplated before.

The world, of course, cannot live on bread alone, but it cannot survive at all without bread. The population explosions taking place everywhere mean that normal economic growth can at best only keep even with present levels of consumption. The geography of hunger demonstrates that the present level is insupportable. The world must adopt effective restraints on undue population growth and at the same time achieve remarkable rates of economic development. Such rates are attainable only by a truly monumental infusion of western capital and technology into the ex-colonial world. To such a task the nations of the western world might turn, utilizing as a vehicle still another cooperative agency beyond the nation-state to which they would contribute their proper shares. In this way they might return some part of the wealth they expropriated throughout some five hundred years of imperial endeavor in Africa, Asia, and Latin America. In so doing, they would help themselves; their own economies would benefit beyond all telling. There is a higher community of interest arching over conflicts of interest in economic relationships. The growth of prosperity elsewhere in the world would contribute not only to international peace but also to continuing economic growth in the West. If arms control is achieved, the great budgets now expended on armaments could be used to subsidize the task of development. No one could predict with total assurance that economic assistance on this scale would accomplish its purpose, but by the same token no other alternative with comparable chances of success has as yet been offered.

The twentieth century was not fated to be a placid epoch; it is a time of troubles. Either we learn to resolve our tensions or we perish. No perfect solutions exist to human problems. Suffering always abides, but so does the task of relieving it. In our own way we suffer deeply in the western world, especially in its most favored isle—America the Beautiful. If we are infrequently hungry, where is happiness? Some among us now claim that our very history is a vast neurosis, that the game we play called civilization has implanted in us all ineradicable psychic disabilities that we cannot hope to extirpate. Doomsday impends. This counsel of total despair may turn out to be correct. It remains to those who hope or believe differently to take arms against that sea of troubles, our contemporary heritage. Each of us helped make the world as it is. Before we surrender to our past, we might attempt to remake the future in a more complaisant image. Arms control leading to general disarmament and massive economic development in the ex-colonial world, achieved through impartial joint agencies, would constitute two giant steps beyond the nation-state system. These steps we must take to make a beginning so that we might sustain a world worth preserving very far beyond today.

Suggestions for Further Reading

The first section lists a large number of sources and authorities for the overall study of the history of American foreign relations. Additional sections discuss the literature for specific periods considered in this book.

GENERAL MATERIALS

Among the principal bibliographical guides to the history of American foreign relations the following are of particular importance: S. F. Bemis and G. G. Griffin, *Guide to the Diplomatic History of the United States, 1775–1921* (1935), an annotated work on most of the literature for the period it covers published to 1935; and *Foreign Affairs Bibliography,* 4 vols. (1933–1964), a list of books published on international subjects on the period since the outbreak of World War I. The extensive bibliography of world history published by the American Historical Association under the editorship of G. F. Howe, *et al., The American Historical Association's Guide to Historical Literature* (1960), lists many relevant titles. A much more detailed listing of all types of materials is found in O. Handlin *et al., The Harvard Guide to American History* (1954), recently reissued in paperback. For abstracts of relevant historical articles see *Historical Abstracts, 1955–,* and *America: History and Life, 1964–,* both published by the American Bibliographical Institute in Santa Barbara, California. For a recent brief bibliographical survey see A. DeConde, *New Interpretations of American Foreign Policy* (1961), a pamphlet issued by the Service Center for Teachers of American History. A thoughtful commentary on the present state of scholarship on the history of American foreign relations by Ernest R. May is in J. Higham, ed., *The Reconstruction of American History* (1962).

A number of useful textbooks cover all or part of the history of American foreign relations. See those by T. A. Bailey (7th ed., 1964); S. F. Bemis (5th ed., 1965); N. M. Blake and O. T. Barck, Jr. (1960); A. DeConde (1963); R. H. Ferrell (1959); R. W. Leopold (1962); and J. W. Pratt (2nd ed., 1965). A number of others concentrate primarily on the twentieth century, notably Jules Davids, *America and the World of Our Time* (1960); F. R. Dulles, *America's Rise to World Power* (1955), a contribution to the *New American Nation Series* covering the period 1898–1954; S. F. Bemis, *The United States as a World Power: A Diplomatic History, 1900–1955,* rev. ed. (1965); J. B. Duroselle, *From Wilson to Roosevelt: Foreign Policy of the United States, 1914–1945* (1963), translated from the French.

Several writers have offered provocative interpretations of American foreign relations. W. A. Williams, in his *The Tragedy of American Diplomacy* (1959), available in a revised paperback edition, interprets our foreign policy in this century in terms of the expansion of an "informal empire" because of economic influences in policymaking and decision, an overall foreign policy that has led to the "tragedy" of the present. In a different vein, G. F. Kennan has also written critically of American foreign policy in his vastly influential work *American Diplomacy: 1900–1950* (1951), available in paperback, attributing the failures of the United States to excessive legalism and moralism. R. Bartlett adopts a middle-ground point of view in his *Policy and Power: Two Centuries of American Foreign Relations* (1963), a more broadly descriptive work than those of Williams and Kennan. Another interpretive work of "liberal" persuasion is D. Perkins' *The Evolution of American Foreign Policy* (1948), also available in paperback. For a work in intellectual history see A. E. Ekirch, Jr., *Ideas, Ideals, and American Diplomacy: A History of Their Growth and Interaction* (1966).

A number of useful collections of documents and readings on the history of American foreign relations is now available, providing convenient texts of critical state papers and samplings of scholarly writing on specific subjects. Among documentary collections are: R. J. Bartlett, ed., *The Record of American Diplomacy*, 3rd ed. (1954); R. A. Divine, ed., *American Foreign Policy* (1960), a useful documentary history in paperback; D. B. Goebel, ed., *American Foreign Policy: A Documentary Survey 1776–1960* (1961); P. E. Gianakos and A. Karson, eds. *American Diplomacy and the Sense of Destiny*, 4 vols. in paperback (1966); N. Graebner, ed., *Ideas and Diplomacy: Readings in the Intellectual History of American Foreign Policy* (1964), an original collection on an important topic; and A. Rappaport, ed., *Sources in American Diplomacy* (1966). Among collections of essays, some of which also incorporate documentary selections are: A. Rappaport, ed., *Issues in American Diplomacy*, 2 vols. (1965–1966); A. Rappaport, ed., *Essays in American Diplomacy* (1967); D. M. Smith, ed., *Major Problems in American Diplomatic History* (1964); and W. A. Williams, ed., *The Shaping of American Diplomacy: Readings and Documents in American Foreign Relations 1750–1955* (1956), also available in a two-volume paperback set divided at 1900.

From a wide variety of works dealing with the activities of various officials and institutions in the United States government concerned with making and executing foreign policy, the following works are of special interest. On the President see E. S. Corwin, *The President's Control of Foreign Relations* (1917), and his other more general studies of the Presidency; E. Plischke, *Summit Diplomacy: Personal Diplomacy of the President of the United States* (1958); and S. Warren, *The President as World Leader* (1964). On the secretaries of state, consult the ten-volume set edited by S. F. Bemis entitled *The American Secretaries of State and Their Diplomacy* (1927–1930), continued more recently under the editorship of R. H. Ferrell, who has added several studies; A. DeConde, *The American Secretary of State: An Interpretation* (1962), a biography of the office; N. Graebner, ed., *An Uncertain Tradition: American Secretaries of State in the Twentieth Century* (1961), a series of chapter-essays by distinguished authorities; N. L. Hill, *Mr. Secretary of State* (1963), by a political scientist; and D. K. Price, ed., *The Secretary of State* (1960), a symposium of contemporary opinions on the office. Works on the Department of State and the Foreign Service include: W. Barnes and J. H.

Morgan, *The Foreign Service of the United States: Origins, Development, and Functions* (1961); J. R. Childs, *American Foreign Service* (1948); R. E. Elder, *The Policy Machine: The Department of State and American Foreign Policy* (1960); G. Hunt, *The Department of State: Its History and Functions* (1914), a useful older study; W. F. Ilchman, *Professional Diplomacy in the United States: A Study in Administrative History* (1961); G. H. Stuart, *American Diplomatic and Consular Practice*, 2nd ed. (1962); and G. H. Stuart, *The Department of State: A History of Its Organization, Procedure, and Personnel* (1949). For works on Congress and foreign policy, see: H. N. Carroll, *The House of Representatives and Foreign Affairs* (1958); C. V. Crabb, Jr., *Bipartisan Foreign Policy: Myth or Reality?* (1957); R. A. Dahl, *Congress and Foreign Policy* (1950); E. E. Dennison, *The Senate Foreign Relations Committee* (1942); D. N. Farnsworth, *The Senate Committee on Foreign Relations* (1961); D. F. Fleming, *The Treaty Veto of the American Senate* (1930); W. S. Holt, *Treaties Defeated by the Senate: A Study of the Struggle Between President and Senate over the Conduct of Foreign Relations* (1933), an imposing study; J. A. Robinson, *Congress and Foreign Policy-Making: A Study in Legislative Influence and Initiative* (1962); and A. C. F. Westphal, *The House Committee on Foreign Affairs* (1942). Miscellaneous works on other important aspects of governmental activity include: E. M. Byrd, Jr., *Treaties and Executive Agreements in the United States* (1960); H. M. Jackson, ed., *The National Security Council* (1965); A. W. MacMahon, *Administration in Foreign Affairs* (1953); J. L. McCamy, *The Administration of American Foreign Affairs* (1950); J. L. McCamy, *Conduct of the New Diplomacy* (1964), on recent practices; J. C. McKenna, *Diplomatic Protest in Foreign Policy* (1960), covering the period 1900–1935; H. R. Ransom, *Central Intelligence and National Security* (1958); and H. M. Wriston, *Executive Agents in American Foreign Relations* (1929). Three books dealing with the American overseas empire are W. H. Haas, ed., *The American Empire: A Study of the Outlying Territories of the United States* (1940); J. W. Pratt, *America's Colonial Experiment* (1950), a work with the intriguing subtitle, *How the United States Gained, Governed, and in Part Gave Away a Colonial Empire;* and W. T. Perkins, *Denial of Empire: The United States and Its Dependencies* (1962).

No study of the history of American foreign relations is possible without extensive reference to the relations between force and diplomacy. Among works on military questions of use to students in this connection, see especially: P. Y. Hammond, *Organizing for Defense: The American Military Establishment in the Twentieth Century* (1961); S. P. Huntington, *The Soldier and the State: The Theory and Politics of Civil-Military Relations* (1957); E. R. May, ed., *The Ultimate Decision: The President as Commander in Chief* (1960), a series of essays on war presidents: W. Millis, *Arms and Men* (1956), a brief but incisive history of American military policy; R. G. O'Connor, ed., *American Defense Policy in Perspective: From Colonial Times to the Present* (1965), a collection of readings; A. Vagts, *Defense and Diplomacy: The Soldier and the Conduct of Foreign Relations* (1956); and T. H. Williams, *Americans at War: The Development of the American Military System* (1960). Works on naval and maritime questions are less plentiful, but see: R. G. Albion and J. B. Pope, *Sea Lanes in Wartime: The American Experience, 1775–1942* (1942); E. B. Potter, ed., *Sea Power: A Naval History* (1960); C. Savage, ed., *Policy of the United States toward Maritime Commerce in War*, 2 vols.

(1934–1936); and H. and M. Sprout, *The Rise of American Naval Power, 1776–1918*, 3rd ed. (1944).

On the history of American foreign relations with the other nations of the western hemisphere see: S. F. Bemis, *The Latin American Policy of the United States* (1943), an older but vastly influential study; H. F. Cline, *The United States and Mexico*, rev. ed. (1963); D. M. Dozer, *Are We Good Neighbors? Three Decades of Inter-American Relations, 1930–1960* (1961); J. W. Gantenbein, ed., *The Evolution of Our Latin-American Policy: A Documentary Record* (1950); S. G. Inman, *Inter-American Conferences, 1826–1954: History and Problems* (1965); E. Lieuwen, *United States Policy in Latin America: A Short History* (1965); J. A. Logan, Jr. *No Transfer: An American Security Principle* (1961), dealing with a poorly understood aspect of the Monroe Doctrine; E. W. McInnis, *The Unguarded Frontier: A History of Canadian-American Relations* (1942); J. L. Mecham, *A Survey of United States-Latin American Relations* (1965); J. L. Mecham, *The United States and Inter-American Security, 1889–1960* (1961); D. Perkins, *A History of the Monroe Doctrine*, rev. ed. (1955), the most useful work on the subject; J. T. Shotwell ed., *The Relations of Canada and the United States*, 25 vols. (1937–1945), a general title for a series containing many studies of specific subjects; G. H. Stuart, *Latin America and the United States*, 3rd ed. (1955); A. P. Whitaker, *The Western Hemisphere Idea* (1954); and W. A. Wilbur, ed., *The Monroe Doctrine* (1965), containing documents and interpretive readings.

Works on relations with European countries include for Great Britain, probably the most important international associate of the United States in the past: H. C. Allen, *Great Britain and the United States: A History of Anglo-American Relations, 1783–1952* (1955); J. B. Brebner, *North Atlantic Triangle: The Interplay of Canada, the United States, and Great Britain* (1945); C. C. Brinton, *The United States and Great Britain*, rev. ed. (1948); F. Davis, *The Atlantic System: The Story of Anglo-American Control of the Seas* (1941); R. B. Mowat, *The Diplomatic Relations of the United States and Great Britain* (1925), covering the period 1783–1914; and A. Wolfers and L. W. Martin, eds., *The Anglo-American Tradition in Foreign Affairs* (1956). For Russo-American relations see: T. A. Bailey, *America Faces Russia* (1950); V. M. Dean, *The United States and Russia* (1948); F. R. Dulles, *The Road to Teheran* (1944); L. Fischer, *The Soviets in World Affairs*, 2 vols. (1951); O. Jensen, ed., *American and Russia* (1962); G. F. Kennan, *Russia and the West under Lenin and Stalin* (1960); M. M. Laserson, *The American Impact on Russia, Diplomatic and Ideological, 1784–1917,* (1950); F. L. Schuman, *American Policy toward Russia since 1917* (1928); B. P. Thomas, *Russo-American Relations, 1815–1867* (1930); P. Tompkins, *American Russian Relations in the Far East* (1949); and W. A. Williams, *American-Russian Relations, 1781–1947* (1952). For other European countries see: C. J. H. Hayes, *The United States and Spain: An Interpretation* (1951); H. S. Hughes, *The United States and Italy* (1953); D. C. McKay, *The United States and France* (1951); and F. D. Scott, *The United States and Scandinavia* (1950). Curiously, there are no overall studies of German-American relations.

For general works on Asia and the Pacific the reader may turn to: L. H. Battistini, *The United States and Asia* (1955); F. R. Dulles, *America in the Pacific; A Century of Expansion* (1932); E. A. Falk, *From Perry to Pearl Harbor: The Struggle for Supremacy in the Pacific* (1943); M. S. Farley, *United States Relations with Southeast Asia* (1955); C. H. Grattan, *The United States in the Southwest Pacific* (1961); A. W. Griswold, *The Far Eastern Policy of the United States* (1938), an influential work; E. A. Speiser, *The United States in the Near East* (1950); and J. A. DeNovo, *American Interests and Policies in the Middle East, 1900–1939* (1963). There are many works on China and Japan but relatively few for other regions. For China, consult: P. H. Clyde, ed., *United States Policy toward China: Diplomatic and Public Documents, 1838–1939* (1940); T. Dennet, *Americans in Eastern Asia* (1922), stressing the nineteenth century; F. R. Dulles, *China and America: The Story of Their Relations since 1784* (1946); J. K. Fairbank, *The United States and China*, rev. ed. (1958); K. S. Latourette, *The History of Early Relations Between the United States and China, 1784–1844* (1917); E. Swisher, *China's Management of the American Barbarians* (1943); P. A. Varg, *Missionaries, Chinese, and Diplomats: The American Protestant Missionary Movement in China, 1890–1952* (1958); and W. W. Willoughby, *Foreign Rights and Interests in China*, 2 vols. (1927). For Japan, see: L. H. Battistini, *Japan and America* (1953); F. R. Dulles, *Forty Years of American-Japanese Relations* (1937); W. L. Neumann, *America Encounters Japan: From Perry to MacArthur* (1963); E. O. Reischauer, *The United States and Japan*, rev. ed. (1957); R. S. Schwantes, *Japanese and Americans: A Century of Cultural Relations* (1955); and P. J. Treat, *The United States and Japan, 1853–1921* (1921), still useful. General works on other countries are rather scattered, reflecting the relative lack of extensive contacts in the region until recent years. Among these studies see: W. N. Brown, *The United States and India and Pakistan* (1953); L. J. Gordon, *American Relations with Turkey, 1830–1930: An Economic Interpretation* (1932); G. A. Grundy and W. E. Livezey, *The Philippines and the United States* (1951); S. Harrison, ed., *India and the United States* (1961); W. Levi, *American-Australian Relations* (1947); L. K. Rosinger, *India and the United States* (1950); G. H. Ryden, *The Foreign Policy of the United States in Relation to Samoa* (1933); N. Shafran, *The United States and Israel* (1963); and L. V. Thomas and R. N. Frye, *The United States and Turkey and Iran* (1951). Unfortunately, there are hardly any works dealing with America and Africa. Two are of some interest: R. W. Bixler, *The Foreign Policy of the United States in Liberia* (1957); and C. F. Gallagher, *The United States and North Africa: Morocco, Algeria, and Tunisia* (1963).

NINETEENTH CENTURY

The most stimulating interpretation of American foreign relations spanning the nineteenth century is R. W. Van Alstyne's *The Rising American Empire* (1960), now available in paperback. It describes the acquisition of both the continental and overseas empires of the United States, stressing the continuity in this process from the colonial period to World War I. Three stimulating studies of the intellectual and emotional justifications of expansion are A. K. Weinberg, *Manifest Destiny* (1935); E. M. Burns, *The American Idea of Mission: Concepts of National Purpose and Identity* (1957); and F. Merk, *Manifest Destiny and Mission in American History* (1963). A brief survey for the period 1800–1860 is W. H. Goetzmann, *When the Eagle Screamed: The Romantic Horizon in American Diplomacy, 1800–1860* (1966). The most recent work on the consequences of the War of 1812 is B. Perkins, *Castlereagh and Adams: England and the United States, 1812–1823* (1964). S. F. Bemis has written the magisterial *John Quincy Adams and the Foundations of American Foreign Policy* (1949), and *John Quincy Adams and the Union* (1956); D. Perkins' three volumes on *The Monroe Doctrine* (1927–1937) analyze that policy in depth for the period 1823–1907. The best work on the period of the Mexican War is N. A. Graebner, *Empire on the Pacific: A Study in American Continental Expansion* (1955). A. Nevins has edited a condensed version of the diary of President James K. Polk, *The Diary of a President, 1845–1849* (1952), and we now have the excellent two-volume biography of Polk by C. G. Sellers, Jr., *James K. Polk* (1957–1966). The careful scholarship of F. Merk on the Oregon question is now collected in *The Oregon Question: Essays in Inter-American Diplomacy and Politics* (1966). For the Civil War see F. L. Owsley, *King Cotton Diplomacy* (1958); and E. D. Adams, *Great Britain and the American Civil War*, 2 vols. (1925). In recent years a number of scholars have drawn attention to the importance of the years between Reconstruction and the Spanish American War, notably W. LaFeber in *The New Empire: An Interpretation of American Expansion, 1860–1898* (1963), an excellent example of sophisticated economic interpretation, and D. Pletcher, *The Awkward Years* (1963). F. R. Dulles provides another of his useful surveys in his *Prelude to World Power: American Diplomatic History, 1860–1900* (1965). Among helpful biographical studies are A. Nevins' study of President Grant's Secretary of State, *Hamilton Fish: The Inner History of the Grant Administration* (1936), and A. F. Tyler's work on the Secretary of State in the Garfield and Harrison administrations, *The Foreign Policy of James G. Blaine* (1927). A useful commentary on the development of government policies is in J. A. S. Grenville and G. B. Young, *Politics, Strategy, and American Diplomacy: Studies in Foreign Policy, 1873–1917* (1966). For the two most celebrated works by members of the "imperial cadre" see J. Strong, *Our Country* (1891), available in paperback, and A. T. Mahan, *The Influence of Sea Power upon History* (1890).

THE SPANISH-AMERICAN WAR

For a general work on the 1890s see H. U. Faulkner, *Politics, Reform, and Expansion, 1890–1900* (1959). Two older works on the Spanish-American War are still useful, W. Millis, *The Martial Spirit* (1931), highly critical of the United States, and J. W. Pratt, *Expansionists of 1898* (1936), an examination of expansionist views at home. LaFeber's *The New Empire* is useful on the origins of the war, as is J. E. Wisan, *The Cuban Crisis as Reflected in the New York Press* (1934). The best one-volume work is E. R. May, *Imperial Democracy* (1961), covering the period 1895–1900. A useful brief summation is found in H. W. Morgan, *America's Road to Empire: The War with Spain and Overseas Expansion* (1965). See also F. Freidel's *The Splendid Little War* (1959). Two recent works on President McKinley, both relatively sympathetic, are M. Leech, *In the Days of McKinley* (1959), and H. W. Morgan, *William McKinley and His America* (1963). On the subject of relations with other countries consult: A. E. Campbell, *Great Britain and the United States, 1895–1903* (1960); C. S. Campbell, Jr., *Anglo-American Understanding, 1898–1903* (1957); J. L. Keim, *Forty Years of German-American Political*

Relations (1919); C. E. Schieber, *The Transformation of American Sentiment toward Germany, 1870–1914* (1923); E. H. Zabriskie, *American-Russian Rivalry in the Far East, 1895–1914* (1946); and P. J. Treat, *Diplomatic Relations Between the United States and Japan, 1895–1905* (1938).

THE IMPERIAL INTERLUDE

Several general surveys of American history treating the period between the Spanish-American War and the American entry into World War I provide useful background information and introductory interpretations of American foreign policy during those years. See in particular S. P. Hays, *The Response to Industrialism, 1885–1914* (1957); G. Mowry, *The Era of Theodore Roosevelt* (1958); A. Link, *Woodrow Wilson and the Progressive Era, 1910–1917* (1954); and R. Wiebe, *The Search for Order: 1877–1920* (1967). For two surveys of imperial diplomacy see F. R. Dulles, *The Imperial Years* (1956), and A. L. P. Dennis, *Adventures in American Diplomacy, 1898–1906* (1928). A considerable biographical literature discusses the careers of the presidents of this era in great detail. For McKinley see the works by Morgan and Leech previously cited. On Theodore Roosevelt consult: H. K. Beale, *Theodore Roosevelt and the Rise of America to World Power* (1956); J. M. Blum, *The Republican Roosevelt* (1954); W. H. Harbaugh, *Power and Responsibility: The Life and Times of Theodore Roosevelt* (1961); and E. E. Morison, *The Letters of Theodore Roosevelt*, 8 vols. (1951–1954). An older, more anti-Roosevelt work is H. F. Pringle, *Theodore Roosevelt* (1931). See also Pringle's extensive work on Roosevelt's successor, *The Life and Times of William Howard Taft*, 2 vol. (1939). For Woodrow Wilson see the extraordinary multi-volume biography by A. Link, now extending to five volumes to the beginning of the American intervention in 1917, *Wilson*, 5 vols. (1947–   ), and his incisive *Wilson the Diplomatist* (1957). Link is also editing the papers of Wilson, of which two volumes to 1884 are now available. The older biography by R. S. Baker, *Woodrow Wilson: Life and Letters*, 8 vols. (1927–1939), is still of use. See also R. S. Baker and W. E. Dodd, eds., *The Public Papers of Woodrow Wilson*, 6 vols. (1925–1927). Other works include: J. M. Blum, *Woodrow Wilson and the Politics of Morality* (1956); H. C. F. Bell, *Woodrow Wilson and the People* (1945); J. Garraty, *Woodrow Wilson* (1956); A. and J. George, *Woodrow Wilson and Colonel House: A Personality Study* (1956); and A. W. Walworth, *Woodrow Wilson*, 2 vols. (1958). Among works on other important personalities of the period see: T. Dennett, *John Hay* (1933); P. C. Jessup, *Elihu Root*, 2 vols. (1938); R. W. Leopold, *Elihu Root and the Conservative Tradition* (1954); H. C. Lodge, ed., *Selections from the Correspondence of Theodore Roosevelt and Henry Cabot Lodge, 1884–1918*, 2 vols. (1925); and C. Seymour, ed., *The Intimate Papers of Colonel House*, 4 vols. (1926–1928), concerning Wilson's most influential counsellor. For studies of relations with European powers in addition to those cited in connection with the Spanish-American War, see: C. D. Davis, *The United States and the First Hague Peace Conference* (1962), and L. M. Gelber, *The Rise of Anglo-American Friendship* (1938). Works on relations with Latin America include: W. H. Callcott, *The Caribbean Policy of the United States, 1890–1920* (1942); C. W. Hackett, *The Mexican Revolution and the United States, 1910–1926* (1926); D. F.

Healey, *The United States in Cuba, 1898 – 1902: Generals, Politicians, and the Search for Policy* (1963); H. C. Hill, *Roosevelt and the Caribbean* (1927); C. Kelsey, *The American Intervention in Haiti and the Dominican Republic* (1922); D. A. Lockmiller, *Magoon in Cuba* (1938), about the American intervention of 1906 – 1909; D. C. Miner, *The Fight for the Panama Route* (1940); D. G. Munro, *Intervention and Dollar Diplomacy in the Caribbean, 1900 – 1921* (1964); N. J. Padelford, *The Panama Canal in Peace and War* (1942); D. Perkins, *The Monroe Doctrine, 1867 – 1907* (1937); and R. E. Quirk, *An Affair of Honor: Woodrow Wilson and the Occupation of Veracruz* (1962). For relations with the Pacific-East Asian region consult: T. A. Bailey, *Theodore Roosevelt and the Japanese-American Crises* (1934); W. R. Braisted, *The United States Navy in the Pacific, 1897 – 1909* (1958); C. S. Campbell, Jr., *Special Business Interests and the Open Door Policy* (1951); H. Croly, *Willard Straight* (1924), about the originator of dollar diplomacy; R. W. Curry, *Woodrow Wilson and Far Eastern Policy, 1913 – 1921* (1957); T. Dennett, *Roosevelt and the Russo-Japanese War* (1925); Tien-yi Li, *Woodrow Wilson's China Policy: 1913 – 1917* (1952); C. Vevier, *The United States and China, 1906 – 1913* (1955); J. A. White, *The Diplomacy of the Russo-Japanese War* (1954); and L. Wolff, *Little Brown Brother* (1961), about the Philippine insurrection.

WORLD WAR I

The biographical works on Woodrow Wilson listed in the previous section are of great importance for the study of American foreign relations during the First Conflict.

An extensive work by F. L. Paxson, *American Democracy and the World War,* 3 vols. (1936 – 1938), is still the only comprehensive general survey of the period. See also the illuminating chapters on the war in W. E. Leuchtenberg, *The Perils of Prosperity, 1914 – 1932* (1958), as well as the work by Wiebe, *Search for Order.* A useful short summation of American foreign relations is D. M. Smith, *The Great Departure: The United States and World War I, 1914 – 1920* (1965). Seymour's work on Colonel House provides a continuing commentary from the perspective of Wilson's adviser.

On the origins of the war the following are representative works: L. Albertini, *The Origins of the War of 1914,* 3 vols. (1952 – 1957); S. B. Fay, *The Origins of the World War,* 2 vols. (1928); the "revisionist" work of H. E. Barnes entitled *The Genesis of the World War: An Introduction to the Problem of War Guilt* (1926); and B. E. Schmitt, *The Coming of the War: 1914,* 2 vols. (1930). Unfortunately there are no general studies of the relation of the United States to the origin and causation of the war.

On the period of neutrality, 1914 – 1917, there is a considerable literature, much of it concerned with explaining the reason for the American intervention of 1917. For the view that the submarine controversy was at the bottom of the intervention see: C. Seymour, *American Neutrality, 1914 – 1917* (1935). Works critical of the intervention from various revisionist points of view are E. M. Borchard and W. P. Lage, *Neutrality for the United States* (1937); C. H. Grattan, *Why We Fought* (1929); and C. C. Tansill, *America Goes to War* (1938). Recent studies of the period, less polemical and more fully documented, are:

E. R. May, *The World War and American Isolation, 1914–1917* (1959); D. M. Smith, *Robert Lansing and American Neutrality, 1914–1917* (1958); and E. H. Buehrig, *Woodrow Wilson and the Balance of Power* (1955). Smith has collected various views in his *American Intervention, 1917: Sentiment, Self-Interest, or Ideals?* (1966). For the German situation see K. E. Birnbaum, *Peace Moves and U-Boat Warfare: A Study of Imperial Germany's Policy Towards the United States, April 18, 1916–January 9, 1917* (1958). For the activities of the American ambassador in London, see B. J. Hendrick, *The Life and Letters of Walter Hines Page*, 3 vols. (1924–1926). Works on the period of belligerency, 1917–1918, are much less plentiful and more scattered in coverage. The most general work is C. Seymour, *American Diplomacy During the World War* (1934). See in particular: T. A. Bailey, *The Policy of the United States Towards the Neutrals, 1917–1918* (1942); L. E. Gelfand, *The Inquiry: American Preparations for Peace, 1917–1919* (1963); R. Lansing *War Memoirs of Robert Lansing* (1935), by the wartime Secretary of State; V. S. Mamatey, *The United States and East Central Europe, 1914–1918: A Study in Wilsonian Diplomacy and Propaganda* (1957); A. Mayer, *Political Origins of the New Diplomacy, 1917–1918* (1959), available in paperback under the title *Wilson vs. Lenin*, an important comparison of the Wilsonian versus the social revolutionary perspective on the war; J. J. Pershing, *My Experiences During the World War*, 2 vols. (1931), by the American commander-in-chief; H. R. Rudin, *Armistice: 1918* (1944); D. F. Trask, *The United States in the Supreme War Council: American War Aims and Inter-Allied Strategy, 1917–1918* (1961); and B. M. Unterberger, *America's Siberian Expedition, 1918–1920: A Study in National Policy* (1956). The American diplomatic correspondence concerning the war is published by the United States Department of State in *Papers Relating to the Foreign Relations of the United States: Supplement, the World War*, 7 vols. (1928–1932). The State Department has also issued in the Foreign Relations series *The Lansing Papers*, 2 vols. (1939–1940). Another published source of interest is E. D. Cronon, ed., *The Cabinet Diaries of Josephus Daniels, 1913–1921* (1963), concerning the activities of the Secretary of the Navy. In connection with the naval war see the memoir of the American naval commander, Admiral William S. Sims, *The Victory at Sea* (1920).

For the peace conference and after the literature is very extensive, centering on why the United States ultimately refused to accept the Treaty of Versailles. The most comprehensive history of the conference is H. W. V. Temperley, ed., *A History of the Paris Peace Conference at Paris*, 6 vols. (1920–1924). The best one-volume study is P. Birdsall, *Versailles Twenty Years After* (1941). For an extensive collection of records see United States Department of State, *Papers Relating to the Foreign Relations of the United States: The Paris Peace Conference*, 13 vols. (1942–1947). Another private collection of great utility is D. H. Miller, *My Diary at the Conference of Paris*, 21 vols. (1924). Miller also wrote *The Drafting of the Covenant*, 2 vols. (1928). An early analysis of the Conference came from R. S. Baker, *Woodrow Wilson and World Settlement*, 3 vols. (1922), favorable to the President and quite in contrast to the negative appraisals of two British writers, J. M. Keynes in his *The Economic Consequences of the Peace* (1920); and H. Nicolson in his *Peacemaking, 1919* (1933). T. A. Bailey has written two influential works, one entitled *Woodrow Wilson and the Lost Peace* (1944), about the negotiations in Paris, and *Woodrow Wilson and the Great Betrayal* (1945), about the refusal of the Senate to accept the Treaty of Versailles. An earlier pro-Wilsonian work on the treaty fight is D. F. Fleming, *The United States and the League of Nations, 1918–1920* (1932). J. Garraty discusses the role of a controversial senator in *Henry Cabot Lodge* (1953). A work on the organization of the conference is F. S. Marston, *The Peace Conference of 1919: Organization and Procedure* (1944). The text of the treaty is carefully edited by D. P. Myers, *The Treaty of Versailles and After: Annotations of the Text of the Treaty* (1947). Two works on important aspects of the treaty negotiations are R. H. Fifield, *Woodrow Wilson and the Far East: The Diplomacy of the Shantung Question* (1952); and S. P. Tillman, *Anglo-American Relations at the Paris Peace Conference of 1919* (1961). The activities of Wilson's fellow plenipotentiaries are considered in R. Lansing, *The Peace Negotiations* (1921); A. Nevins, *Henry White* (1930); and D. F. Trask, *General Tasker Howard Bliss and the "Sessions of the World," 1919* (1966). The leading work on the origins of the league concept is R. Bartlett, *The League to Enforce Peace* (1944).

THE LONG ARMISTICE

Two general works on American history during the interwar period in the *New American Nation Series* are: J. D. Hicks, *Republican Ascendancy, 1921–1933* (1959); and W. E. Leuchtenberg, *Franklin D. Roosevelt and the New Deal, 1932–1940* (1963). See also the latter's *Perils of Prosperity.* A crisp survey is in D. A. Shannon, *Between the Wars: America, 1919–1941* (1965). Two recent works on the foreign policy of the period by S. Adler are *The Isolationist Impulse* (1957), and *The Uncertain Giant, 1921–1941: American Foreign Policy Between the Wars* (1935). A sparkling analysis for the general history of international relations is in E. H. Carr, *The Twenty Years' Crisis, 1919–1939: An Introduction to the Study of International Relations* (1946). Another impressive analysis is S. Neumann, *The Future in Perspective* (1946), in which the concept of a modern Thirty Years' War in this century is advanced. A. Nevins has contributed two useful studies, *The United States in a Chaotic World: 1918–1933* (1950), and *The New Deal and World Affairs: A Chronicle of International Affairs, 1933–1945* (1950). Among works on specialized topics of general interest across the period see: F. P. Walters, *A History of the League of Nations,* 2 vols. (1952); W. I. Cohen, *The American Revisionists: The Lessons of Intervention in World War I* (1967); and G. A. Craig and F. Gilbert, eds., *The Diplomats, 1919–1939* (1953).

For works dealing with general issues and the personalities of the Twenties, the following are of importance. On the United States relation to the League of Nations see C. A. Berdahl, *The Policy of the United States with Respect to the League of Nations* (1932), and D. F. Fleming, *The United States and World Organization, 1920–1933* (1938). On economic questions consult: B. H. Williams, *Economic Foreign Policy of the United States* (1929); H. Feis, *The Diplomacy of the Dollar: First Era, 1919–1932* (1950); J. Brandes, *Herbert Hoover and Economic Diplomacy: Department of Commerce Policy, 1921–28* (1962); and G. Soule, *Prosperity Decade* (1947). On important statesmen see: D. R. McCoy, *Calvin Coolidge: The Quiet President* (1967); M. J. Pusey, *Charles Evans Hughes,* 2 vols. (1951); D. Perkins,

Charles Evans Hughes and American Democratic Statesmanship (1956); L. E. Ellis, *Frank B. Kellogg and American Foreign Relations, 1925–1929* (1961); M. C. McKenna, *Borah* (1961); and J. C. Vinson, *William E. Borah and the Outlawry of War* (1957).

For works on the problem of neutrality during the Thirties see: R. A. Divine, *The Illusion of Neutrality* (1962); M. Jonas, *Isolationism in America, 1935–1941* (1966); J. E. Wiltz, *In Search of Peace: The Senate Munitions Inquiry, 1934–1936* (1963); W. S. Cole, *Senator Gerald P. Nye and American Foreign Relations* (1962); and E. M. Borchard and W. P. Lage, *Neutrality for the United States* (1937). Works dealing with the coming of the war include: C. Grove Haines and R. J. S. Hoffman, *The Origins and Background of the Second World War* (1947); J. W. Gantenbein, *Documentary Background of World War II, 1931–1941* (1948); C. C. Tansill, *Backdoor to War: The Roosevelt Foreign Policy, 1933–1941* (1948); C. Beard, *American Foreign Policy in the Making, 1932–1940* (1946), along with Tansill revisionist in nature; D. F. Drummond, *The Passing of American Neutrality, 1937–1941* (1955); W. L. Langer and S. E. Gleason, *The Challenge to Isolation, 1937–1940* (1952), the most comprehensive work; A. J. P. Taylor, *The Origins of the Second World War* (1961); and L. C. Gardner, *Economic Aspects of New Deal Diplomacy* (1964), a stimulating work of economic interpretation.

Works on President Herbert Hoover and his administration include: R. H. Ferrell, *American Diplomacy in the Great Depression* (1957); W. S. Myers, *The Foreign Policies of Herbert Hoover* (1940); W. S. Myers, *The State Papers and Other Public Writings of Herbert Hoover,* 2 vols. (1934); H. Hoover, *The Memoirs of Herbert Hoover: The Cabinet and the Presidency, 1920–1933* (1952), and *The Memoirs of Herbert Hoover: The Great Depression, 1929–1941* (1952). On Hoover's Secretary of State, Henry L. Stimson, see: E. E. Morison, *Turmoil and Tradition: A Study of the Life and Times of Henry L. Stimson* (1960); R. N. Current, *Secretary Stimson: A Study in Statecraft* (1954), a critical appraisal; H. L. Stimson and M. Bundy, *On Active Service in Peace and War* (1948), a memoir; and R. H. Ferrell, *Frank B. Kellogg/Henry L. Stimson* (1963). The biographical literature for President Franklin D. Roosevelt is overwhelming. For a representative sample of different views see: A. M. Schlesinger, Jr., *The Age of Roosevelt,* 3 vols. (1957–), taking the story to 1936; F. Freidel, *Franklin D. Roosevelt,* 3 vols. (1952–), taking the story to 1933; J. M. Burns, *Roosevelt; The Lion and the Fox* (1956); J. Gunther, *Roosevelt in Retrospect* (1950); E. E. Robinson, *The Roosevelt Leadership, 1933–1945* (1955), a critical work; and S. I. Rosenman, ed., *Public Papers and Addresses of Franklin D. Roosevelt,* 13 vols. (1938–1950). For Roosevelt's Secretary of State, Cordell Hull, see: J. W. Pratt, *Cordell Hull, 1933–1944,* 2 vols. (1964); and C. Hull, *The Memoirs of Cordell Hull,* 2 vols. (1948).

The problems associated with the Pacific-East Asian region have attracted considerable attention. For the Washington Naval Conference of 1921–1922 consult: R. L. Buell, *The Washington Conference* (1922); C. L. Hoag, *Preface to Preparedness: The Washington Conference and Public Opinion* (1941); J. C. Vinson, *The Parchment Peace* (1956), dealing with Congressional questions; and H. and M. Sprout, *Toward a New Order of Sea Power* (1940). Works on the Twenties include: G. E. Wheeler, *Prelude to Pearl Harbor: The United States Navy and the Far East, 1921–1931* (1963); and D. Borg, *American Policy and the Chinese*

Revolution, 1925–1928 (1947). See also R. G. O'Connor, *Perilous Equilibrium: The United States and the London Naval Conference of 1930* (1962). On the Manchurian Crisis of 1931 and after see D. Borg, *The United States and the Far Eastern Crisis of 1933–1938* (1964); A. Rappaport, *Henry L. Stimson and Japan, 1931–33* (1963); S. R. Smith, *The Manchurian Crisis, 1931–1932: A Tragedy in International Relations* (1948); and D. J. Lu, *From the Marco Polo Bridge to Pearl Harbor: Japan's Entry into World War II* (1961). On Joseph Grew's role as Ambassador to Japan see: W. Heinrichs, *American Ambassador* (1966), and J. Grew, *Ten Years in Japan* (1944). For two important documentary collections see United States Senate, *Conference on the Limitation of Armaments* (Senate Document No. 125, 67th Congress, 2nd Session) (1922); and United State Department of State, *Japan, 1921–1941,* 2 vols. (1933).

United States-Latin American relations are considered in: A. DeConde, *Herbert Hoover's Latin-American Policy* (1951); J. R. Clark, *Memorandum on the Monroe Doctrine* (1930), the famous critique of the Theodore Roosevelt Corollary to the Monroe Doctrine; D. M. Dozer, *Are We Good Neighbors? Three Decades of Inter-American Relations, 1930–1960* (1961); B. Wood, *The Making of the Good Neighbor Policy* (1961); E. O. Guerrant, *Roosevelt's Good Neighbor Policy* (1950); G. Beckett, *The Reciprocal Trade Agreements Program* (1941); E. D. Cronon, *Josephus Daniels in Mexico* (1960); and J. Fred Rippy, *The Caribbean Danger Zone* (1940). For specialized works on relations with Europe see: C. Lasch, *The American Liberals and the Russian Revolution* (1962); R. P. Browder, *The Origins of Soviet-American Diplomacy* (1953); H. G. Moulton and L. Pasvolsky, *War Debts and World Prosperity* (1932); R. H. Ferrell, *Peace in Their Time: The Origins of the Kellogg-Briand Pact* (1952); F. J. Taylor, *The United States and the Spanish Civil War* (1956); A. Guttmann, *The Wound in the Heart: America and the Spanish Civil War* (1962); B. Harris, Jr., *The United States and the Italo-Ethiopian Crisis* (1964); and J. W. Wheeler-Bennett, *The Pipe-Dream of Peace: The Story of the Collapse of Disarmament* (1935).

WORLD WAR II

By far the most extensive body of literature concerning the United States and World War II deals with the process by which the United States was drawn into the war. Some of these works are listed in the previous section. The most recent brief survey of the subject is R. A. Divine, *The Reluctant Belligerent: American Entry into World War II* (1965). The following works are generally favorable in varying degrees to the diplomacy of the administration: B. Rauch, *Roosevelt: From Munich to Pearl Harbor* (1950); H. Feis, *The Road to Pearl Harbor* (1950); W. L. Langer and S. E. Gleason, *The Undeclared War, 1940–1941* (1953); and W. Millis, *This Is Pearl!* (1947). Various types of revisionist history are presented in a collection of these works edited by H. E. Barnes, *Perpetual War for Perpetual Peace* (1953). Full-length inquiries include: C. A. Beard, *President Roosevelt and the Coming of the War 1941* (1948); C. C. Tansill, *Backdoor to War* (1952); G. Morgenstern, *Pearl Harbor: The Story of the Secret War* (1947); P. W. Schroeder, *The Axis Alliance and Japanese-American Relations 1941* (1958), a "power realist" critique argued quite differently than most revisionist works;

and F. R. Sanborn, *Design for War: A Study of Secret Power Politics, 1937–1941* (1951). The official record of the Pearl Harbor investigation after the war which unearthed massive evidence pertaining to the entrance into the war, is in United States Senate, *Pearl Harbor Attack*, 39 parts (79th Congress, 2nd Session) (1946). Other works of interest in connection with the period of neutrality are: R. J. C. Butow, *Tojo and the Coming of the War* (1961); W. S. Cole, *America First: The Battle Against Intervention, 1940–1941* (1953), about the leading isolationist group; W. Johnson, *The Battle Against Isolation, 1940–1941* (1944); and R. Wohlstetter, *Pearl Harbor: Warning and Decision* (1962), on the intelligence breakdown associated with the successful Japanese attack.

Among the general histories of wartime diplomacy the two most extensive are H. Feis, *Churchill, Roosevelt, Stalin: The War They Waged and the Peace They Sought* (1957); and W. H. McNeill, *America, Britain, and Russia: Their Cooperation and Conflict, 1941–1946* (1953). A convenient short study is J. L. Snell, *Illusion and Necessity: The Diplomacy of Global War 1939–1945* (1963). A brief but excellent account is G. Smith, *American Diplomacy During the Second World War, 1941–1945* (1963). Winston Churchill's massive *The Second World War*, 6 vols. (1948–1953), is an indispensable work, but it must be used with caution. W. L. Neumann provides a brief account of wartime diplomacy in his *Making the Peace, 1941–1945* (1950). The biographical literature on President Roosevelt and his circle is given in the previous section. See also, for the war period, R. L. Walker and G. Curry, *E. R. Stettinius, Jr./James F. Byrnes* (1965), about two Secretaries of State; R. E. Sherwood, *Roosevelt and Hopkins* (1948), of special importance; J. F. Byrnes, *All in One Lifetime* (1958), a memoir by Truman's first appointee as Secretary of State; W. D. Leahy, *I Was There* (1950), by Roosevelt's personal chief of staff; and J. G. Winant, *Letter from Grosvenor Square* (1947), by the wartime Ambassador to Great Britain. For President Truman see the first volume of his *Memoirs*, 2 vols. (1955–1956).

For specialized works on various aspects of wartime diplomacy see: A. Armstrong, *Unconditional Surrender: The Impact of the Casablanca Policy upon World War II* (1961); R. H. Dawson, *The Decision to Aid Russia, 1941* (1959); P. Goodhart, *Fifty Ships That Saved the World: The Foundation of the Anglo-American Alliance* (1965), on the destroyer-for-bases deal of 1940; D. D. Eisenhower, *Crusade in Europe* (1948), the memoirs of the Allied Commander-in-Chief; J. R. Deane, *The Strange Alliance: The Story of Our Efforts at Wartime Cooperation with Russia* (1947); P. Kecskemeti, *Strategic Surrender: The Politics of Victory and Defeat* (1958), on the wartime surrenders; J. L. Snell, *Wartime Origins of the East-West Dilemma over Germany* (1959); E. R. Stettinius, Jr., *Lend-Lease: Weapon for Victory* (1944); E. R. Stettinius, Jr., *Roosevelt and the Russians: The Yalta Conference* (1949), edited by W. Johnson; J. L. Snell, ed., *The Meaning of Yalta* (1956), a useful collection of various views; H. Feis, *Between War and Peace: The Potsdam Conference* (1960); R. J. C. Butow, *Japan's Decision to Surrender* (1954); and H. Feis, *The Atomic Bomb and the End of World War II* (1966). Feis, the most prolific writer on the diplomacy of World War II, has also contributed *The China Tangle: The American Effort in China from Pearl Harbor to the Marshall Mission* (1953). Works on the development of the atomic bomb include: R. C. Batchelder, *The Irreversible Decision, 1939–1950* (1962); J. P. Baxter, *Scientists*

Against Time (1947); R. G. Hewlett and O. E. Anderson, *The New World, 1939– 1946* (1962), the first volume of a history of the Atomic Energy Commission; and F. Knebel and C. W. Bailey, *No High Ground* (1960). On preparations for peace consult: L. W. Holborn, *War and Peace Aims of the United Nations, September 1, 1939-December 31, 1942* (1943), and *War and Peace Aims of the United Nations, 1943–1945* (1948); R. B. Russell, *A History of the United Nations Charter: The Role of the United States, 1940–1945* (1958); and United States Department of State, *Postwar Foreign Policy Preparations, 1943–1945* (1949).

Documentary collections of great importance issued by the United States Department of State include: *A Decade of Foreign Policy, Basic Documents, 1941– 1949* (1951); *Japan: 1931–1941*, 2 vols. (1943); *Participation in International Conferences, 1941–1945* (1947); *The Conferences at Cairo and Teheran, 1943* (1961); *The Conferences at Malta and Yalta* (1955); *The Conference of Berlin (Potsdam), 1945*, 2 vols. (1960); *The United States and Italy, 1936–1946* (1946); and *United States Relations with China with Special Reference to the Period 1944–1949* (1949), the famous China "white paper."

SINCE 1945

It is impossible to provide here even a rough survey of the voluminous and often ephemeral literature available on the extraordinarily complex course of American foreign relations and world politics since the end of World War II. The following list of the more important general materials provides an introduction to the subject.

For American history since 1945 there are several useful summaries and interpretations: O. T. Barck, Jr., *A History of the United States since 1945* (1965): H. Agar, *The Price of Power: America since 1945* (1957); and E. Goldman, *The Crucial Decade and After: America, 1945–1960* (1961). For surveys and interpretations of world history see: G. Bruun and D. E. Lee, *The Second World War and After* (1964); H. Gatzke, *The Present in Perspective: A Look at the World since 1945*, 2nd ed. (1961); and J. W. Spanier, *World Politics in an Age of Revolution* (1967). Surveys of American foreign relations include: W. G. Carleton, *The Revolution in American Foreign Policy: Its Global Range* (1963); J. Spanier, *American Foreign Policy since World War II*, Rev. ed. (1965); and N. A. Graebner, *Cold War Diplomacy: American Foreign Policy, 1945–1960* (1962). For a useful collection of foreign impressions of the United States see A. F. Westin, ed., *Views of America* (1966). For annual surveys of policy development see *The United States in World Affairs* and accompanying documentary collections published by the Council on Foreign Relations. See also the following publications of the United States Department of State, *A Decade of American Foreign Policy, Basic Documents, 1941–1949* (1950); *American Foreign Policy, 1950–1955: Basic Documents*, 2 vols. (1957); and *American Foreign Policy: Current Documents, 1956–* (1959–   ), issued for each year. The most convenient history of the United Nations is C. Eichelberger, *UN: The First Twenty Years* (1965).

Works on the history of the Cold War are available in some quantity, reflecting various points of view. Among these are: J. Lukacs, *A New History of the Cold War* (1966); D. F. Fleming, *The Cold War and Its Origins, 1917–1960*, 2 vols.

(1961), notably critical of the United States; M. F. Herz, *Beginnings of the Cold War* (1966); I. Deutscher, *The Great Contest: Russia and the West* (1960); Z. K. Brzezinski and S. P. Huntington, *Political Power: USA/USSR* (1964); K. Ingram, *History of the Cold War* (1955); J. P. Morray, *From Yalta to Disarmament: Cold War Debate* (1961); P. Seabury, *The Rise and Decline of the Cold War* (1967); F. L. Schuman, *The Cold War: Retrospect and Prospect* (1962); and H. Seton-Watson, *Neither War nor Peace: The Struggle for Power in the Postwar World* (1960).

Works on the Truman years are available in relative plenty. For the activities of the President see H. S. Truman, *Memoirs,* 2 vols. (1955–1956). See also W. Hillman, *Mr. President: The First Publication from the Personal Diaries, Private Letters, Papers and Revealing Interviews of Harry S. Truman* (1952). Three works on the Truman years of general interest include L. W. Koenig, ed., *The Truman Administration: Its Principles and Practice* (1956); C. Phillips, *The Truman Presidency: The History of a Triumphant Succession* (1966); and B. J. Bernstein and A. J. Matusow, *The Truman Administration: A Documentary History.*(1966). Works on Truman's secretaries of state are: R. L. Walker and G. Curry, *E. R. Stettinius, Jr./James F. Byrnes* (1965); J. F. Byrnes, *All in One Lifetime* (1958); R. Ferrell, *George C. Marshall* (1966); D. Acheson, *Strengthening the Forces of Freedom: Selected Speeches and Statements of Secretary of State Acheson, February, 1949, to April, 1950,* 2 vols. (1950); and M. Bundy, ed., *The Pattern of Responsibility* (1952), a collection on Acheson's activities. Also see General Services Administration, *Public Papers of the Presidents: Harry S. Truman, 1945–1953,* 9 vols. (1961–1965).

For the Eisenhower Presidency consult: D. D. Eisenhower, *The White House Years,* 2 vols. (1963–1965); General Services Administration, *Public Papers of the Presidents: Dwight D. Eisenhower, 1953–1961,* 8 vols. (1958–1961); R. J. Donovan, *Eisenhower: The Inside Story* (1956); M. W. Childs, *Eisenhower: Captive Hero* (1958); R. H. Rovere, *Affairs of State: The Eisenhower Years* (1956); S. Adams, *Firsthand Report: The Story of the Eisenhower Administration* (1961); and E. J. Hughes, *The Ordeal of Power: A Political Memoir of the Eisenhower Years* (1963). Works on the Secretary of State are: J. R. Beal, *John Foster Dulles* (1957); A. H. Berding, *Dulles on Diplomacy* (1965); R. Drummond and G. Coblentz, *Duel at the Brink: John Foster Dulles' Command of American Power* (1960); R. Goold-Adams, *John Foster Dulles: A Reappraisal* (1962); H. Finer, *Dulles over Suez: The Theory and Practice of His Diplomacy* (1964); and D. and D. Heller, *John Foster Dulles: Soldier for Peace* (1960). Vice-President Richard Nixon's recollections are chronicled in his *Six Crises* (1962).

For President John F. Kennedy the materials are more limited but highly informative. See his collections of speeches entitled *The Strategy of Peace* (1960), and *To Turn the Tide* (1962); General Services Administration, *Public Papers of the Presidents: John F. Kennedy, 1961–1963,* 3 vols. (1962–1964); J. M. Burns, *John Kennedy: A Political Profile,* 2nd ed. (1961); P. Salinger, *With Kennedy* (1966); T. Sorensen, *Kennedy* (1966); A. M. Schlesinger, Jr., *A Thousand Days: John F. Kennedy in the White House* (1965); and T. White, *The Making of a President, 1960* (1961).

The literature on President Lyndon Johnson is as yet quite sparse. See R. Evans and R. Novak, *Lyndon B. Johnson: The Exercise of Power* (1966); and P. L.

Geyelin, *Lyndon B. Johnson and the World* (1966). His public materials are being collected in General Services Administration, *Public Papers of the Preident: Lyndon B. Johnson, 1963–* (1965–   ).

For information on the critical question of nuclear arms control see: H. K. Jacobson and E. Stein, *Diplomats, Scientists, and Politicians: The United States and the Nuclear Test Ban Negotiations* (1967); H. W. Baldwin, *The Great Arms Race* (1958); B. G. Bechhofer, *Postwar Negotiations for Arms Control* (1961); D. G. Brennan, ed., *Arms Control, Disarmament, and National Security* (1961); United States Department of State, *Documents on Disarmament, 1945–1960,* 3 vols. (1960–1961); and A. H. Dean, *Test Ban and Disarmament: The Path of Negotiation* (1966).

Among the more useful early works on the war in Vietnam are: J. Lacouture, *Vietnam: Between Two Truces* (1966); D. Pike, *Vietcong: The Organization and Techniques of the National Liberation Front of South Vietnam* (1966); F. Trager, *Why Vietnam?* (1966), favorable to the policies of the Johnson administration; A. M. Schlesinger, Jr., *The Bitter Heritage* (1967), critical of the Johnson administration; R. Shaplen, *The Lost Revolution: The U.S. in Vietnam, 1946–1966,* rev. ed. (1966); and *The Vietnam Hearings* (1966), a report on the hearings of the Senate Committee on Foreign Relations concerning Vietnam in 1966.

Index